Best wishes,

journeymen

journeymen

24

Bittersweet Tales of
Short Major League
Sports Careers

BY KURT DUSTERBERG

ORANGE FRAZER *PRESS*
Wilmington, Ohio

Orange Frazer Press
P.O. Box 214, Wilmington, OH 45177
Telephone 1.800.852.9332 for price and shipping information.
www.orangefrazer.com

art direction & cover Jeff Fulwiler
technical assistance Chad DeBoard

Library of Congress Cataloging-in-Publication Data

Dusterberg, Kurt William, 1965-
 Journeymen : 24 bittersweet tales of short major league sports careers / By Kurt William Dusterberg.
    p. cm.
 ISBN 978-1-933197-36-4
1. Professional athletes--United States--Anecdotes. 2. Professional sports--United States--Anecdotes. I. Title.
 GV697.A1D87 2007
 796.0922--dc22
 [B]

                         2007011351

This book is dedicated to Kim, Karen, and Conner

Robin Jennings, Cincinnati Reds

contents

preface

When an acquaintance introduced me to Peter LeBoutillier at a restaurant, she mentioned that LeBoutillier was a former professional hockey player. I recalled his name, but nothing else about his career. So I asked, "Did you ever play in the NHL?" He looked at his feet and answered almost reluctantly, "Yeah, I played about 35 games." In fact, LeBoutillier played exactly 35 games, making him an ideal subject for *Journeymen: 24 Bittersweet Tales of Short Major League Sports Careers.*

I later asked him why he seemed embarrassed to tell me he played in the NHL. He said, "When people ask me how many games I played, I think, Oh, here we go. They don't always understand."

He's right. As fans, we don't see the whole picture when it comes to journeymen players, the ones whose careers are measured in games rather than seasons. Mostly, we just assume the guy didn't get the job done—he couldn't pick up a first down, hit major league pitching or sink the open jumper. There is bound to be some truth in those assumptions; the best players make the most of their chances. But usually the stories of near-miss careers are far more complex. They are about timing and relationships and personal maturity. And bad breaks.

Sometimes a player is put in a no-win situation. Take Robin Jennings, for example. In five minor league seasons in the Chicago Cubs organization, he hit for power and average as an everyday player. But when he reached the majors in 1996, his first 18 appearances came as a pinch hitter. Jennings went from batting four times each night in the minor leagues to batting once every few nights against the top relievers in the major leagues. Is it any wonder Jennings hit .224 with the Cubs that season? Despite his potential, he had one strike against him.

There are countless behind-the-scenes events that can sidetrack a promising career. In sports like baseball and hockey, where a prospect can spend years in the minors, the obstacles are similar to those faced by young professionals in the corporate world. Players have to please bosses at each level, and the higher-ups may have separate agendas. Fred Knipscheer was a young Boston Bruins forward when he was traded to the St. Louis Blues. The Blues had no real interest in acquiring Knipscheer—but the organization's minor league coach did. The farm team's bench boss thought Knipscheer would make an ideal leader. In an instant, Knipscheer's career had jumped the tracks.

All 24 athletes profiled in *Journeymen* live with a collection of mixed feelings. They made it to the top, but they did not find a lasting place on the major league stage. For the rest of their lives, people will ask about their careers in professional sports. A neighbor or a colleague will say, "Did you play in the major leagues?" But the subsequent questions are the tricky ones: Were you any good? Did you get a decent shot? Why didn't you play longer?

The answers tap into deep emotions, even in retirement. Some stories are heartbreakingly unjust. You will learn about Tom Flick, an NFL quarterback who seemed destined for stardom. That was before an innocent misunderstanding with his head coach put his career on a path to oblivion.

The stories share certain commonalities, regardless of the sport. All the players learned quickly that professional sports is, first and foremost, a business. High-dollar draft picks are given every opportunity to prove themselves. Late rounders—many of whom you will meet in *Journeymen*—rarely receive the star treatment. The players also agree that, when it comes to earning a major league roster spot, the first audition is the most important one. Once you've been traded, released or sent to the minors, you're no longer a prospect.

The greatest source of frustration among the players? The lack of communication from the front office. Above all, the players wanted to know where they stood with the organization—Did they have a shot at the majors, or were they simply filling out a minor league roster? Most players grew frustrated by the lack of feedback.

But *Journeymen* looks beyond the complicated climb to the peak of professional sports. The stories are a celebration of the major league dream. For most of the players, the newness never wore off. Their fondest memories are the same ones we imagine ourselves embracing: meeting a superstar, playing in a famous stadium, having that one glorious moment that makes all the struggles worthwhile. And some of the best memories are hapless ones, like the goalie who hitchhiked to his first NHL game. Or the kicker who was stuck in a kindergarten class when he finally got the call to the NFL.

To a man, these retired athletes have learned valuable lessons that they now apply to life after sports. Not just simple platitudes, but actual wisdom they gathered from their playing careers. They have learned the finer points of perseverance, humility, personal growth and gratitude. What is noteworthy is how their perspectives change with the passing years. Several of the players were interviewed within a couple years of their last professional games. For them, the specific issues that diminished their careers are still very fresh in their minds. The players who have been retired for a decade or more tend to view their star-crossed careers in the larger context of their lives.

There is one more thing they all have in common. All the players genuinely believe they were blessed to reach the major leagues.

—*Kurt Dusterberg, summer, 2007*

journeymen

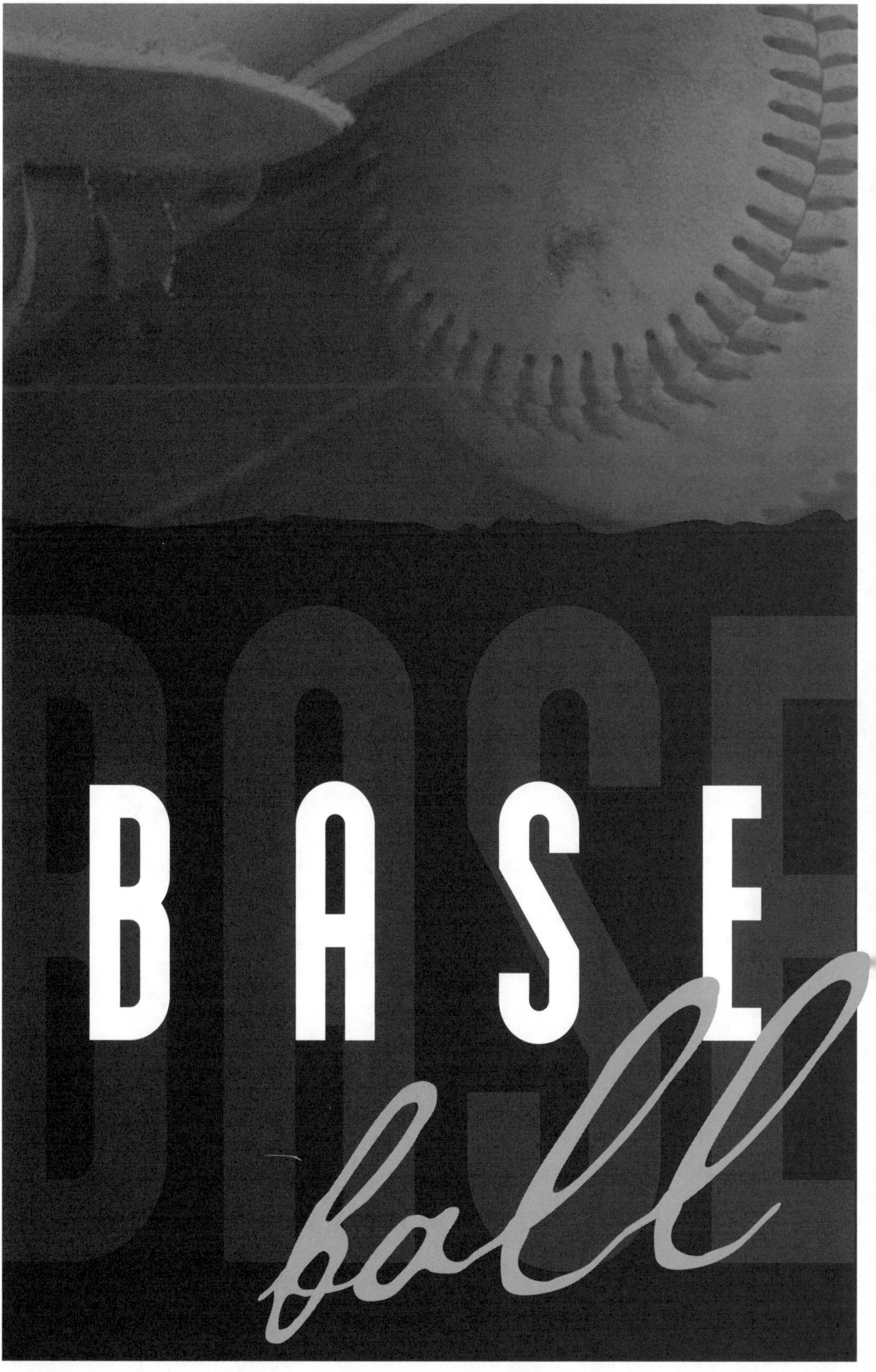
BASE
ball

STEVE FIREOVID

A starter finds relief

A lengthy AAA career left Steve Fireovid searching for a way to bow out gracefully.

There was little at stake when San Diego met Cincinnati during the last month of the 1983 baseball season. But Padres pitcher **Steve Fireovid** viewed his relief appearance as more than mop-up work. In his second September call up, he was hoping to finally convince the Padres he was ready to stay in the majors.

"We were in our own ballpark, it was late in the game, and there's a hum in the stadium," Fireovid explains. "And it's becoming really loud, and I can't figure out for the life of me what is going on."

The fans were buzzing about Johnny Bench, who was swinging a bat in the Cincinnati on deck circle. The Reds catcher was planning to retire at the end of the season, and the impending pinch-hitting appearance was shaping up to be Bench's farewell in San Diego.

"They pried him off the bench and sent him up, and I threw three fastballs right by him," he says. "He swung at the last two, and the crowd booed like crazy. I get into the dugout and Terry Kennedy, who was our catcher, says, 'Did you notice how I was sitting right down the middle of the plate? I wanted to see Bench hit one 500 feet.' I said, 'That's really nice of you, Terry.'"

And just so there is no misunderstanding, Fireovid clarifies the intent of Kennedy's remarks.

"He wasn't kidding."

The fact that the Johnny Bench story is the most impressive in Fireovid's body of work speaks volumes about his career. Striking out a hall of famer in a late-season relief appearance is a nice memory, but it tells you that his list of big moments is a little thin. The Bench story also shows where Fireovid's hapless career path meets up with his wave-the-white-flag humor. When you put in 15 years of work for 71 innings in the majors, a sense of humor is required. "I had a really strange career," he says. "There's not too many people that can say they never came close to accomplishing what they wanted to, but yet they played longer than they wanted to."

At 49 years old, Fireovid is a financial planner in his hometown of Bryan,

Ohio. When he reflects on his baseball career today, his delivery comes with a sigh and a chuckle. Even his current line of work provides a reminder of the cost of doing business in the minors for 15 seasons. "Look what I could have had in my 401K!" he says with a weary laugh. "What a waste of 15 years! How many years of my life I gave to baseball with that little to show. I walked away with nothing financially. What am I ever going to have to show for that?"

Throughout the 1980s, Fireovid was regarded as the best AAA pitcher in baseball. As he neared the end of his career in the early 1990s, he was reminded by sports writers that he surely had more AAA pitching wins than anyone in the previous decade. It would take some effort to prove it, but that's just as well. It's a distinction that makes Fireovid want to hurl—and we're not talking about a baseball. "Golly, who else would be stupid enough to have more than I did?" he asks, triggering his reflexive laugh. "I read that too many times for it to be wrong. That's certainly nothing I'm real proud of. To me, that's kind of a lesson in futility. That was never any feather in my cap. I was embarrassed by it."

"The last three years, I didn't want to play. You didn't want to tell people that too much because, first of all, they weren't going to feel sorry for you. I kept that very much to myself. I was sick of it when I was playing."

By almost any measure, the futility outweighed the feathers by the time he retired in 1993. He reached the majors with five teams but passed through nine organizations. The fact that he was consistently successful at AAA was only part of the reason that he was in demand. The scouting report on Fireovid included plenty of attributes outside his pitching repertoire. He was viewed as the consummate professional, a guy who set a good example for young pitchers. He followed the rules, maintained his training regimen, stayed out of trouble off the field and never rocked the boat with the team.

Today, he is most comfortable observing the absurdity of his baseball journey. But the longer you listen to his tale, the less it sounds like baseball and the more it sounds like everyday life. Name a thinking man's issue, and Fireovid has explored it—self-doubt, taking responsibility for your actions, being grateful for what you have. Pitching every fifth day leaves plenty of down time for contemplation.

"I knew full well what the situation was. The type of career I had forced me to look at my place in this world. I had to look at it from that perspective or I would have gone nuts. And it wasn't like I had to fool myself by giving myself little pep talks. I really did believe that I was very fortunate. Other players weren't forced to. They didn't have to look as hard to count their blessings."

After a steady climb through the Padres organization, Fireovid made his major league debut in 1981. He made four starts over the final weeks of the season. His 2.73 ERA was dramatically better than any of San Diego's regular starting pitchers. But in spring training the next season, he "never got a sniff." He spent the entire 1982 season with AAA Hawaii. "I didn't deserve to go up," he says. "I chipped my ankle, playing basketball the winter prior. I remember being kind of disenchanted with the game at that time."

By the time San Diego came calling again late in 1983, Fireovid was ready. He had won 14 games as a starter in AAA, and he expected to get a long look with the pitching-poor Padres in the final weeks. Instead, he made three relief appearances totaling five innings. It's not that the Padres were reluctant to audition a AAA pitcher; Greg Booker, who was promoted with Fireovid, pitched in twice as many games. Booker happened to be the son-in-law of San Diego general manager Jack McKeon. "So there's a little nepotism for you," Fireovid says. "Nothing against Greg. He's a great guy. What's he supposed to say? No thanks, I can't do that? You almost can't make that up—the GM's son-in-law."

Although Booker finished the season in San Diego with an ugly 7.71 ERA, he earned a spot on the Padres roster for the next six years. By contrast, Fireovid posted a sparkling 1.80 ERA. He was dealt to Philadelphia at the end of the season.

"At that point, I knew Cooperstown was out of the question," he deadpans.

"I knew I wasn't going to be a 20-game winner. But I didn't doubt that I could help somebody. I thought I could still start. I definitely knew I could be a long or middle reliever. At that time, I was already 27. You're really at a point there where you need to make something happen."

He could not have come much closer than he did with the Phillies. Fireovid was so clearly in Philadelphia's plans that he appeared in the 1984 opening day team photo. But the picture was taken a couple days before bad luck knocked him off the team. "They were trying to trade away Kevin Gross to keep me, and that fell through. I had a phenomenal spring, I was excited, I was with new blood. But they had to send me out to Portland, and I sulked a little bit, I think, subconsciously."

It didn't help his state of mind when he checked Philadelphia's box scores in the newspapers. While Gross appeared in 44 major league games, Fireovid struggled as a starter in Portland and was sent to the bullpen. Soon, however, he found his rhythm and allowed just one run over two months. The Phillies called him to the majors near the end of the season, but he spent most of his time watching from the bullpen.

On the final day of the season, Fireovid pitched well in both games of a doubleheader, lowering his ERA to 1.59. A Phillies coach told him that he was already in the team's plans for 1985. "I left there feeling pretty good. I felt that maybe this was OK. Lesson learned, I'll come back next year and do it over again, and I'll break camp with them. And of course, that didn't happen. They let me go a month after the season. That was the first time I'd ever been released. That's a little bit of a blow. Boy, I felt rejected."

Fireovid signed with the Chicago White Sox in 1985 and spent the majority of the season in AAA Buffalo. He did earn a call-up in July, but the opportunity quickly fizzled. He had spent the first half of the season in Buffalo's starting rotation, but the White Sox put him in the bullpen and used him just four times in four weeks. On the day Fireovid was sent back to AAA, Chicago manager Tony LaRussa accepted some of the blame for the pitcher's so-so outings, admitting he did not give Fireovid enough outings. "I really respected

him for saying that," he says. "It was hard to get mad at him for saying part
of it was his fault too."

Fireovid earned his first extended stay in the majors in 1986. After signing with Seattle, he spent all but six weeks in the majors, pitching out of the
Mariners bullpen. But there was little joy in the experience. Dick Williams, his
former manager in San Diego, had taken over the Mariners in May. Fireovid
had already witnessed Williams' confrontational personality, so he knew the
importance of keeping a low profile. Plus, when it came to pitching, there
was little work to be done. He appeared in just 10 games. "Mostly I just sat
there. But at that point in my career, it was more important to me just to be
in the major leagues than it was to put up great numbers in AAA. I'd rather be
screwed in the major leagues than be on all-star teams in AAA."

For a brief time that season, Fireovid appeared on the verge of a breakthrough. Seattle's season was going badly after the all-star break, and Williams shook up the starting pitching. To Fireovid's surprise, he was included
in the rotation. In his first start at Oakland, he limited the Athletics to two
singles in three innings. But in the fourth inning, he developed a blister on his
middle finger and had to come out of the game. The performance may have
been short, but it was nearly flawless. A few days later, Williams announced
he would return to his previous rotation. With no explanation, Fireovid was
sent back to the bullpen. He made three more relief appearances the rest of
the season. "I was never so happy to have a season end. I was on the road
within 10 minutes of the last pitch. That's when I wanted to get released.
They said, 'No, no, no, we've got big plans.' And I'm thinking, Give me a break."

The following spring training confirmed his suspicions. The Mariners had no
plans for Fireovid. He was released three weeks into spring training. By then,
being released was no big deal. What upset him was the timing. "They let me
go, just out of the blue. I was never a troublemaker. I was never a thorn in
anybody's side. I kept my mouth shut. Why wouldn't you let me go at the end
of the previous season?"

After his release from Seattle, he landed a short-term assignment with an
injury-depleted AAA team in Syracuse. But he knew the job was temporary

and his heart was never in it. He was ineffective in 10 relief outings before his release a month later. Fireovid was out of work and wondering how his career had come apart so quickly. "One year you're in the majors most of the year," he says, "and the next year you're playing softball."

Fireovid returned to baseball in 1988 and quickly resumed his role as AAA's go-to guy. He posted two winning seasons for Kansas City's farm team in Omaha, followed by a year with Montreal's affiliate in Indianapolis. While in Indy, he posted a 2.63 ERA, the best mark of his AAA career. But his most impressive achievement that year came with a pen in his hand. Fireovid chronicled his season in diary form in *The 26th Man: One Minor League Pitcher's Pursuit of a Dream*, a widely-acclaimed account of the ups and downs of minor league life.

He moved on to Pittsburgh's farm system in 1991 and crafted an ERA below 3.00 for the second straight year. Normally that would make someone a lock to pitch in the majors the following year. But Fireovid was 34 years old. He had not faced a big league lineup in five years.

So when Fireovid made the Texas Rangers out of spring training in 1992, it was an unexpected surprise. In fact, he earned the opening day win, coming on in relief in a 12-10 victory over Seattle. "I didn't throw very well," he admits. "I was the last pitcher standing when we went ahead." He took no measure of satisfaction in earning the pitching decision. The way he looked at it, he was only wearing a Rangers uniform because he had not figured out how to quit the game. "I felt like an outsider," he says. "That was nothing I was going to admit to anybody.

"The truth was, I was using them every bit as much as they were using me the last few years. If I could have found another career back here at home, I was gone. The last three years, I didn't want to play. Once I got there I adjusted all right, but I would have loved to have had a career in something that would have enabled me to not play. You didn't want to tell people that too much because, first of all, they weren't going to feel sorry for you. And you didn't want to come across like a spoiled little brat. I kept that very much to myself. I was sick of it when I was still playing."

After three relief appearances with the Rangers in April, he returned to Oklahoma City for yet another productive season in AAA. Fireovid finally found his way out of baseball in the spring of 1993. A mysterious neck injury prevented him from turning his head without pain. So after a couple outings at Oklahoma City, he went home for good.

Fireovid had no plan for getting on with life, but he was relieved that the baseball safety net was gone—no more pitching jobs were waiting on the other side of winter. During most baseball offseasons, he had worked for the city of Bryan, Ohio, supplementing a minor league salary that averaged around $40,000. But the work also delayed the future, a thought that plagued him one winter while testing sewer lines for the city's engineering department.

"They would give me dye and a map of the sewer lines in the town," he recalls. "There were some concerns back then that some of the sewer lines and sanitary lines were not right." So he trudged around town putting drops of orange dye in downspouts. Then he followed the water flow through neighborhoods and pried open manhole covers, "waiting to see if the orange water showed up." The job did not help Fireovid discover a career path, but he ruled out sewer testing. "It was kind of a circular thought process. I would think, What am I doing this for? And then it would lead to, If I don't want to do this, what am I playing baseball for? So it was like ping pong. There's a lot of soul searching that can go on while you're checking downspouts."

When Fireovid left the familiar footing of the pitchers mound for good, he found his way into the investment business with the help of a high school classmate. "I didn't know the difference between a stock and a bond, and I didn't care either," he says, recalling how grateful he was to focus on something other than baseball. "I became a broker. Probably for the first year, the people who came in to talk to me about their money, they knew more about money than I did. That's a bad situation for both of us. But I stayed with it and paid some dues."

Today his financial planning operation includes his second wife, Michelle, who contributes her marketing knowledge to his work. "We're quite successful here. If I'd have known I was going to land on my feet the way I did,

I would have had a lot less sleepless nights the last five years of my career. You've got to be an absolute moron to not worry about how you're going to support a family when you're in your 30s and you're still playing AAA."

Finding a rewarding profession helped Fireovid come to terms with his star-crossed career. Baseball may have antagonized him at times, but its charms far surpass anything that happens while managing money. "It's not even close. This is not a passion," he says. "I grew up as a boy throwing balls against the wall. That's all I did. I was in my mid 30s before I stopped doing it. That's all I wanted to do. I don't wake up in the morning and start getting all giddy because I get to go to the office. There's a little adrenaline there if I've had a good day or I bring on a new client. But it doesn't compare to even a normal day in the minors."

Fireovid believes he would have been successful in the majors over the long haul, but he's not about to grandstand. He never feared the free swingers of his era. "The guys who used to drive me nuts were the contact hitters. They just fight everything off. The kind of stuff I had, they didn't have any trouble fighting it off."

And that reminds Fireovid of one of the many lessons he learned along the way. There was nothing wrong with his pitches—a fastball in the 90s and a decent slider—but he never upgraded his arsenal. "That was me having just enough success to not learn a really good change-up," he admits. "I should have developed a really good one, and I was a good enough athlete to do that. That's something I have to take to the grave with me. That was on my shoulders. If I had gotten knocked around a lot earlier, I might have been better in the long run. I could have had a pretty decent career. I can't blame the coaches. That was me."

Other lessons were more hopeful. He learned about gratitude from relief pitcher Tug McGraw. The two pitchers crossed paths with Philadelphia in 1984. The flamboyant McGraw was in the final season of his 20-year career. "Every single day when he would come into the clubhouse, he would throw the doors open and scream, 'Another day in the big leagues!' This guy had been doing this for two decades, and he still had all that enthusiasm."

With each glimpse of big-league life, Fireovid discovered the importance of judging people for himself. "Steve Carlton had the reputation for being surly and self-centered, and nothing could have been further from the truth. He was a neat guy. The next year I was in Chicago with Tom Seaver. He had the golden boy image, and he's the guy who wouldn't give me the time of day."

When your dream is just out of reach for most of 15 years, you need to draw something positive from the pursuit. That is why he values the lessons. "I always just tried to be appreciative for what I had. I never wanted any pity," says Fireovid, who has five children. "I'm pretty grateful I had the type of career I had. I'm very happy now. I certainly appreciate what I have now. If I would have been making $300,000 a year for the last seven or eight years of my life before I did this, I wouldn't appreciate what I have now. Maybe I'm a little hungrier than I would have been otherwise. I think things worked out just fine. I don't harbor any bitterness at all."

There are no baseball photos on the walls of Fireovid's office, nothing designed to impress clients. There is just one souvenir, a single baseball. Late in his career, Fireovid pitched a season of winter ball in Puerto Rico, opting for a decent payday and a break from working for the city back home. For one night, while pitching for the Bayamon Metros, everything came together just right. Fireovid tossed a two-hit shutout. Ten strikeouts, no walks. "I felt like I was 25 again," he says.

The next morning, he checked the box scores from around the Puerto Rican league. His pitching performance was far and away the best of the night. That was important. Years earlier, Fireovid had set a goal: One day in your life, be the best in the world at what you do. "I didn't think about it until I got back to my apartment that night. I thought, This was your night. Although it was in the dead of winter, you were the best in the entire world at what you did one day in your life."

His only regret was forgetting to save the ball from the final out. But when he returned to the stadium the next day, there it was, tucked in the web of his glove. Today the dirty old ball sits on a shelf across from his office desk, a reminder of everything great about playing baseball.

Reality check

Although Riccardo Ingram
felt cheated by baseball,
the hurt didn't
last long.

When **Riccardo Ingram** has something to say, good or bad, he punctuates his words with a smile that swells into a chuckle. Friendly is his default setting. There is a place for that kind of enthusiasm when you manage a single-A baseball team.

Managers are supposed to make 21-year-old kids believe in their abilities. But Ingram is also a realist. So at some point, he is going to deliver his reality-check message—the one that makes his Fort Myers Miracle players stop in their tracks and listen to the gospel according to Riccardo.

"Everything can be a desire, but it can't be a goal," says Ingram. "Goals are something you can control. In the arena of professional baseball, it can be a desire to be in the big leagues. I treated it as a goal, like if I hit .350 in AAA, they've got to play me in the big leagues. Not necessarily."

It is the ultimate wet-blanket message for a kid in his early 20s, but Ingram prefers to lay out the truth for his prospects in the Minnesota Twins organization. His speech boils down to this: Sometimes being good enough isn't good enough. Be ready for that.

Coming out of Coffee High School in Douglas, Georgia, Ingram had no idea what to expect along the road to athletic stardom. He was good enough to earn scholarship offers in baseball and football. Georgia Tech football coach Bill Curry won the recruiting battle against the University of Georgia by offering Ingram a chance to play both sports. "I was thinking football," Ingram says. "I liked playing baseball. I just didn't want to give it up if I had a chance to play both." As a junior, Ingram hit .426, leading the Atlantic Coast Conference with 99 RBIs. In the fall, he was an all-ACC selection at safety. At the end of his junior year in 1987, the Detroit Tigers selected Ingram in the fourth round. But he had unfinished football business, so he stayed at Georgia Tech to play his senior season.

Although he attended the NFL combines in 1988, he knew that people would question his commitment to football. "I scared a lot of teams off by being a dual-sport athlete. Is this guy going to pull the Bo Jackson thing?

They were nervous because I hadn't made a decision, and they knew I had been drafted in baseball. Nobody wanted to draft me." A half-dozen teams called as soon as the draft ended, hoping to lure Ingram to the NFL as a free agent. But with a $40,000 signing bonus on the table in baseball, Ingram decided to become an outfielder in single-A ball, first in Fayetteville, North Carolina, then in Lakeland, Florida.

 **"It takes a while for the swelling to go down. You don't just walk away from something you did all of your life and say, 'OK, change gears.' It's still in there. The only healer is time."**

When his average hovered around .200 with Lakeland, Ingram began to wonder if he had made a terrible mistake. The Tigers were at least three minor league jumps and several years away. But just 30 minutes down the road, the Tampa Bay Buccaneers were gearing up for the NFL season. He figured he could make a quick impression on Buccaneers coach Ray Perkins, who had led Alabama against Ingram's Georgia Tech teams. As he pondered his future, Ingram realized he had never really come to terms with leaving football. So he left the minor leagues and thought it over for a few days. "I was a little bit tortured because I had played football all my life," he says. "I thought I could be a good strong safety in the NFL. I'd seen guys I'd played against in previous years playing in the league.

"The minor leagues, after being in a program where you were a two-sport star, that was like the real world. It was an awakening. I was like, Man, I've gotta do this for however many years it takes to make it, versus going over there (Tampa) and maybe making the club. I really considered it, but my mom basically talked me out out of it. She said, 'You committed to the Tigers, and you have to honor your contract and see what happens.' When I came back, I knew I had to go at it whole-heartedly, follow the program and do whatever they ask."

Ingram spent another season in Lakeland, followed by a full season with AA London, Ontario. But despite being a high draft pick, Ingram had a hard time getting on the fast track with the Detroit organization. After three years in the minors, he was still not an everyday player. "I was not happy with the way I was treated by those guys. They didn't really clarify what they expected of me. It was like, You're here, just play. I don't think I was treated like a fourth-round guy who was a prospect. I don't think I was being developed correctly."

In his second season in London, Ingram became a fixture in the lineup, and he rewarded the organization with 17 home runs and a .271 average. He earned a promotion to AAA Toledo in 1992, inching slowly toward a major league opportunity as his batting average improved. In 1994, Ingram's third season with the Mud Hens, manager Larry Parrish gave Ingram the right kind of encouragement. "He said something to the effect of, If you hit 15 to 20 home runs and drive in this many runs, you'll be in the big leagues," Ingram remembers. "I thought, OK, there's a goal, there's a direction. That year I got off to a good start. That gave me the focus I needed."

As the summer heated up, so did his bat. Ingram's average climbed to .330 as Toledo battled Richmond for first place. It wasn't the major leagues, but Ingram was focused on the here and now. So when the Mud Hens blew a particularly painful game—Ingram stood in left field and watched a game-winning home run sail over his head into the seats—he came unglued. "I was fuming. I was one of the veteran guys, one of the leaders. I picked a water cooler up and slammed it." Then he called out the team's bullpen closer, who served up the decisive pitch on an 0-2 count. When Ingram's tirade was finished, Parrish called the outfielder into the manager's office. Regardless of his standing as a valuable veteran, Ingram knew he had overreacted, so he braced himself for the skipper's wrath.

"You've been a good leader and you've played well," Parrish told him. "But...you're going to the big leagues."

After seven years in the minors, he was ready to taste the big-league life. In Detroit, manager Sparky Anderson welcomed Ingram and immediately gave him a chance to get his feet wet, pinch running for Cecil Fielder. The next night Ingram started in left field at Seattle. "My first at-bat, I was so nervous," he says. "I remember going up there facing a lefty junk baller (Dave Fleming). I worked the count pretty good but I was so excited that I ended up jamming myself and breaking my bat. But I got back in the flow.

"The second at bat I hit a deep fly ball to center. I thought it was out of the park. But then there was Mr. Griffey, who brought it off the wall with one of those spectacular catches. I thought, That ball is crushed! How did he catch that ball? I got back in the dugout and Tony Phillips said, 'Hey son, there's no money out there in center.'"

For the next month, Ingram settled into a supporting role with the Tigers. He started five games, scattering five hits in 20 at bats. His best day was a 2-for-3 effort against Texas pitcher Kenny Rogers. Otherwise, Ingram was on call as a pinch runner and late-inning defensive replacement. For a guy knocking the cover off the ball in AAA, it was not much of a showcase. That was the part Ingram could not understand. Outfielder Eric Davis was on the disabled list, and Detroit's backup outfielders were struggling at the plate. The door appeared wide open for an experienced prospect who had mastered the minor leagues. Ingram felt a bit cheated. "Internally, you're not happy about what's going on, but you can't show too much outward emotion," he says. "You're in the big leagues finally. You're happy to be there. You could always be in AAA. The competitive nature inside you makes you want to get out there and contribute and have a chance to help the team and show what you can do.

"People always say they get screwed. I hate to say that because sometimes that's overused and used as an excuse. But I couldn't figure it out. I didn't complain about it, but in the back of my mind I thought, This doesn't seem right. I felt like I was a good teammate and a good guy."

With the major league baseball strike looming near the end of the 1994 season, the Tigers sent Ingram back to Toledo to finish the season. At the end of the year, he became a free agent, confident that he was on the verge of landing in the majors for an extended stay. He was already acclimated to the big leagues, and he had nothing left to prove in the minors. "It was a combi-

nation of my mind was right and the focus was right. I'm thinking, I've got to do it now. I'm 28. I know I can do it. I need to get off to a good start, stay hot all year and hopefully get up there and get an opportunity to play. And then maybe get two or three years in the big leagues and finish up a good career."

Ingram signed with the Minnesota Twins in 1995. He was so confident in his ability that he barely flinched when he was sent to Salt Lake City at the end of spring training. After bashing AAA pitching for half a season, the Twins brought him up. Like Detroit, Minnesota had every reason to give Ingram some starts in the outfield. The Twins had a 25-50 record, and aside from Kirby Puckett, the team's outfield consisted of little more than untested youngsters. With the season slipping away, Minnesota had the perfect chance to evaluate Ingram, the leading hitter in the AAA Pacific Coast League.

But the Twins rarely called on Ingram during his first two weeks. He served as the designated hitter twice and made a pair of pinch-hit appearances. In ten trips to the plate, he singled and walked twice. On a road trip in early August, Twins general manager Terry Ryan phoned him at the team hotel. Minnesota was shopping for a pitcher. They needed to free up Ingram's roster spot. "You might as well take it," Ingram told Ryan. "I'm not using it."

He returned to Salt Lake City still determined to make some noise. "That's what I learned from the year before," he says. "Don't go down and sulk." He won the PCL batting title with a .348 mark while driving in 85 runs. But being the best hitter not in the big leagues was little consolation. "I guess that was the straw that broke the camel's back." His voice trails off, looking for an explanation. "I felt like there was nothing else I could do. I needed to get some (major league) at bats to show what I could do, but it didn't happen."

Ingram did his homework in the off-season, looking for a team that needed outfield depth in the majors. He chose the San Diego Padres. At the end of spring training, he had a .361 average, better than starting outfielders Tony Gwynn, Rickey Henderson and Steve Finley. "I had an outstanding spring. In my mind, I made that club. I actually even played in an exhibition game in San Diego. The next game was opening day in Chicago. They sent me down that night. That was harder than anything I ever dealt with."

Ingram told general manager Kevin Towers and manager Bruce Bochy he was ready to go home. For good. Towers and Bochy told him to take a couple days off and think about it. But what was there to think about? Ingram had won the previous season's AAA batting title, and now he had out-hit two future hall of famers in spring training. If that wasn't good enough to earn a roster spot, why spend another year knocking around the minors?

But he did agree to report to AAA Las Vegas. In the end, it was not so much a baseball decision as a personal one. Mike Sharperson, a veteran infielder and former Dodgers third baseman, had struck up a friendship with Ingram in spring training. Sharperson's pitch to Ingram was simple: If I can muddle through another AAA season at age 34, so can you. "He basically talked me into coming back. After that, we were roommates on the road. I kind of knew this was going to be it. I had had a couple good years in AAA. I had the awesome spring. I figured I might as well finish it out and see what happens."

After a few weeks in Las Vegas, Sharperson got the call from the Padres. San Diego third baseman Ken Caminiti was hurt, and Sharperson was in the right place at the right time, leaving Ingram to fend for himself in AAA. As the Las Vegas players made plans for Sharperson's call-up party, the two friends sat talking in the clubhouse. Ingram was happy for his friend, and in turn, Sharperson assured Ingram that his day was coming. "You're starting to come on now," he said. "You'll come up there and join me soon." Ingram appreciated the words of encouragement, but he told his buddy he would pass on the party that night, preferring to go home to his family. The two friends hugged, and Sharperson promised to call the next day when he joined the Padres in Montreal.

Several hours later, Ingram's phone startled him from his sleep. Sharperson had swerved off the concrete edge of the highway and into an embankment. "So I'm getting up to get dressed and go to the hospital to see what's going on," Ingram says. "They called back in about 10 minutes and said he didn't make it."

Sharperson's death was the beginning of the end of Ingram's playing days. He no longer had the energy to make peace with baseball's fickle fortunes.

"That was the culmination, when Sharperson died. That was a major blow for me. I think I was just frustrated by the whole scenario. I wasn't into it. I just couldn't believe what had happened. Things became so minuscule after that. I wasn't thinking about the game. It was more than I had ever dealt with." He finished the year hitting .249, ready for a different challenge. "I felt like I could do something else and let the stress go away," he says.

After four months as a sales rep for Coca-Cola in Toledo, Ingram returned to Georgia Tech and completed his undergraduate degree. It was time to put his education to work. So when the Minnesota Twins called, it seemed like a cruel joke. The organization was looking for a minor league coach. They wanted to know if Ingram could teach hitting. Were they serious?

Too much pain. Too many hard memories. That's what went through Ingram's mind. That's what he wanted to tell them. His eight at bats with the Twins are part of the reason he refers to his major league career as "a sip of coffee," rather than the traditional cup. But the opportunity was exciting, and he signed on for a season of single A in Fort Wayne, Indiana. It was the first of six seasons as a hitting instructor or manager in the Twins organization.

It is several hours before game time on a hot summer afternoon in Fort Myers. Ingram is relaxing in the manager's office in Hammond Stadium, the home of Minnesota's Gulf Coast League team. The players are trickling into the clubhouse, and Ingram is still a couple hours from filling out the evening's lineup card. He leans back at his desk and tries to explain the differences between sitting in the manager's office and facing the daily stress of proving your mettle as a player.

"It's worlds apart," he says without hesitation. "As a player, you care about your team, but you worry, more or less, about your individual accomplishments. The pressure is always on you to get it done. As a coach or a manager, your focus is to develop, to help, to teach, to prepare for what lies ahead. I'm just going to try to get these guys ready for the next level. That's my only job."

The job is made a lot easier when the players are buying what Ingram is selling. "You teach the guys who want to learn. You teach the guys who trust in what you're telling them. You can't convince everyone. If someone wants to think, Hey, he didn't do anything up there (in the majors), and they don't want to listen to me, I can't control that."

If any of these single-A players want to look up their manager's major league statistics, they will find six hits and a .194 average. "It's probably their first impression—he wasn't very good, he couldn't get it done," Ingram admits. "People will take what they will out of it. If people know the game, they know you didn't just wake up and go up there for 16 games. I don't feel bad about it. It doesn't upset me. I didn't get a shot. But you can't explain that. People don't want to hear that."

So Ingram is not about to serve up excuses. In fact, he takes a moment to think about his statistics as objectively as he can, wondering exactly what someone might say at first glance. "That's brutal," he says, breaking into a laugh.

After such a brief major league showcase, it would have been easy to get bogged down in bitterness. But Ingram's frustration faded quickly after joining the coaching ranks. "It takes a while for the swelling to go down. You don't just walk away from something you did all of your life and say, 'OK, change gears.' It's still in there. The only healer is time. After my first full year of coaching, I was convinced that it was water under the bridge. It's gone. I can't worry about it. I can't reflect on it too much. Now I am in the environment in a different role. That's what helped me."

On the other hand, when you begin coaching in your early 30s, all the playing skills are still in place. Surprisingly, he never had the urge to step into the batter's box and start hacking until one night a few seasons ago. He was the hitting instructor in Fort Myers, and the players were in a collective slump. Frustrated, Ingram picked up a bat and headed for the field. "This is ridiculous," he told them. "What's so hard about hitting the ball?" He ripped the first six batting practice pitches around the field. The seventh one went sailing out of the park. "And their jaws dropped, like, What are you doing?" says Ingram, still with great amusement. "That's something that's with you all your life."

As long as he is surrounded by bats and men willing to throw batting practice, Ingram can wonder. Most of the time, he doesn't. He is content to know there is still a AAA batting champion in there somewhere. "I feel like if you give me a month to train, I probably could go play at AAA at 38 and maybe do OK if I could hold up physically."

The realist in Ingram knows that will never happen. If he is going to reach the major leagues again, it will be on a coaching staff. He would like to manage in the majors someday. But Ingram is not banking on anything. He has learned a lot, watching how a baseball life plays out.

"It's my desire to be a manager in the bigs," he says. "Sure, I want to. But it's not a goal."

RICCARDO INGRAM

ROBIN JENNINGS

One fair shot

26

Robin Jennings put up big numbers in the minors, but major league breaks were hard to come by.

 In the spring of 2004, **Robin Jennings** was only halfway through his rehab from shoulder surgery. Still, he was taking his best shot at winning an outfield job with the Tampa Bay Devil Rays. Things were not going well. "Every throw was killing me," Jennings says. "My arm felt like it was going to fall off."

When the Devil Rays released him, Jennings called it quits. Today, when people learn that he once played in the major leagues, Jennings can wrap up the story by mentioning the shoulder injury and the retirement. That can be the end of it.

But in reality, Robin Jennings retired because of a broken baseball heart.

In the end, too many higher-ups made too many decisions that took their toll on him. After 12 years of professional ball, Jennings was no longer a prospect—not a guy with upside. "I always hear, You're young, I can't believe you're not playing anymore. You're only 32," says Jennings, just one year removed from his tryout with the Devil Rays. "They don't realize if you're not a starter in the big leagues at 32, you are done. You're actually an old AAA player."

Jennings began his minor league career as a lightly-regarded prospect, drafted by the Chicago Cubs out of Manatee Junior College in the 33rd round in 1991. He spent three seasons hitting .300 in single A, followed by a breakout AA season that included 17 home runs. He began the 1996 season at AAA Iowa, where he made an immediate impression. In the first week of the season, Jennings hit three home runs in one game. That feat earned him an immediate call to Chicago for his major league debut.

What happened next sent Jennings down an irreversible path. His first action with the Cubs came as a pinch hitter. Two days later, he pinch-hit again. Then again. After four-plus seasons as an everyday player in the minors, the Cubs were asking Jennings to make the jump to the major leagues by batting a couple times a week against the top relief pitchers in the game. He spent a month in Chicago, batting 14 times, each time as a pinch hitter. "They knew I was going to sit on the bench," Jennings says. "I went up to fill in for the left-handed hitter off the bench, Dave Magadan. It was kind of ridiculous. That's not really a confidence builder for a young player. It's not really pro-ductive to come in as a 24 year old and hit against setup men and closers."

Jennings returned to Iowa in May and resumed his role as an everyday outfielder. In September, the Cubs brought him back to the majors. After four more pinch-hit appearances, the Cubs finally handed Jennings the keys to right field for the final two weeks of the season. In his last eight starts, Jennings hit .346. Finally, he had shown the front office what he could do, but he was left with mixed feelings. "I was extremely disappointed (after the season)," he says. "There was never any communication, never a call into the office saying, Hey, you're a young player, we're sorry we're not playing you but we know you work hard. It was silence and intimidation. Be happy to be here—you might not be here tomorrow. It's not the way you bring up a young player."

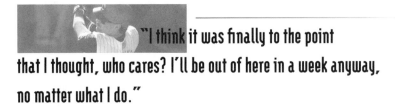

"I think it was finally to the point that I thought, who cares? I'll be out of here in a week anyway, no matter what I do."

In the spring of 1997, Jennings' hopes were dashed by a torn wrist liga-ment, forcing him to play his way back in AAA. But after another strong performance in Iowa, his second September call-up was more of the same: nine appearances, six of them as a pinch hitter.

Despite the frustration, Jennings was coming to terms with his role in the Cubs organization. As a player drafted in the 33rd round, he knew he stood at the back of the line among Chicago's prospects. Like all teams, the Cubs wanted their top draft picks to reach the majors. Scouts and general managers look like great talent evaluators when the blue-chip players pan

out, instead of the guys who sign for gas money. Chicago had plenty of top-end outfield talent in the mid-1990s, including Pedro Valdes (12th round, 1990 draft), Doug Glanville (1st, 1991), Brant Brown (3rd, 1992) and Brooks Kieschnick (1st in 1993). "In the time that I was still young enough to be an everyday player, they made it very clear that I wasn't going to be (a top prospect) with them. I always knew I had to work extremely hard and still wait for Brant or Brooks to fail before I was going to get an opportunity. So it wasn't a rosy outlook for me in the Iowa years."

But at least Jennings knew what he was up against. After playing the 1998 season entirely in the minors, he owed the Chicago organization one more year. He was determined to look out for number one. "That was the toughest year, trying to play for yourself," he says. "Realizing as a minor leaguer that you have to play for yourself and not for your organization was something I was never accustomed to. My parents taught me to respect authority. And when you put up good numbers and you love your organization and you want to play well for them, finding out it doesn't matter how you play is very disheartening."

The 1999 season reminded Jennings why he was itching for free agency. After hitting .309 in Iowa, he made just five more pinch-hit appearances in Chicago. As his days in the Cubs organization came to a close, he tried to dwell on some of the positives. Luis Gonzalez and Mark Grace had made him feel welcome in the big leagues. Dave Magadan, the injured player Jennings replaced on the roster, shared his home. But before he left the Cubs organization, Jennings spoke his mind to the key decision makers in Chicago. "I went to (manager) Jim Riggleman and (general manager) Ed Lynch and said, 'The way you handled my career over the last three years is an absolute debacle.'"

With that, Jennings set out to renew the dream that got bogged down in Iowa. At 28, there was still time to carve out a career in the majors. Jennings signed with the Minnesota Twins in 2000 and was assigned to AAA Salt Lake City. This time, however, Jennings had a bit of leverage. His contract stipulated that he could become a free agent if he did not play for the Twins by July 1. When the date arrived, Jennings was hitting .310, leading the Pacific Coast

League in runs, hits and RBIs. The Twins, meanwhile, were 12 games under .500 and had no interest in bringing him to the majors. Jennings packed up and left. "I went to my agent and said, 'Where does it stop? I can't do any better than I am right now and apparently it's not good enough.'"

Three days later, he joined the Cincinnati organization at AAA Louisville. Jennings says the Reds told him he would be brought up to Cincinnati within two weeks. Wanting nothing left to chance, Jennings made it easy for Cincinnati to keep its word. He raised his game a notch, scorching the pace he had set in the Twins organization. But two weeks came and went. So did the month of September, when major league rosters expand. All the while, Jennings was tearing the cover off the ball. In 32 games at Louisville, he hit .377 and drove in 27 runs. In a cruel twist, Jennings' old Cubs nemesis, Brooks Kieschnick, parlayed his .277 average at Louisville into twelve hitless at bats in Cincinnati.

"Once again," Jennings says, "I just got blatantly lied to by an organization."

At the end of the season, Reds player development director Tim Naehring told Jennings that Reds manager Jack McKeon had not wanted any minor leaguers called up. Jennings responded, "Tim, what I did for your team and what I did on the year merited a call-up. I don't care who you want to put it on."

When Naehring made overtures to Jennings about coming back the next year, Jennings knew better. What was he supposed to do? Hit .400? He added Cincinnati to his growing list of organizations that could take a flying leap. "Maybe I shouldn't have been so headstrong in a few situations, but hindsight is always 20-20. And it wasn't as though I ever got into an altercation or a yelling match. I just simply stated the way I felt to the people who lied to me."

Jennings had high hopes for the 2001 season. He signed with Oakland and drove in 16 runs in the exhibition season, second only to Jason Giambi, the reigning American League MVP. "I had an incredible amount of hope to be in the big leagues and still be a starter, even after all the tough years," he says.

Jennings made the opening day roster with Oakland. But before he could

establish himself, the situation turned sour. "Once again politics took over," says Jennings. "There was just no way around it. Jeremy Giambi (Jason's younger brother) was going to be in the outfield. I had coaches on the staff and players saying, 'You should be the starting right fielder.'"

Jennings hit .250 in 20 games, but Oakland sent him to AAA Sacramento, where he spent six weeks driving in runs and hitting better than .300. Then he was on the move again, traded to Colorado for veteran slugger Ron Gant. The Rockies assigned him to AAA Colorado Springs, his fifth AAA team in less than two seasons. He was now the undisputed poster boy for the almost-major leaguer.

But the wild ride continued when Colorado brought him to the majors after 11 AAA games. To Jennings, it looked like a decent opportunity. Gant was gone, and the Rockies needed another outfielder with some pop in his bat. Jennings joined the team in San Francisco, where he was immediately inserted in the lineup, playing left field and batting seventh. "I show up and I'm starting. So I was thinking, Wow, am I actually going to get a chance to start in the big leagues? It was crazy."

Jennings went 0-for-3 in his debut. It was also his farewell. The next morning, Colorado manager Buddy Bell broke the news to Jennings that he had been traded. His Rockies career was over in less than 24 hours. Despite all the false starts, Jennings tried to be optimistic. After all, three teams had now acquired his services in 2001, and the season was barely half over. Maybe his stellar hitting in AAA over the past two seasons was creating some buzz among major league general managers.

Then Bell told Jennings where he was traded—Cincinnati. It made perfect sense that the Reds would bring back a player who hit .377 in their system the previous season. Maybe Cincinnati wanted to give him the opportunity that he was denied in 2000. But once again, he was sent straight to AAA. "So I got to Louisville and did the same thing I was doing the year before. I was playing for myself at that point and scratching my head at what was going on."

But Jennings had an idea that things might be different the second time around with Cincinnati. Bob Boone had replaced Jack McKeon as manager, and Boone had been high on Jennings for years after watching him play in the Arizona Fall League in 1995. So after 28 games in AAA, Jennings got another call to the majors. As he flew to Montreal to join the Reds, he had no idea what to expect. He was joining his sixth team of the season, and he already had reason to distrust the organization. "I think it was finally to the point that I thought, who cares? I'll be out of here in a week anyway, no matter what I do."

When Jennings walked into the visitors' clubhouse in Montreal, Boone greeted him with three little words: You're hitting fifth. It was exactly what Jennings wanted to hear. Still, his enthusiasm was tempered by the memory of the same scenario in Colorado, where the honeymoon ended before the next morning's breakfast.

But this trip to the majors started with a bang. In his first game, Jennings knocked around the Expos pitchers for a single, two doubles and a triple. He put up a 4-for-6 night with three RBIs. Five nights later, the Reds returned to Cincinnati to face Pittsburgh. He introduced himself to the locals with a bases-loaded triple off the center field wall in the third inning. In the fourth inning, Jennings came to the plate with the bases loaded again. When Pirates reliever Damaso Marte left a 3-2 fastball high and inside, Jennings got all of it, adding a grand slam to his home debut. "The ball went over the fence," he says, "and I was in shock."

After four games, Jennings had two home runs and 10 RBIs. He had finally made his breakthrough. As the Reds stumbled through the final weeks of a 66-96 season, Jennings played on a regular basis. He hit .286. His 14 RBIs projected to 80-plus over a full season. The Reds rewarded him with a guaranteed major league contract for 2002 worth $310,000, the first big payday of his career.

By his own admission, Jennings had a poor spring training the following year, compounded by personal issues away from the field. Before heading north from Florida, the Reds told Jennings they had acquired another outfielder, hoping to add more speed to the team. The player was Reggie Taylor,

who had one major league hit and one stolen base to his name in 18 at bats in the majors. Jennings was headed back to Louisville. "Once again, I couldn't believe it. That might have been the straw that broke the camel's back. I went down that year, and I just couldn't put it together. I just had a horrendous year. I think that was the start of the end of my career."

His third stint in Louisville was a nightmare. Collecting a major league salary did not ease the pain. In fact, the big checks only made it worse. "As cliched as it sounds, I had never played for the money. The whole year I was playing poorly in Louisville, everyone from the manager to the bullpen catcher knew how much I made. And they were saying, 'You're laughing all the way to the bank.' I wasn't laughing about anything," Jennings says. His voice grows a bit agitated, clearly still frustrated with the memory. "I was playing pathetically. I didn't care about the monetary amount. I was embarrassed about my performance on the field."

Physically, Jennings was suffering too. He endured 18 cortisone injections for a bad back, and he finished the season with a .222 average. After his eye-opening performance one year earlier, he suddenly found himself a struggling minor league veteran with an injury.

He closed out his playing days in 2003 on another sour note, dislocating his shoulder while diving for a ball in Louisville. To add insult to injury, when he asked for his release in order to retire, the Reds demoted him to AA Chattanooga. It was a final, lonely reminder of the politics of professional sports. "Guys like me don't get demoted," he says somberly. "We get released."

Today, Jennings and his wife Kristen make their home in Park City, Utah. They fell in love with the surroundings when he played half a season in Salt Lake City. For Jennings, the first year out of baseball was a welcome look at normal family life. "I had the greatest summer of my life, doing everything I hadn't done in 12 years," he says. "Taking the kids to the pool, barbecues, bike rides, hikes on the trails, taking my dog on runs—everything I could do to be away from baseball and be with my family."

But when you have played the game forever, it is hard to walk away entirely. When Jennings was asked to lend his know-how for a local baseball clinic, he wondered how he would feel. He had not picked up his glove since bowing out with Tampa Bay almost a year earlier. "I thought, I'm still in good enough shape to play, but I don't want to. And I was fine with that. I like the fact that I'm done."

Professionally, Jennings is keeping his distance from the game. He opened a perfume studio in Park City, a resort town that caters to skiers and snow-boarders. Vacationers can come in and custom blend a perfume or cologne right there in the store. Obviously, there is no overlap between the perfume business and professional baseball. It is a clean break, exactly the way Jennings wants it.

"I'm only 32 now, and everybody thinks I'm young and in good shape. But I've had six invasive surgeries before the age of 32. It doesn't matter how I look aesthetically. It's more trauma than most people will have in their lifetime. I'm happy I can do other things. I love snowboarding, I love tennis. I love outdoor things. I find other ways to get the competitive spirit out."

Being just one year removed from professional baseball is far different than getting a decade under your belt. By then, families and careers have been built, difficult personal decisions have been made. But for now, some of the injustices of Jennings' career remain fresh in his mind. So far, that's not a problem. "I was very proud of myself for the work ethic I upheld through some of the adversity I faced in my career," he says. "I really, truly loved the game of baseball for 85 percent of my career. It wasn't until the last couple years that I lost my desire to play the game.

"But there's always going to be the perfectionist in me that says I could have done better. I do still wish I could have played better under certain circumstances, and I wish my (major league) career was longer. I felt like mentally I let myself get beat a couple of times. Otherwise I look back and have nothing but good memories."

Mostly, though, Jennings looks ahead.

"That was the first third of my life. I still have two thirds to go. That's the way I'm taking it."

The fictional king

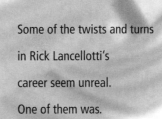

Some of the twists and turns in Rick Lancellotti's career seem unreal. One of them was.

Ask **Rick Lancellotti** about most any episode in his base-ball career, and you spark a new ember of total passion.

"I was infatuated with the game," says Lancellotti, brimming with the conviction of an infomercial pitchman. "I loved it. I couldn't get enough of it."

Fifteen years have passed since he took his last cut in a major league batter's box, but Lancellotti can easily piece together the events of his 17-year professional career. The facts are right there at his fingertips, while all the emotions bubble just below the surface. That part is a double-edged sword. There are moments in his career that take strength to revisit. If he were wired differently, he might have been swallowed by regret.

Good thing he loves baseball.

Lancellotti was never a sure bet to be a professional. As a high school player, he was a singles hitter with little promise. But he filled out a bit at Glassboro State College and learned to use his legs in his hitting stroke. As a sophomore and junior, he reached double digits in home runs. "All of a sudden the ball just started to go," he remembers.

The Pittsburgh Pirates drafted him in the 11th round in 1977. After two seasons in single A, the left-handed hitting Lancellotti was ticketed for AA Buffalo, where he made the most of the stadium's short dimensions down the right field line. He slugged 41 home runs to lead the Eastern League.

He moved to AAA Portland, Oregon in 1980, but when he failed to put up more eye-popping numbers, he was sent back to Buffalo. Demoralized, Lancellotti began to stew. "They give you three days to report, and for three days, I'm like, What am I doing? I might as well just quit. This sucks. If (hitting 41 home runs in Buffalo) wasn't good enough, what am I supposed to do?"

Lancellotti had to face a cold reality. Like most minor leaguers, he was no longer on the fast track to the majors. He was becoming one of the many players sifted into the general talent pool. He didn't like it, but he intended to

do something about it. "It was right then and there that I realized there were much stronger forces than I could have imagined that controlled the game," he says. "It's not about, You did good and you're going to go up. It's a cold-blooded, ruthless way of life. If you don't adapt to that, it will eat you alive. That's when the blood started running colder and I started getting more intense about the game. I realized that people could take it away from me in a heartbeat."

His awakening about professional baseball came just in time. The emotional tests were just beginning. Shortly after his return to Buffalo, Lancellotti was traded to San Diego. At first the Padres told him he was headed to AAA Hawaii, but he wound up in AA Amarillo. "Here I am sitting in the stands with my suitcase about two hours before anyone shows up, and I'm just watching some guy water the field. It's like a dust bowl of a town. I've just hit rock bottom. I figured this is probably the end. But you get the uniform on, you start to make some friends, you start to have some fun and all of a sudden it starts to come back to you again. The game just messes with your emotions so much that it's hard to move on. It's a very mental game."

Lancellotti graduated to Hawaii the following year and hit 20 home runs, renewing his status as a big-league prospect. A year later, as he finished a second AAA season, Hawaii manager Doug Rader called the team together and reminded the players to keep their focus over the last few weeks. In turn, the manager promised to help the players reach any realistic statistical milestones. But Rader warned Lancellotti that he would not get a crack at 100 RBIs, even though he was just five short.

"Why?" Lancellotti barked at his manager. "Are you gonna hold everybody up at third?"

"No," Rader answered. "I'm sending you to the big leagues." Lancellotti's teammates were in on the surprise. They mobbed him like he had hit a walk-off grand slam.

When he arrived in San Diego's clubhouse the next day, Padres manager Dick Williams told Lancellotti he was penciled into the lineup that night at first base. "This is like yesterday," Lancellotti says, recalling those first hours in the majors. "I was standing in the on deck circle. I've got my San Diego Padres uni on. I'm in the big leagues. I'm 26 years old. I'm looking out at everything. I'm trying to take this all in. I closed my eyes and thought, If I die right now, I'm OK. I died a big leaguer."

For his first at bat against St. Louis pitcher Joaquin Andujar, Lancellotti kept his objective simple. Whatever you do, he told himself, don't you dare strike out. "So I've got two strikes on me, and I'm digging in, and I strike out. I walk back to the bench and I'm fuming. And a guy's going, 'Rick, don't worry about it. It's just your first at bat.' And I go, 'That's the problem! It's my first at bat, and I have to tell my grandkids their grandfather struck out his first time up!'"

Padres manager Dick Williams walked up to Lancellotti "like he's arguing with an umpire. He starts laying into me for five straight minutes. 'Who the f--- do you think you are? Do you think this is the f---in' minor leagues? Do you think you can do whatever you want?' And he just wouldn't let up."

Saddled with a messy 0-for-4 after his first game, Lancellotti found his groove in his second start. With the bases loaded, he drove an outside fastball to left-center for a bases-clearing double. "I round first, my helmet flies off. I'm standing at second. (St. Louis manager) Whitey Herzog comes to the mound, pulls Ken Forsch. The place is going crazy. They got my name in lights—Rick Lancellotti's first major league hit. I'm like, Oh my God, shoot me now!"

The pressure was off. It was time to show the Padres he belonged in The Show. A few games later in Cincinnati, Lancellotti started in left field. With the Padres leading 4-2 in the eighth inning, Reds second baseman Ron Oester drove a pitch over Lancellotti's head. "I jumped as far and high as I could stretch out, and I hit the wall. Cincinnati's fence didn't have padding. I hit it so hard that it crushed my shoulder. I was on all fours and my head was

tucked in between my legs. I opened my glove and the ball was in the glove."

After the game, his shoulder was black and blue. Williams told Lancellotti abruptly, "You make sure you're here for treatment at two o'clock tomorrow." Knowing that Williams was famous for his no-nonsense attitude, Lancellotti set out for Riverfront Stadium at 1 p.m., giving himself twice the time he needed to get to the ballpark. Soon, however, he was forced to detour around construction and he missed the stadium exit. By the time he arrived in the visitors' clubhouse, it was 2:15. "I come in and there's two clubhouse guys and Williams, and they're playing cards. I said, 'I'm sorry. I got in traffic and construction and I missed the exit. I'm sorry.' Williams didn't say a word."

Lancellotti could feel the tension in the air. By the time he climbed on a table for treatment, the trainer was whispering at him through a scowl. "He's going, 'Rick, where the hell have you been? He's been in here every five minutes and the more he comes in here the more pissed he's getting.' All of a sudden Williams walks up to me like he's arguing with an umpire. He starts laying into me for five straight minutes saying, 'Who the f--- do you think you are? Do you think this is the f---in' minor leagues? Do you think you can do whatever you want?' And he just wouldn't let up.

"And I said, 'Do you think I'd do this on purpose? I've been waiting my whole life for this. I'm sorry. I got lost.' And he said, 'There's only one excuse for being late and that's being dead. And if you think you're playing for me again, you're wrong.'

"My whole life just sunk at that moment. Here I was the hero of last night's game and 12 hours later I'm just being crucified."

Lancellotti had bounced back from hard times before, but this was different. In the final weeks of the season, the shoulder injury kept him out of the lineup, making it difficult to judge the extent of Williams' wrath. But everything became clear one day after the season ended. Lancellotti was traded to Montreal.

The Expos organization was a bad fit from the start. He was assigned to AAA Wichita, a team with a glut of outfielders. Soon he was released and looking for work. He called Doug Rader, his old Hawaii manager, who was now managing the Texas Rangers. Rader cleared the way for Lancellotti to report to AAA Oklahoma City. It was just the break he needed—a minor league job with the blessing of the organization's major league manager. But when Lancellotti stopped in the manager's office to introduce himself, he felt the cold shoulder of Tom Burgess. The Oklahoma City skipper had been passed over for the Texas job in favor of Rader.

"So we know how that works. I'm the bad guy," says Lancellotti. "He goes, 'I don't know who you are, where you've been or what you've done. We got a couple of guys hurt. When they get better, I can't promise you a job. Your uniform is in your locker. Get on the field in 15 minutes.' I'm like, OK, Tom, great to meet you."

When the injured players returned to the lineup, Burgess sent Lancellotti packing. He headed home to his Buffalo apartment, thinking his career might be over. In desperation, he did something that seemed unthinkable less than a year earlier. He called San Diego general manager Jack McKeon. Padres first baseman Bobby Brown had broken his thumb, and Lancellotti figured the team might be in a bind. McKeon told him, "Get on the next plane. You had a little misfortune over here. Maybe things can turn out better."

The bitter confrontation with Williams still bothered Lancellotti, but it didn't really matter. He needed a place to play baseball, and AAA anywhere was better than nothing. San Diego's affiliate had moved from Hawaii to Las Vegas, but playing with familiar teammates felt like old times for Lancellotti. He hit nine home runs in August, which prompted San Diego's minor league director to offer a contract for the 1984 season. Lancellotti had just one question: "Do I get to go to big-league camp?"

"You know better," he was told.

That was all Lancellotti needed to know. Williams was still calling the shots, and he had a long memory. Despite the bad blood, Lancellotti decided to stay in the Padres organization. "I loved playing in the (Pacific) Coast League, and I loved playing in Vegas. And I thought, You're using me, I'm going to have to use you. I'm going to pick a park I feel really comfortable in."

Lancellotti made the right call. He drove in a league-high 131 runs for Las Vegas. But as long as Williams had a say in the matter, he was going nowhere.

The Padres boss made that clear each week when Las Vegas manager Bob Cluck phoned in progress reports to the organization. Cluck once told Lancellotti, "I shouldn't tell you this, but I have to. Every time I put your name in, he says, 'I don't want to f---in' hear about him again.'"

In the spring of 1985, Lancellotti was traded to the Mets, who assured him he would get a shot at backing up first baseman Keith Hernandez. But Lancellotti played poorly at AAA Tidewater, where he felt pressure to repeat his performance one year earlier. "I swung myself into frenzy," he says. Halfway through the season, the San Francisco Giants bought his contract, and he finished the season in Tucson, his seventh AAA town.

He re-signed with San Francisco in 1986 and got off to a solid start in Tucson. He earned a 10-day call-up to the Giants in June, but he pinch hit just once before returning to AAA. Lancellotti finished the PCL season with 31 home runs, good for his second minor league home run title—and another shot with the Giants in the month of September.

Even in a star-crossed career, there are moments when everything falls together. September of 1986 proved to be Lancellotti's pinnacle experience in the majors. After two weeks of pinch-hitting duty, he came off the bench in the top of the ninth against Atlanta. With the Giants leading, Lancellotti took a big hack at a pitch from reliever Jeff Dedmon. "And I'm watching (right fielder) Dale Murphy running back...Keep running Dale, keep running, keep running. I'm jogging down to first base and it drops over the fence, and I'm like, Amen! I got around the bases in about 3.5 seconds. Shoot me again! I'm good to go! Everything—good and bad—all melted away. It was all gone for that moment."

Two nights later, he delivered an encore, launching a three-run homer at Cincinnati. That's when he became a side show. His teammates wanted to see three home runs in three pinch-hit appearances. The opportunity came 24 hours later. Houston fireballer Nolan Ryan had overpowered the Giants all night when Lancellotti came to the plate in the eighth inning. The all-time strikeout king made him the last of 12 whiffs that evening, finishing him off on three high fastballs.

Lancellotti batted .222 in 18 at bats with the Giants, but he had shown them that he could, at the very least, provide a big stick coming off the bench. For the first time, it appeared he was in a team's plans going into the offseason.

So what happened next seems almost cruel. A Japanese team in Hiroshima had begun pursuing him in September. Long known for luring American power hitters for big money, the Japanese figured Lancellotti, with his sputtering career, was an easy target. And the money was serious: a two-year deal worth $475,000. It was far more than he had ever made in professional baseball.

But nothing could have been more troubling to Lancellotti. Playing two seasons in Japan until the age of 32 would be career suicide for a guy with 57 career at bats. The decision to stay at home was easy—until friends and family members began weighing in. Take the cash, they told him. Have something to show for all the dead-end years. That logic only made Lancellotti upset. Couldn't anyone else see that this was a deal with the devil? "I was so confused. I couldn't sleep. I couldn't eat. I was so torn. I had 10 years in the minor leagues and I had $10 to show for it. If I go back to San Francisco and they send me back to the minors, I've got nothing. So here I am faced with this."

He turned to San Francisco manager Roger Craig for help. Craig offered encouragement and assured him that he was an ideal guy to drive in runs in the late innings.

"On the other hand," Craig said, "that's an awful lot of money."

Three days later, Lancellotti met with the Japanese officials and signed the contract. "I felt empty. I felt like a whore. I felt like I sold myself out. I hated myself. It was a very bad time."

The two years in Japan were the worst of his life. Hiroshima issued him uniform number 45, the number of round-trippers they expected him to hit. "I couldn't believe I actually was there. I didn't want anything to do with it. I was playing strictly for money. I went into a shell. I grew a beard and I hid behind it." But Lancellotti did deliver on the expectations. With 39 home runs in his first season, he won the third home run crown of his career.

In spring training of 1989, he was cut by the Yankees but caught on with Boston's AAA team in Pawtucket. Having endured every hard-knock reality

the game could throw at him, Lancellotti's career crossed over to fantasy. The movie *Bull Durham* had been a box office hit over the previous year. The story of Crash Davis, a career minor leaguer with 21 days in the majors, had a familiar ring for Lancellotti. In the movie, Davis was a power hitter, playing out the final days of his career. The storyline included the slugger's chase of the all-time minor league home run record of 246. Back in real life, somebody started doing the math on Lancellotti's career. As luck would have it, he had just passed 246 home runs a couple weeks earlier.

This was big news. Move over, Crash Davis. Rick Lancellotti was the new feel-good story in baseball's backwaters. Interview requests poured in from everywhere. It all seemed a bit much to Lancellotti. He enjoyed the attention, sure, but there was one little problem. The record for minor league home runs was not 246. Several players had been documented with more. Some as many as 400. The media did not seem to care that 246 was just an arbitrary number used in the movie.

But Lancellotti played along when the limo picked him up in New York and delivered him to the set of NBC's *Today Show*, where Bryant Gumbel asked him about breaking the mark. "That was pretty wild," says Lancellotti, who doubts that Gumbel ever understood that the record was fictional. "I answered a lot of things in joke form. OK, if you guys want to play, I'll play along. It's so easy to make fun of myself. I tried to make it semi-serious."

So there was Lancellotti, his 15 minutes of fame now defined by absurdity, still searching for a breakthrough in the real baseball world. He returned to Pawtucket for the 1991 season, where he continued to play well. Then in early August, PawSox manager Johnny Pesky delivered the news that Lancellotti had been called to the big leagues. He immediately hopped in the car and made the short drive to Boston. Since the Red Sox were off that day, Lancellotti gave himself a quick tour of Fenway Park to soak in the atmosphere. That's when Boston general manager Lou Gorman caught up with him. Gorman explained that Red Sox outfielder Mike Marshall had not cleared waivers, which tied up the roster spot intended for Lancellotti.

Dejected and angry, Lancellotti got in his car and drove back to Pawtucket.

In less than one day, he had been called up to the majors and returned to the minors. The PawSox game was just ending when Lancellotti strolled into the manager's office to tell Pesky what happened. "You know what Lance?" the former Boston great told him. "I've been in this game for over 50 years, and I've never seen that happen to anybody. But if I thought it would happen to somebody, you'd be the guy."

A week later, the Red Sox made good on the call up. He joined the team in Seattle, where he went 0-for-8 over three games. A few days later, his modest dream—"All I wanted was one at bat in Fenway"—came true. Back in Boston, he delivered a sacrifice fly against California. Then it was back to Pawtucket, where he put the finishing touches on the fourth home run title of his career.

But his days of hovering near the major leagues were over. He played two more season in Italy, slowly weaning himself from baseball. Lancellotti knew it was time to move on. Once baseball ended, he had little to fall back on financially. The $475,000 from his Japanese contract was gone, lost in a bad real estate investment. He returned to Buffalo with his wife, Debbie, and borrowed money to open Rick Lancellotti's Buffalo School of Baseball. Today, thousands of kids pass through the doors of the school each year, some of them headed for success. "I see it every day because I teach it. Some kids are extremely talented, and you wonder how far they're going to go."

For Lancellotti, there is unabashed joy on memory lane. Not only can he still see his first home run sail beyond the reach of Dale Murphy, he still feels it. The same goes for the rest of his baseball emotions. That part is tough. You don't bash home runs all over creation and just accept that you were meant to be a lifer in the minors. You struggle with it. "If you look at certain moments, you know it was a crossroads," he says. "If this had just gone this way, or someone could have had more faith in me, or the trade would have happened. If this, if that. It's not a good way to live. It's over, and I can't go back and change it."

Lancellotti is wading into the emotional turmoil now. And that leads him back to the episode with Padres manager Dick Williams. How can it not? Most managers would have forgiven his tardiness and accepted his explanation.

But those fateful 15 minutes changed everything. Had he not missed the stadium exit in Cincinnati and incurred the wrath of the manager, Lancellotti would not have been traded the day after the season ended. Maybe he would have won a job in San Diego the next spring and started hitting homers in big league parks. And then what? That is the story Lancellotti can only imagine.

"For the life of me, I couldn't ever imagine doing that to somebody," says Lancellotti, his voice softening. "It was beyond me that someone could be that cruel and insensitive and downright bad. It's a story that haunts me, and I don't ever enjoy telling it. I would just like to corner him and say, 'Why did you do that to me?'"

Near the end of his career, he had his chance. At a Boston sportswriters dinner in 1990, Lancellotti spotted Williams making his rounds.

"I was trying to get to him, and he was lost in the crowd. Then I went to a party at the hotel, and Williams was there. I saw him walk through the door, and my blood just went cold. He's looking around the room and he sees me, and he just beelines out the door. I'm thinking, Do I go after him? Yes, I should. But by the time I got in the hallway, he's gone. I didn't know if I was going to kill him, which I was afraid I might do."

He pauses, then finishes his thought.

"I was just a kid."

If Lancellotti had his way, he would bury the Dick Williams story once and for all. But if you want to know why things never worked out in the big leagues, it's part of the presentation.

"Deep in my soul, I know I could have played 10 or 15 years in the big leagues," he says. "And that makes it easier to do my day-to-day stuff. What keeps me going is at least I did it. It helps me sleep at night to know I played in the major leagues. At least I got there. I kind of hang on to that."

If you tap into Lancellotti's few precious moments of major league success, you learn why the game sustains him. Ask him about his first hit, the one that cleared the bases. See if he will tell you about the back-to-back pinch-hit homers. That's when Rick Lancellotti's adrenaline rushes right back.

Shoot him, all over again.

Worth the wait

Dale Polley's prospects were often hopeless, but his pitching payoff was worthy of Hollywood.

When **Dale Polley** finished college, he pinned all his hopes on being drafted by the Cincinnati Reds. It had nothing to do with growing up in nearby Georgetown, Kentucky. It's just that the Reds were the only team that had ever heard of him.

Polley pitched for Kentucky State University, a small school with a Division II program. The Reds had worked him out a couple times, giving him some hope on draft day in 1987. But the phone never rang. "I was very disappointed. I waited by the phone for Cincinnati," says Polley. "So I just assumed that was it."

Career over. No free-agent offers, nothing. So when a friend called a few weeks later, looking for someone to fill in on the mound for a summer-league game, Polley figured, why not? He tried not to dwell on the fact that the game was in Cincinnati and that scouts would be everywhere, sizing up the college players that he would pitch to. He wouldn't let that torment him. He was pitching for his buddy's team, and that was that.

Then he pitched a one-hit shutout. After the game, a college coach told Polley that he might want to make plans to be in Cleveland the next weekend. The major league scouting bureau was holding a tryout camp. With nothing to lose, Polley put in some empty hours, first driving to Cleveland, then sitting around a field for several hours with 250 other dreamers. Finally, his name was called. The lanky left-hander took the mound, fired off 15 or 20 pitches, then took a seat. A couple minutes later, Braves scout Tony Stile approached Polley. "He signed me on the spot for $2,000. I would have signed for nothing at the time," Polley says, with an affable chuckle. "Two days later, I was on a plane to Pulaski, Virginia. If it wasn't for that game at that point, it never would have happened."

Polley got off to a fast start with Atlanta's rookie league team, posting a stellar 1.75 ERA as Pulaski's closer. Later in the summer, he moved up to single A and posted a 2.88 ERA in the starting rotation. In 1988, he continued his quick rise with a strong year at AA Greenville, South Carolina. When the season ended, Polley tried to maintain his momentum by playing in the Venezuelan winter league. He pitched all the way through the Caribbean World Series. After the longest season of his career, he was worn down.

"After a whole season of baseball, and a full season of winter ball, I was headed to spring training a week later. I think it just caught up with me," says Polley, who went 6-15 despite a 3.35 ERA during his second season in Greenville. "I had some bad luck. It was a season to just check your character. You go through a lot of adversity, and that was my year of being down. It was definitely a down year."

 **After he retired, it took a couple of years before he could watch a game on TV. "I think it was just me being in a kind of depression, knowing I was finished and it wasn't going to come back."**

At the same time, it was clear that the Braves were developing some of the best pitching prospects in baseball. Three number one draft picks—Kent Mercker (1986), Derek Lilliquist (1987), and Steve Avery (1988)—were ready for the majors. All three were southpaw starters. Making matters worse, Atlanta already had left-handers Tom Glavine and Charlie Leibrandt in the starting rotation. Polley was at the back of a lefty log jam. Even when he made the AAA all-star team with Richmond in 1990, he knew he was becoming an afterthought in Atlanta. The top draft picks were on the fast track, while the undrafted free agent was merely going in circles. "They had their boys throw innings (in Atlanta)," he says. "I knew that being a left-handed pitcher in that organization at that moment was a tough haul."

Polley went into a two-year holding pattern, pitching effectively out of the Richmond bullpen in 1991 and 1992. But in the spring of 1993, the Atlanta

organization began to lose interest. "The last day of spring training we got ready to break, and they called me in and said, 'It's a numbers game. We're going to take a look at some other players in AAA that haven't had that opportunity. We're going to start you out back in Greenville.' I didn't like it. I had met my wife (Angela) the year before. We had planned on getting married in Richmond, and our plans got changed.

"So we got married in the backyard of the courthouse in Greenville, South Carolina," he says, pausing a moment to laugh at the memory. "That's how we got married. We have our pictures, standing in front of a tree with the justice of the peace and a lady with a cigarette in her hand."

Polley returned to Richmond late in the season, but he was a spare part. He pitched only when games were out of hand, sometimes going more than a week between appearances. "I really had to stop and think where my career was going at that point. It was a letdown. These guys had given up on me."

As spring training approached in 1994, Angela was due with their first child. Her pregnancy had been difficult, and Polley knew she would need help at home. "I was 30 years old. I had played a while, and I loved the game, of course. But I was at a crossroads in my career. It was a hard decision to give it up."

He returned to Kentucky, where he pitched in around the house and at the family's tool and dye business in Georgetown. Then after a year away from baseball, the phone rang one evening. It was Braves executive Rod Gilbreath, wanting to know if Polley wanted to play again. Major league players were on strike in the spring of 1995, and teams were filling their rosters with replacement players. Gilbreath offered $5,000 just to come to spring training. Polley said no thanks. A couple days later, Gilbreath sweetened the deal. This time, the offer was $15,000 just to show up. No strings attached. "Even if I never played a game," says Polley. "Angela and I talked about it. I said, 'Maybe we'll come down for a two-week vacation.' We packed up and headed to West Palm Beach, Florida."

The up-front money sealed the deal, but the circumstances of his return were less than ideal. "Even when I was down there, it was still a tough decision. I knew why I was there. If I got to the big leagues for a week, it might be my claim to fame. I had worked hard and spent a lot of days trying to get there, and I had seen a lot of guys pass me up. If I could get to the big leagues that way, that was how it was going to be."

On the eve of opening day, the strike was settled. The major leaguers agreed to start the season a few weeks late, leaving the replacement players out of the picture entirely. Polley's dream was dashed for a second time. But the Braves had one more proposal. The organization needed to field enough players to open the AAA season. They offered him $10,000 per month to play in Richmond—more than twice his previous best salary. Polley signed on for the 1995 season, and he made the AAA all-star team for the second time, crafting a career-best 1.56 ERA.

But his chances of earning a call-up were more remote than ever. The issue was Polley's status as a replacement player. Even though the Braves were light on left-handers in the bullpen, they made do without him. "There wasn't a thought in my head about that being the reason," he recalls. "I had been so used to waiting for that call. About a month and a half before the end of the season, I realized that's why I wasn't being called up."

The scenario became clear to Polley when Atlanta promoted four other left-handed relievers for the month of September. No team wanted to test team chemistry by adding a replacement player to the roster. "Here I am just absolutely killing it in AAA," Polley says, "and it was not going to happen. I wasn't going to get called up. I knew the consequences. But I was making 10 grand a month, and that made it easier to swallow."

It also helped that Polley was approaching free agency for the first time. Left-handers were always in demand, and Polley had a nasty go-to pitch—a sharp-breaking curve that cut across the plate rather than down. When the New York Yankees and Los Angeles Dodgers showed interest during the winter, Polley made a practical decision. Angela was pregnant with the couple's second child, and New York's AAA team was in Columbus, just a few hours from their home in Kentucky.

After two months in AAA, Polley was on top of his game, striking out nearly a

batter per inning. On June 10, Columbus Clippers manager Stump Merrill pulled Polley aside and told him the Yankees were releasing veteran reliever Steve Howe. Polley was going to join the Yankees on the road. He packed his car and made the three-hour drive to Cleveland. "Of course, petrified," he says.

The clubhouse was empty when he arrived, game time still several hours away. With bags in each hand, he looked around until Yankees manager Joe Torre came to welcome him. After a few moments of small talk, Torre told Polley about one last hurdle that stood in the way of becoming a major league player: Howe had not yet been told of his release.

"So Torre says, 'If you don't mind, could you take your stuff into the bathroom? Steve Howe is coming in my office as soon as he gets in the clubhouse.' So I take my equipment, and I go in the bathroom, and wait for them to release Steve Howe. I was standing in the shower, and I just waited for him to pack his stuff and leave before I brought mine out."

Finally with full clubhouse clearance, Polley eased into life with the Yankees. He knew his status as a replacement player could be an issue, but he already felt enough pressure making his debut with baseball's most famous franchise. "I pretty much kept to myself. I was in awe," he says.

His fears about acceptance quickly faded. Whatever ill feelings the Yankees harbored were kept to a minimum. At 32 years old, Polley was the second-oldest Yankees rookie in history. Perhaps the veteran players knew he had paid his dues. "I can't complain one bit about the way I was treated. I know there was some animosity there, but no one said, 'Get away from me, scab.' They treated me like someone who was supposed to be there. And the longer I stayed there, the better they knew my situation and the more they accepted me."

Yankees closer John Wetteland took Polley under his wing, helping the rookie feel at home among stars like Bernie Williams, Wade Boggs and rookie sensation Derek Jeter. Even New York's utility players—Darryl Strawberry, Tim Raines, Dwight Gooden—were legends. And if the roster didn't intimidate a newbie, there was always Yankee Stadium. "One of a kind," says Polley. "The atmosphere is like no place you've ever been. The ground shakes when that place rocks. Just talking about it sends cold chills down my arms."

He managed to block out the circus atmosphere whenever duty called. Torre used Polley effectively, calling on him to get key outs in the middle and late innings. His first four appearances were flawless, recording five outs without allowing a baserunner. He earned the win in his second appearance, retiring one batter in the eighth inning before Williams homered in the ninth for a 2-1 win over Minnesota.

But short relief appearances are a recipe for statistical disaster. Give up a couple runs, and your numbers skyrocket. By season's end, Polley was saddled with a 7.89 ERA. "I had a few runners get on base on me, and I would come out of the game. It seemed like every time I left a runner on base, whoever came in behind me gave it up," Polley says. "Twenty one innings, it doesn't take long."

That was it. Just 21 innings over 32 appearances in 1996. Because it is such a small body of work, Polley can recall nearly all of it. Like the day in Seattle in late August when he faced the heart of the Mariners batting order. Alex Rodriguez, Ken Griffey Jr., Edgar Martinez, and Jay Buhner combined to hit 155 home runs that year. A-Rod notched his 38th against Polley. "I'm not ashamed of it," he laughs.

While Polley was chalking up big league memories a couple hitters at a time, New York was clinching the American League East. When the play-offs began, however, he became a sort-of Yankee. Torre chose hulking lefty Graeme Lloyd as the last pitcher on the playoff roster. Polley was sent to the team's spring training complex in Florida to stay sharp in case he was needed. He remained out of sight through the American League playoffs, but when the Yankees reached the World Series against Atlanta, Polley earned an upgrade.

Although he was not added to the active roster, he dressed and sat in the bullpen for every game. He also made a small contribution to the Yankees fortunes. He pitched batting practice to his teammates on the day Tom Glavine pitched for the Braves, giving the Yankee hitters a lefty preview. Otherwise, Polley sat back in the bullpen, feeling nothing but tension until New York finished off the Braves in six games. "I can remember running from the bullpen,

jumping on the pile in the middle of the field. We took a victory lap around the field. I can remember being totally out of breath, totally exhausted from running around the field from the adrenaline. The joy of the moment was unbelievable."

A few days later, the joy of winning the World Series came to an abrupt halt. His role as a replacement player with Atlanta had come back to haunt him. Because replacement players were not allowed to join the Major League Baseball Players Association, Polley was at the mercy of his teammates when it came to receiving a share of the World Series winnings. A full share was worth a whopping $216,870. His teammates voted to give him nothing.

"Sure I wanted the money," he says. "It did bother me. But what do you do? The thing they can't take away is the World Series championship and the ring." Shortly after the snub, Polley received a check for $20,000 from a teammate. He identifies the player only as "a good friend of mine and a great-hearted person." Later, the Yankees management also gave him an extra $20,000.

The afterglow of the World Series wore off quickly. The following spring, Polley was returned to Columbus. "I was so disappointed that I wasn't in New York. Maybe I just put too much pressure on myself. Then when I knew I wasn't pitching well enough to get back, it was real discouraging." After a full season in AAA, Polley was faced with a family crisis that made retirement the only realistic choice. Dale and Angela's second child, Chad, was diagnosed with autism.

At 32, he returned to Georgetown once and for all. He went to work with his father and brother at Polleycraft Tool, a company that supplies metal and plastic machine parts for the local Toyota factory. These days, business is good. Just as he worked well from the starting rotation or out of the bullpen, Polley is versatile at work, operating every machine in the shop.

But Polleycraft Tool is not baseball. It took a couple years before he could watch a game on TV. "I think it was just me being in a kind of depression, knowing I was finished and it wasn't going to come back," he says. "I'm content that I got to the big leagues and I got a World Series ring, but I felt I was better than 32 games in the big leagues. Personally, I felt like I would have gotten a shot quicker in another organization, but it's something you have to live with."

Polley does have one regret. For most of his summer as a Yankee, he played it cool with his many superstar teammates. Years later, he sounds every bit like the kid from tryout camp when he reveals the one do-over he would like.

"Why didn't I get his autograph?" says Polley, referring to any number of players. "I was right there playing with him. What an opportunity I blew, as far as getting memorabilia." But he didn't exactly leave empty-handed. He saved his full Yankees uniform, as well as a bat from the World Series, signed by everyone on the team. He did ask Jeter and Strawberry for signatures. "Strawberry was a nice guy," he says. "He treated me super." And Polley was semi-brave enough to get Mark McGwire's signature. "I sent the bat boy over to get his autograph," he says.

He may not have cornered the market on signed Yankees merchandise, but the story line for his career would stand up against any of Hollywood's great baseball movies. Even the theme resonates years later. "Baseball is so full of failures," he says. "You learn to deal with whatever comes along. It helps you deal with the good and bad things in life."

Polley stays plenty busy in life after baseball. He and Angela have their three boys, Matt, Chad and Evan. Summers are spent shuttling between the kids' baseball games, and Dad lends a hand coaching when he can. It keeps him connected to the game he loves. At the same time, Polley is 41 years old, and there is still some pitcher left in him. If he wants to, he can still put a great spin on a curve ball. He just can't put one on retirement.

"I'll be honest with you," Polley says, sounding upbeat. "It's still hard to this day. I still have dreams about pitching in the big leagues. And I wake up and I wonder if I can still do it. I think, Man, I was back in the big leagues for a minute."

Then he laughs, and you sense what is coming.

"It's kind of disappointing when I wake up."

Best seat in the house

Scott Pose toiled

in the minors for years

before finding his niche

in his baseball twilight.

Scott Pose was not much in the mood for a pep talk. It was the spring of 1993, and he was just a few weeks removed from being the first batter in Florida Marlins history. Now he was trying to keep his chin up, playing AAA ball in Edmonton. "Where Santa Claus lives," he says.

So when his teammate, Nick Capra, offered a bit of advice, Pose suffered him politely. He had little use for the wisdom of a 35 year old with just 54 major league at bats.

"As long as you have a uniform," Capra told him, "you have a chance."

By the time Pose turned 35, he had worn 16 uniforms, each representing another chance. "It's just the kind of player I was," he says. "I was fighting tooth and nail all the way."

Pose knew where he stood the day he arrived in professional baseball in 1989. The Cincinnati Reds drafted him in the 34th round from the University of Arkansas. As the 885th overall pick, Pose knew that the organization would not spend much time worrying about his progress. If he was going to get anywhere in baseball, he would have to make some noise on his own. "All I wanted was a chance. Once you get between the lines, it doesn't matter. Either I was naive enough or focused enough that it didn't bother me. I was going to make the most of it."

At the start of his career, Pose played like a blue-chipper. He was an all-star outfielder in 1989 and 1990, first in rookie ball, then in single A. He made his mark by doing the little things well. He was a singles hitter who relied on speed, hustle and baseball smarts.

Two seasons later, at the age of 25, Pose looked like a big league prospect. He hit .342 at AA Chattanooga. "I knew the culling point was AA. At that level, there's talk about the major leagues. And at that time we knew expansion was coming up."

With the Florida Marlins and Colorado Rockies set to join the major leagues

the following season, Pose hoped to get a shot with the Reds if they lost any outfielders in the expansion draft. Then came a big surprise. He was left off of the team's 40-man protected roster. Reds general manager Jim Bowden told Pose he had become a liability on the base paths, reminding him that he was caught stealing as often as he was successful in Chattanooga. "There are so many numbers you can find to justify any position you want to take," Pose says. "You've gotta just hang in there and take a shot. That's the way it is."

As an unprotected player with three seasons in the minors, Pose was placed in baseball's Rule 5 draft. The Marlins selected him and put him on their 40-man roster. Right away, he tapped into a vibe that only a minor league player can truly appreciate. "They sent me a jersey in the offseason. It was number 2, a single-digit number. Normally guys like me are 68 or 80 or something. I got a real number."

He also had a real chance to make the team. Chuck Carr had a bit of big league experience and was penciled in as the starter in center field. But Marlins manager Rene Lachemann told Pose he would get a look. Soon, Pose was thriving and Carr was struggling. The day before the season began, Lachemann called the two outfielders into his office and announced that Pose would start on opening day. "I was dumbfounded," he says. "I felt this weight in my chest. What have I gotten myself into?"

For starters, he was about to enter the history books: Florida Marlins first batter—Scott Pose, April 6, 1993. Before the game even started, it was clear he had made a name for himself. "In the tunnel, (ESPN's Chris) Berman comes by and says congratulations. It's one of those surreal moments. The little things got me going. In spring training that year, I got excited because I had my own bats with my own name on it. I'm excited because I'm talking with Berman and he knows who I am. That kind of stuff. It says, You've arrived. You're here."

When Pose finally dug in at the plate, he saw Dodgers star Orel Hershiser staring back from the mound. Then on a 2-1 count, Pose smacked a pitch off Hershiser's glove and beat the throw from second baseman Jody Reed. Pose had his first major league hit in his first at bat. As tradition dictates, the ball was tossed into the Florida dugout, a souvenir of Pose's big moment. Moments later, the official scorer ruled the play an error. The hit was gone, the celebration halted. "But the next time up, I did get a hit. And they threw the ball out of play again. It made Orel mad," he laughs.

At the end of the opening home stand, Pose looked like a keeper. The unheralded rookie had started all six games, posting a .308 batting average. As the team flew to San Francisco on Easter Sunday, he got word that Carr would get the start in the series opener against Giants left-hander Bud Black. Pose made a pinch-hit appearance in the first game, then went hitless the rest of the series. Normally, an 0-for-10 stretch is not much cause for concern—a mini-slump, just part of the game for everyday players. But it mattered to the Marlins. Pose did not start another game. A week later he was sent to Edmonton and taken off the 40-man roster.

"That was devastating to me," he says.

He was given no explanation for his demotion or his removal from the 40-man roster. By contrast, Florida right fielder Junior Felix went 0-for-14 the same week, dropping his average to .115. He remained in the starting lineup for three months.

Just as he had felt the joy of his first hit evaporate before him, Pose saw his dream vanish before he could really enjoy it. "As soon as I hit .308, I started thinking, Hey, I belong here. As soon as I believed it, the rug was pulled out from under me. I never wanted to buy into that again. You don't know how long it is going to last. It was very humbling. Each day can be your last."

Pose reported to Edmonton, where the combination of cold weather and hurt feelings made for a slow start. "It was hard to get back in the saddle right away," he says. He went on to hit .284 in his first AAA season, but he sensed it would take a miracle to impress the Marlins.

The following spring began with renewed hope. After the 1993 season, Florida had sent him to the Arizona Fall League, an instructional league for baseball's top prospects. Pose dominated in Arizona, winning the batting title. As a result, he was invited to major league spring training and seemed to be back in the good graces of the organization. But in the exhibition season,

Pose batted just 20 times, mostly as a pinch hitter. Not only did he miss out on making the team, this time the Marlins wanted to send him to AA. With his career going backwards, Pose asked to be released.

"That started the odyssey," he says.

He signed with Milwaukee and spent the season at AAA New Orleans, hitting .282 as an everyday outfielder. Despite finishing last in the American League Central, the Brewers were content to leave him in the minors all year. That experience taught Pose a lesson. In the future, he would only sign with teams that looked like playoff contenders. Good teams were more likely to call up a player with major league experience when they had a short-term need. Also-rans like Milwaukee were inclined to audition their prospects.

At the start of the 1995 season, Pose was 28 years old and he needed to find a path to the major leagues. Having failed to gain traction in three organizations, he signed with the Los Angeles Dodgers. Immediately, he became entangled in politics. The major league players were on strike, and teams were fielding replacement squads comprised of minor leaguers. "You can call it what you want," Pose says, "but if the best players aren't in the game, it's not the major leagues, and I didn't want to play in it."

But by steering clear of the replacement team, Pose got caught in a numbers game. Like other teams, the Dodgers had made deals with some of the replacement players, offering guaranteed minor league jobs when the strike ended. So when the major leaguers returned just before opening day, Los Angeles needed to free some roster spots in the minors. Pose, who was hitting .188 after seven games at AAA Albuquerque, was released.

Now Pose had nowhere to go. He had married his wife, Laurie, during the previous offseason, but they had no year-round residence. For the short term, they moved in with Pose's parents in Des Moines, Iowa. For six weeks, he worried that his career could be over. Then baseball came calling. Minnesota Twins outfielder Alex Cole had broken his leg. The Twins replaced him with a prospect, leaving an opening for an outfielder at AAA Salt Lake City. "I looked at it as a new lease on life. I was catching bullpens. I didn't care. If I saw my name wasn't in the starting lineup, big deal. I got a uniform, I got a chance."

As an outsider, Pose knew he was not in Minnesota's plans. But by hitting .301 in AAA, he was back on baseball's radar. He signed with the Cleveland Indians in 1996, where he figured to play at AAA Buffalo for Brian Graham, his manager in the Arizona Fall League back in 1993. But two days into camp, Cleveland had a change of plans. Minor league director Mark Shapiro told Pose the organization needed the AAA roster spot for a player who was going to be sent down. Instead of feeling cheated, Pose was grateful for the honest explanation. Not only was Shapiro forthright, but he also found Pose another job. The Toronto Blue Jays needed an everyday outfielder, so Shapiro swapped minor leaguers. "I thanked him up and down," Pose says, "because otherwise I would have been sitting (in AAA Buffalo)."

 **"I begged them not to put me on the disabled list. Because I knew once I was on the disabled list, that was the kiss of death. Once I was sent out, I was never coming back."**

Instead of making a fresh start, Pose barely kept his head above water at AAA Syracuse. He injured a hamstring in June and finished the season hitting .271, "which was death to me," he says. He resolved to move to Raleigh, North Carolina, where he and Laurie had met early in his playing career. It was time to put down some roots. As for baseball, he was a realist. Since his debut with the Marlins, he had played nearly four full seasons of AAA ball. He was 30 years old and no longer a prospect. If he did not receive an invitation to a major league camp for the 1997 season, he was going to call it quits.

So when his favorite childhood team, the New York Yankees, invited him to camp, Pose was thrilled. "I've got no shot at making the team. But I know that and I don't care. I'm wearing the pinstripes. I'm No. 67."

Pose saw plenty of Grapefruit League action, but as spring training drew to a close, he sensed his demotion was imminent. He had no control over the

situation, but he could at least try to stave off the bad news. In one of New York's final exhibition games, Pose hit a triple and scored before being taken out of the game. "I didn't want the reaper to find me, so I scored the run, showered and got out of there as quick as I could," Pose says, breaking into a loud laugh. "I didn't want him to find me. I just wanted another day."

In the end, Yankees manager Joe Torre shared the inevitable news, sending Pose to AAA Columbus. But his message motivated Pose: "You are a major leaguer. Don't you forget that. Just be ready if I need you."

In May, the Yankees paid a visit to Columbus for an exhibition game. As Pose renewed spring training friendships before the game, the big-league players kept asking him if he had heard the news—that Pose was getting called up after the game. First, Jorge Posada mentioned it, then Paul O'Neill. Pose wondered if it was a prank. Finally, he got the word from Columbus manager Stump Merrill. Indeed, Pose was going to be a Yankee.

First, however, he had a dress rehearsal. He was scheduled to play in the exhibition game that night—as a Yankee, not a Clipper. He needed only to get through the game without a catastrophe. But early in the game, Pose collided viciously with second baseman Luis Sojo while chasing a fly ball. "I was seeing double. It was a hard collision," Pose says. "Luis came out of the game. I was feeling pretty funny, but I didn't say a word. It's taken this long to get a call up. I'm not going to tell them. The grogginess left after about three innings."

In a bit of a stupor, Pose boarded the team plane, grateful to be back in the big leagues. He stayed on the roster the rest of the year, batting 87 times in 54 games with a .218 average. Torre called on him when he needed a defensive replacement or a pinch runner for players like Cecil Fielder and Daryl Strawberry. Pose was a spare part and loving it. "I didn't care how much I played or what happened," he says. "I'm now on the Yankees. If we're up by 10 or down by 10, I get to go in."

And since those blowouts were rare, Pose decided to get something more out the Yankees experience than a dugout view of a hall-of-fame lineup.

"Somebody could come off the disabled list one day, and I could be gone. So I took in every bit I could. I started a tradition. Forty minutes before the game started, I would go out to the bench and just sit and take it all in. The guys had their routines and they were getting ready. They didn't need me in their way. (Yankees bench coach) Don Zimmer would come out, and I'd say, 'Zim, who was the best second baseman you ever saw?' It was like fantasy camp in a way. I'd go into Camden Yards (in Baltimore) where Cal Ripken plays, and I'd go stand at shortstop and see what he sees every day. I was going to take in whatever I could."

Pose signed with the Yankees again in 1998, hoping to reprise his utility role. This time, the best he could do was earn a starting job in the Columbus outfield. He hit .297 and stole 47 bases, numbers that made him a deserving choice for a late-season opportunity in the Bronx. But the Yankees were in the midst of a brilliant season. Torre was reluctant to tinker with team chemistry, even when the rosters expanded in September.

Pose moved on to the Kansas City Royals in 1999, and he was ticketed for AAA Omaha at the end of spring training. Then he caught an unexpected break. One day later, Kansas City traded veteran outfielder Jeff Conine to Baltimore. The Royals were committed to three young stars in the outfield. What they needed was a player who could be content to watch from the bench and make no waves. Scott Pose was their man. He broke camp with the Royals.

As the season wore on, he quietly assumed the same role he enjoyed in New York. He would chat up Royals greats George Brett and Frank White and soak up all the baseball knowledge he could. But this time around, he did far more than collect an anecdotal history of baseball. Pose played in 86 games, mostly coming off the bench. Yet he was most productive in the starting lineup. In 24 starts, he batted .338. He finished the year with a .285 average, by far his most successful stint in the major leagues. As grateful as he was for the opportunity, Pose had a hard time enjoying it. Omaha always looked too close for comfort. "That's just the reality of the type of player I was, the type of ability I had," he concedes. "What happened with the Marlins, I promised I would never buy into it again or get complacent because it hurt too bad."

Pose made the Royals roster again in 2000, but his strong 1999 season may

have undermined his chance to earn more playing time. The Royals already knew that Pose excelled in a limited role, and he did it without complaining. In his second season in Kansas City, he started just four games, none after mid June. He batted just 48 times in 47 games and batted .188.

"We weren't winning. You had Jermaine Dye in right field, Carlos Beltran in center, and Johnny Damon in left. Who were you going to sit to play me?" he asks. "I understood that role. I pinch hit a lot in the ninth. I'd sit for five days, and then I'd lead off the ninth and be facing Mariano Rivera or Troy Percival. I was facing closers. I was thankful for being there, but I knew it could end at any time."

When the Royals passed on bringing Pose to camp in 2001, he signed with the Houston Astros. His season turned sour quickly when he was shipped to AAA New Orleans and tore his MCL. His season was over. He returned to his family in Raleigh for his first heavy dose of life without baseball. Now 34 years old, he knew it would be difficult to revive his career after a major surgery. In addition to rehabbing his injury, he completed his undergraduate degree in accounting. "I was home at six o'clock at night in July, barbecuing with the kids, not worrying about batting practice or what pitcher I was going to face. I really got to see how much I was missing."

He returned to baseball in the spring of 2002. The Astros released him in spring training, but as always, Pose was in demand somewhere else. This time the Los Angeles Dodgers had room on their AAA team in Las Vegas. Only this time, there was something missing. "Here I am in AAA, not seeing my kids," he says. "And I know what it's like in the big leagues."

Accustomed to the major leagues and longing for family life, Pose could see the end of the baseball trail. After 23 games, he was hitting just .203. The Dodgers cut him loose. Without any fanfare, Pose returned to Raleigh, ready to put baseball behind him. He found some part-time construction work and began sending out resumes. But before he could find a fit in the working world, baseball placed one more call. Oklahoma City, the AAA team for the Texas Rangers, was in a pennant race and needed help. Pose figured he might be able go out on a nicer note than he had in Las Vegas. "Kind of my swan song in AAA," Pose says. "It was better than working in construction. I was getting paid to play, and I could maybe help a team."

When Oklahoma City lost in the first round of the playoffs, Pose was truly ready to retire. He soon went to work as a pharmaceutical sales representative with Pfizer. Today, he is satisfied with his new life, calling on doctors and pitching Detrol LA, Celebrex and Zoloft. But at 38, Pose stays close to the game. He helps out with the USA Baseball program, and he does color commentary for AAA games on regional cable TV. And for baseball at an uncomplicated level, Pose watches his son, Chase, play Little League. "I can't get it out of my blood. I need a shot in the arm, but in a different sense," he says. With his playing days behind him, Pose has found a new athletic outlet. "I took up hockey. I'm awful."

Pose has always known his limits as an athlete. That's why he never felt any shame in accepting bit parts on the baseball stage. It also explains why he was the rare marginal player whose best days came at the end of his career. Many others would have retired long before Pose, realizing that a long AAA tenure is rarely an asset.

Once he had a foothold in the majors, Pose knew enough about the business of baseball to recognize how easily he could lose his grip. In his final season in Kansas City, he strained a groin muscle. The team suggested he go on the disabled list. Knowing the Royals would fill his roster spot with a prospect, Pose grew nervous. "I begged them not to put me on the disabled list," he says. "Because I knew once I was on the disabled list, that was the kiss of death. Once I was sent out, I was never coming back."

Some careers are prolonged by potential, while others are curtailed by skepticism. The latter may explain Pose's fate. Baseball executives crave players who can hit for power. With just six home runs in 14 professional seasons, Pose may have given scouts and general managers just enough reason to pass on his stellar .293 career minor league average. After all, there is always another prospect around the corner—and he just might have a more promising skill set. "I knew going into it there was a different set of standards for me compared to most players. I knew I wasn't a phenom. So I got a leash

of 10 at bats in Florida, where a bona fide prospect would have gotten more. In my case, that wasn't it, so why complain about it? That's the way life is. That's the way baseball is. I'm grateful for every chance I got."

Coming to terms with the long odds was a necessity as a player. In retirement, he is happy to let go of the pressure. "I don't miss having to get two hits a night to stay around," he says. "I know in my heart I could compete up there."

When you are drafted in the 34th round, you take what the game gives you. That's why Pose is thankful for each opportunity in the major leagues—even when his uniform number was better suited for an offensive lineman.

"Never once in my backyard did I envision myself being a scrub. I never worked out so hard in the offseason to be a bench guy. I don't know of anybody who trained to be the journeyman. It's just how it worked out."

Scott Pose does not lose any sleep over it. Instead, when he closes his eyes at night, he sees what Cal Ripken saw.

SCOTT POSE

FOOT *ball*

Plenty left in the tank

R.J. Bowers took a
swing at baseball
before he landed
in the NFL.

R.J. Bowers was less than a year into retirement when the Carolina Panthers called, looking for a running back to fill out the roster. At age 30, he was still young enough to revive his career.

"But I wasn't ready to work out," Bowers says. "When you do that stuff your whole life, you want to take a break and relax. So I told them to keep me in mind and I would start to work out. If you have a need, give me a call."

By the time those words were out of his mouth, he knew the Panthers had turned to the next name on their list. "To an NFL scout, that's not going to fly," he says.

The flirtation with Carolina in 2004 gave him the incentive to get back in training mode. "My head tells me I can play, but my body really doesn't," says the 32-year-old Bowers. "About a year ago, I started running and I pulled a hamstring. I thought that was a fluke. Then I started lifting, and I pulled a muscle in my neck. I thought, Oh boy, maybe I am done."

Fortunately, he had already made it to the NFL. His modest contributions are noted in the league's rushing logs, but the statistics don't reveal the unlikely path he followed.

Raymond Keith Bowers Jr.—as a kid, he was called R.J. by his toddler neighbor—excelled at both football and baseball at West Middlesex High School in Pennsylvania. The University of Akron offered a full football scholarship, while the Houston Astros selected him in the 11th round of the 1992 draft. "I felt I never gave baseball my full attention. At 18 years old, it was an opportunity to turn pro and get a signing bonus," says Bowers, whose contract included $20,000 up front and $28,000 for college. "I just felt I could get better at baseball faster than I could at football."

He put in a couple years as an outfielder with Houston's rookie-league team, followed by four seasons of single A ball split between Davenport, Iowa and Kissimmee, Florida. After six seasons of minor league baseball, his career average was hovering around .250. He knew he was no longer on track to make it to the big leagues. "A lot of things came easy to me in high school, and I never developed the work ethic that I needed to make it to the major leagues. I did what I had to do, and that was about it. I didn't commit myself to the extra hitting.

"I was always a pull hitter, and I would never listen to the coaches and use the whole field," says Bowers, a right-handed hitter. "That outside pitch I grounded out to shortstop instead of taking it to the right-center gap for a double. Little things like that. Not that I didn't listen to what coaches said. I was just stubborn and I wanted to hit everything out of the ballpark. That just doesn't happen. The people who make it to the major leagues are the ones who use the whole field. I just didn't make the adjustments necessary."

"I hit the hole and I saw nothing but green grass in front of me. I crossed the goal line and I did a little fist pump. I wasn't much for celebration, but when I hit the goal line and did that fist pump, it was like everything I worked so hard for my whole life just kind of came together."

He asked for his release from the Astros in the summer of 1997 and played one more season in an independent league. Soon he was back in touch with his old high school football coach, Tom Trimmer, who had moved on to coach the offensive line at Grove City College in Pennsylvania. The school played Division III football, but Trimmer wasted no time giving his former star the recruiting pitch. Several years earlier, Bowers would have scoffed at play-ing non-scholarship football. But now he was ready to listen. "There was no doubt I wanted to play," he says. "But after being away for five years, I wasn't exactly sure."

Bowers decided to give football another chance. In his debut against Kenyon College, he ran tentatively in the first half. Then early in the third

quarter, he took a screen pass and raced 95 yards for a score. He was a football player again. Regardless of his low profile, he was determined to make the most of his opportunity. He renounced his sloppy baseball work habits and turned up the intensity on his football rebirth. "I never lifted weights until I was 24 years old. I went from 210 to 230. I got bigger, faster, and stronger than I'd ever been. My sophomore year was really fun and really easy."

When you lead the country in rushing yardage, how could it be anything else? Bowers was a one-man wrecking crew among the non-scholarship class. By his senior year, he had established 11 Division III records. None of them raised many eyebrows until Bowers became the leading rusher in college football history with 7,353 yards. When you pass guys like Walter Payton and Ricky Williams, people take notice. "I look at the records as something I had to do to get the attention of the scouts," he says. "Yes, I take pride in the record. But do I see it as a huge deal? Not really. It was Division III."

He knew that NFL scouts would evaluate his achievements with skepticism. He had done his best work against schools such as Thiel and Bethany— names that don't even register in pro football circles. Not once did he test his skills against Big Time State or Football U. He erased some of the doubt after playing in two college all-star games following his senior season. His workouts at the NFL combines helped too. But his name was never called in the 2001 NFL draft. "My age (27) didn't help me," Bowers says. "And the D-3 stigma didn't help me either."

The Carolina Panthers took a flier on the runner, signing him as a free agent. Carolina's fullback-friendly offense looked like a good fit for Bowers, who was a solid 230 pounds. But the jump to the NFL caught him off guard. In his first practice, he blew a blocking assignment. Then he ran the wrong pass route. The learning curve was steep and time was short. "I thought I knew a lot about football. But once I got there, I realized how much I didn't know. As a running back, you get the ball and you go. But as a fullback, you have blitz pickups and release assignments. If it's zone, you do one thing. If it's blitz, you do another. It's not about calling a play and running it."

A couple weeks into camp, Bowers learned his fate in a quick, impersonal meeting. Panthers coach George Seifert gathered all the players to be cut and dropped the ax on them all at once. "I'll never forget the day I left. Honestly, I cried," he says. "It was hard. I remember getting in the car and driving home, thinking I had to call my mom and dad. I've got to tell my wife when I get home. What am I gonna do now? Reality really sets in. It all kind of hit me at once. All the hard work and all the things you did, and you let it slip away."

Within 24 hours, Bowers was back in the NFL. The Pittsburgh Steelers offered to sign him to their practice squad. The kid who grew up 60 miles north of Pittsburgh was about to join his local team—although hardly his favorite. "No way, man!" he says. "I was a Cowboys fan. I grew up idolizing Tony Dorsett."

Once he put on the black and gold of the Steelers, his loyalties changed quickly. "Pittsburgh had great chemistry that year. It didn't matter who you were, you were part of that team. The defense respected me too, because when we practiced, I was the (next week's) opposing running back. I watched film with them to make sure I was doing what I needed to do to get them ready for Sundays. No way did I feel I was treading water."

Although he was relegated to the scout team, he was happy to spend his days soaking up wisdom from Jerome Bettis, the premier power runner in the NFL. "Jerome told me, 'R.J., if you never listen to anything else I have to say, listen to this: Fight the battles you know you can win. If you have any doubt, live to fight another day. That's the key to longevity.'"

It was good advice for someone who takes a pounding from NFL defenses, but Bowers had spent all his Sundays in street clothes. In December, however, he caught a break. Cleveland Browns coach Butch Davis called with an offer to sign him for the last few games of the season. Bowers ran the offer past Pittsburgh head coach Bill Cowher. With Bettis nursing an injury, Cowher told Bowers he could play the upcoming home game against Detroit. "Coach Cowher told me he saw me in a Steelers uniform for years to come. So I called Cleveland back and I said, 'I'm going to stay here. Sorry it didn't work out this time, but hopefully in the future it will.'"

The Detroit game set up well for his debut. In the fourth quarter, the

Steelers were cruising to a win that would run their record to 12-2. The waning moments of the game provided a perfect chance to give Bowers a look. But the scenario was hardly ideal for Bowers. The Steelers led the Lions, 47-14, and they were not digging very deep into the playbook. The Lions defense surely wanted to salvage some pride, too. "They know you're going to run the ball because you're trying to run out the clock," he said. "You look across the line, and you've got everybody looking at you. You're thinking, This is gonna hurt."

If it did, he doesn't remember. Only the euphoria left a lasting impression. "The hits were a little bit harder than Grove City, but it was so much fun. It's something I will never ever forget." He rushed seven times for a modest 17 yards against the Lions, a first impression that earned him another game the following week in Cincinnati. Against the Bengals, however, he was limited to blocking and tackling on special teams.

Having already qualified for the playoffs, the Steelers turned to Bowers once more in the home finale against Cleveland. His breakthrough NFL moment came in the fourth quarter. On third down and one, the Steelers called a running play designed for Bowers—39 Boss.

"I started to bounce outside, and I saw it open up, so I hit up inside. I basically wanted to get up in there and get a first down. Then it just kind of opened up. I hit the hole and I saw nothing but green grass in front of me. I crossed the goal line and I did a little fist pump. I wasn't much for celebration, but when I hit the goal line and did that fist pump, it was like everything I worked so hard for my whole life just kind of came together at that point."

It was 21 yards of pure joy. The rest of his day was not too bad, either. He finished with 67 yards on 11 carries.

But the playoffs were a different story. Like most teams, the Steelers turned to their veteran players, leaving Bowers to run with the scout team. Then at the 2002 draft, Pittsburgh selected a running back with a similar skill set. "When they drafted Verron Haynes in the fifth round, I kind of knew the writing was on the wall for me to be the odd man out," he says. "Not to say that was truly the case. They gave me a fair shot."

Because he played sparingly in the first weeks of the exhibition season, Bowers asked for his release. It was a risky move, but it paid off when he was claimed by Cleveland. But the Browns did not rely heavily on the fullback position. Despite dressing for the first four games, Bowers never got his hands on the ball. Cleveland then took him off the active roster for the rest of the season. "I was always hoping to get some touches, based on what I did the prior year, especially against them," he says. "It was frustrating in Cleveland. We had a lot of problems picking up third-down-and-one or fourth-and-one. I wanted the ball bad. But you couldn't say a whole lot up there. Not under coach Davis. You didn't want to say too much because you didn't want to ruffle the water."

His third NFL season began with even less promise. He went on the injured list for eight weeks after he tore a knee ligament doing leg squats in training camp. Already a square peg in the Cleveland offense, Bowers spent his weeks looking for some advantage that could make him more valuable when he returned to the field. He watched tapes of NFL fullbacks, trying to get a handle on the finer points of the role. But when he returned in the ninth game at Kansas City, his first play at fullback was one to forget. Quarterback Kelly Holcomb gave him a chance to catch his first NFL pass. He dropped it. "I tried to run before I caught it," he says. Two plays later, he atoned for his mistake, catching a two-yard toss for a touchdown. It was instant redemption.

It was also the last great memory of his football career. A few plays later, he tore the ligaments in his right ankle. His season was over. One dropped pass, one touchdown catch, one major disappointment. On the day before Christmas Eve, the Browns cut him loose. The timing felt cruel and he did not want to bow out with an injury, but Bowers knew right away it was time to retire. "There comes a time in your life when it's more important to be a daddy and a husband than it is to play in the NFL. I know that sounds crazy to some, but to me it wasn't that big of a deal, I guess.

"For a guy like me, after being in the league for three years, I was never secure in my job. You never knew if you were going to be on the team from one week to the next. It was tough family-wise. We had bought a house in

Pennsylvania, and there I was staying in Cleveland pretty much all week. I was seeing my wife and little boy once a week. It just kind of got old."

He makes a convincing case for retirement—injuries, family separation, lack of job security. His explanation is very practical. But two years after his last NFL game, he does not try to convince you that retirement comes easily. "It's not something that happens overnight. I'm still adjusting to this day," he says.

With football behind him, he now works as a sales representative for ABF Freight System, a trucking company. He likes the world of face-to-face meetings. As luck would have it, his territory is divided between Steelers country and Browns country. If his name rings a bell on a sales call, so much the better. "It definitely opens a lot of doors, and it's quite flattering when somebody does recognize the name," he says. "Generally, it's not something I bring up. But if they do bring it up, then we do talk about it. I don't walk through the door saying, 'I'm R.J. Bowers.'"

Even if he did, he knows his name might not register like it did a couple years earlier. Fans tend to forget the guys who played limited roles. "Life changes very quickly. It's hard to adjust to," he admits. "There I was in the spotlight, and now I'm working for a trucking company. You're no longer the center of attention. When you walk into a restaurant, you're not being hounded for autographs. I miss that. My wife doesn't miss it because now we can eat in peace and talk."

Because there is no blueprint for retiring from the best job in the world at 29, Bowers tries to roll with his conflicting emotions. He knows he can't play the game anymore, but some days he is stuck with his football mentality. "I'm a competitor, period. And that's something that I don't think will ever be out of my blood. My wife kind of gets upset at times because I'll turn normal household things into a race. Something has always got to be on the line for me. That's just how I am."

This is a transition time for Bowers, one which allows him to feel the pulse of perfect memories at the same time he adjusts to a working man's life. Along the way, he has encountered people who see him only as a retired

football player. "The biggest thing I get is, Why are you working now?"
he says. "Because I have to pay bills just like you do. I made a good living
and I was able to put some money away, but I don't want to spend what
I put away."

No one gets rich playing in eight NFL games, being bumped on and off
the active roster. But it's not the money that matters now. For years to come,
Bowers will feel his heart race when he thinks back to game days. Not game
checks.

"A lot of people would give anything to play for one day, or even have
the opportunity to work out in front of scouts. I was there and I did it, and
that's something very, very few people get to do. I wish everybody had the
opportunity to run out in front of 60,000 people just once in a lifetime. You
want to talk about a hair-raising experience. It's unbelievable. It's just
awesome."

Bowers might return to football as a coach one day. Until then, he is
happy with his memories. He has a tape of his 21-yard touchdown run. He
can watch the line of scrimmage open up and hear the fans roar and feel the
rush of that fist pump. "I don't watch it a lot anymore, but when I do, I have
the remote in my hand," Bowers says. "I've probably put it in twice since I
retired, but I probably watched it 20 times each sitting."

And you know how that makes him feel.

"I think I want to do it again."

Half full,
Half empty

Anthony Dilweg had
tremendous highs and
devastating lows in the NFL.
And he knows why.

 As the 1989 NFL draft approached, **Anthony Dilweg** was something of an unknown at quarterback. The experts had the Duke University signal caller slotted in the second round. Or maybe the sixth.

"I was labeled as the most overrated, underrated player by (ESPN's) Mel Kiper," Dilweg says with a laugh. "Before the season I was projected to be a free agent at best, so there wasn't a high expectation."

In fairness to the draft gurus, Dilweg was a work barely in progress. His experience as starting quarterback consisted of one season at Walt Whitman High School in Bethesda, Maryland and a fabulous senior year at Duke. The latter was Steve Spurrier's first as the Blue Devils coach. Together, they put each other on the college football map with the coach's pass-happy offense.

Dilweg made a strong showing in the college all-star games, including an MVP performance in the Hula Bowl. The Green Bay Packers were intrigued enough to select him in the third round. For Dilweg, there was a bit of good karma in going to Green Bay. His grandfather, Lavie, played offensive line for the Packers from 1927 to 1934.

But his rookie year provided little excitement. Third-year quarterback Don Majkowski had taken over the starting job the previous season, earning the nickname Magic for his comeback heroics in a 10-6 season. "We both had a very productive preseason," Dilweg says. "There was some consideration that I might start as a rookie, but they went with Don. Our stats were very similar."

By the end of the year, Dilweg was lucky to have any stats at all. If not for Majkowski getting the wind knocked out of him at Detroit, the rookie would have worn a baseball cap all season. Instead, Dilweg came off the sidelines facing third-down-and-five. "It was a little stop route at seven yards, and I elected to just try to get the first down. I think the corner route was open for a touchdown. It was my one pass, we got a first down, and that was it." One game, one play. But he was quick to look on the bright side.

"I focused on the quarterback rating," he jokes. "Hey, look at my quarterback rating! It was top five in the league."

Majkowski passed for an NFL-high 4,318 yards, earning a trip to the Pro Bowl. But when a contract holdout in 1990 spilled into the preseason, the Packers' fortunes suddenly rested with Dilweg and his one seven-yard completion. He was named the opening day starter, needing only to get through the final exhibition game at Kansas City. "I was terrible," he says of his performance against the Chiefs. "Four interceptions. All of a sudden, Don's in camp on Monday. But (head coach) Lindy Infante had named his starter and he was going to stick by it. So from the first game, I knew it was a game-to-game situation."

The script for the opener was pure Hollywood. The kid gets a shot against the heavily-favored Los Angeles Rams. One slip, and Green Bay turns to its newly-rich veteran waiting in the wings. So when the Packers fell behind the Rams in the first half, Dilweg was already on the ropes. "I remember I jammed my thumb and I was putting ice on it. Lindy comes up and says, 'Hey, can you go?' My paranoid side says, 'Coach, I'm fine! Don't worry about me!' I didn't want Don sliding in there. I'm glad I sucked it up."

He completed 20 of 32 passes for 248 yards and three touchdown passes. The Packers beat the Rams, 36-24, and Dilweg was named the NFC's player of the week. "I had a chance to throw five touchdown passes in that game," he says. "I had two guys wide open for touchdowns. And Lindy reminded me in films, 'Hey, you could have tied the record for Green Bay in your first start.'"

He started the following game against Chicago, but the storybook plot quickly fizzled. He was benched in the course of a 31-13 loss. Majkowski took the reigns on offense, but this time some of his magic was missing. Green Bay muddled through to a 4-5 record until Majkowski separated his shoulder against the Arizona Cardinals. With less than seven minutes left and the Packers trailing, 21-10, Dilweg engineered two scoring drives. The game winner came with 16 seconds left. "At the time, it was one of the top five comebacks in Green Bay history, so I'm thinking I'm destined for greatness," he laughs.

With his confidence brimming, he tossed three touchdown passes the next week to beat Tampa Bay at Lambeau Field. Green Bay was 6-5 and aimed squarely at the playoffs. Dilweg's next mission was a critical one. The Packers visited division rival Minnesota for the Sunday night game on national television. He could not only put the Packers in the thick of the playoff race, but he could show the entire NFL that he was a rising star.

It never happened. His poise was not to be found in Minnesota. "Just a complete collapse," he calls it. "It was just brutal and punishing."

"I was as close to being a fan as anybody. I saw the game as a spectator for 95 percent of my time as a backup quarterback. I never had a heavy dose of football in my life."

Against the Vikings, he could no longer get by on youthful exuberance. Dilweg needed to rely on savvy and patience, and he had none in reserve. Instead of working through the mess in Minnesota, he threw three interceptions in a 23-7 loss. "For some reason, there was a disconnect on knowing that you're never out of the game," he says. "There was a chance that I could have thrown a touchdown pass in the fourth quarter. I blew that call. I was already defeated at halftime. That was the emotional side that I should have shed better.

"I think if I would have had better experience dealing with adversity during games, I would have handled it better. I was immature enough that things were sticking with me. I think I watched my decisions deteriorate during the course of the game, and I let my emotions get caught up into to it."

On the sidelines, his teammates peppered him with upbeat chatter— There's plenty of time left. We're not out of it. We're with you. But his mental funk left him completely out of sync with the rest of the Packers.

"I wasn't listening," Dilweg says flatly.

A day later, his emotional state was no better. While receiving treatment in the trainer's room, he endured another steady stream of optimists. Put it behind you, they told him. We're still in the playoff hunt. We can beat Seattle this week. To Dilweg, that kind of talk was ridiculous. "It was almost too much," he says, recalling his skepticism. "Are you for real? We just got our ass handed to us. I think because I was immature, I didn't have a lot of that experience."

His troubles came to a head against the Seahawks. With the Packers down 20-0, the Lambeau crowd let him have it. "One of the offensive line veterans said, 'Hey Dilweg! Why don't you throw another interception and really piss them off?' He said it in a joking way, meaning, don't worry about those guys. But I took it personally and it magnified itself. I ended up getting benched. Blair Keil came in."

Dilweg injured his foot the next week against Philadelphia but returned for the season finale. With the Packers out of the playoff picture, he completed 15 of 23 passes for 208 yards in a loss to Denver. "I felt like I recovered in that last game," he says.

When training camp opened in 1991, Infante declared the starting quarterback job up for grabs among Majkowski, Dilweg, Kiel and former Bears quarterback Mike Tomczak. After two strong performances in the preseason, Dilweg turned in a bad outing and an average one. He was released by the Packers without much explanation. To this day, he wonders how he became the odd man out. "The simplest way to find out is to pick up the phone and call Lindy Infante and say, 'What do you think?' But it hasn't been such a strong part of my life."

Then Dilweg leans forward across the conference table. "I have a theory," he says. "Don Majkowski was fragile. Blair Keil, he's not going to win the game for you, but he'll keep you in the game. Tomczak had enough experience. I think I was looked at as a wild card. You may get a great performance or a terrible performance. If I'm a head coach and my job is on the line, I don't have time to wait for Anthony to get mature."

His 1990 statistics were satisfactory for an inexperienced quarterback—a completion rate of 52 percent, along with eight touchdowns against seven interceptions. While the statistics don't lie, Dilweg doesn't either. He will tell you that his promise was offset by his mercurial play and lack of poise. "I had some pretty big swings and volatility in my play. When I was cut from Green Bay, every team's comment to my agent was, 'Is there something we don't know? We saw him play. Why did Green Bay cut him?'"

A few weeks after Dilweg's release in Green Bay, Arizona brought him in for a tryout. The Cardinals needed quarterback help, and the coaching staff still had vivid memories of his fourth-quarter comeback against them the year before. As he walked through the team's locker room, he noticed his name and number were already affixed to a locker. Team officials were openly talking about a two-year contract. All that was left for Dilweg was tossing a few passes to wide receiver Ricky Proehl in an informal workout.

When he reached the field, he immediately recognized Cardinals offensive coordinator Jerry Rhome. In his college days, Dilweg had spent a day with Rhome, who was the Washington Redskins quarterbacks coach at the time. The Duke coaching staff had asked Rhome to help the young quarterback improve his throwing motion. "Here is the same guy I went up to see with the Redskins. He said, 'Hey, didn't you come up to visit?' I said, 'No, that wasn't me.' I thought he was going to equate me with the hitch in my motion."

By Dilweg's estimation, his workout performance was average. A short time later, Rhome called Dilweg's agent and said the team was not interested. Immediately, the quarterback wondered if his response had backfired. After all, Rhome remembered him right way. Did the coach think Dilweg was egotistical? Ungrateful? A liar? Years later, he thinks the Arizona job may have gone up in smoke simply because "I was scared to say this guy helped me out with a bad motion one time."

Before the end of the season, Dilweg worked out for Philadelphia, Detroit and San Francisco. His best shot came with the 49ers. San Francisco offensive coordinator Mike Holmgren planned to sign him if 49ers starter Steve Young had to go on the injured list. But Young checked out OK, and Dilweg remained unemployed. He found no takers all season.

His luck changed in 1992. A strong workout with the Los Angeles Raiders led to a contract. In the process, he got a glimpse of how he was viewed by the NFL establishment. Al Davis, the unpredictable owner of the Raiders, spelled it out the way he saw it.

"The word on you is you're either half empty or half full," Davis told him. "No one really knows." In order to find out, the Raiders allocated Dilweg to the World League of American Football, the NFL's developmental league. But after two games with the Montreal Machine, he hurt his knee. Told that he had a torn meniscus, he rehabbed the knee and got ready for Oakland's training camp.

At first, he earned plenty of practice reps. But after the first week, he found himself watching Jay Schroeder, Vince Evans and Todd Marinovich divvy up all the snaps in practice. He remained a bystander through the first couple exhibition games. Finally, he went to Davis and pressed the issue. Dilweg wanted playing time.

"I don't make the decisions," Davis told him. "You have to talk to Art Shell." Shell, the head coach, completed the runaround. He blamed Davis.

It was clear the Raiders had no intention of letting him show off his arm during the preseason. So Dilweg came up with an air attack of his own. During an exhibition game, he chartered a plane to fly over the stadium with a message banner: "AL DAVIS, GIVE ME A CHANCE. DILWEG."

"That was just my mind trying to be creative and have fun with it," he says. "All the coaches were pulling for me. I had nothing to lose. What was the worst thing they could do, cut me?"

USA Today ran a photo of the plane, trailing its clever plea. While the stunt scored points with readers and fans, it failed to tickle the organization's funny bone. The Raiders released Dilweg, adding a third strike against him after an injury and a year out of football. "I'm like the plague now," Dilweg says. Making matters worse, the Raiders had misdiagnosed the knee injury. In reality, he had a torn ACL. He figures the Raiders knew the severity of the injury, and they did not want to pay a $340,000 salary to a quarterback who needed surgery and a long rehab. He ended up filing a grievance against the Raiders before reaching a settlement.

After ACL reconstruction surgery in October, Dilweg made one last attempt to catch on in the NFL. He reached an agreement with the Cincinnati Bengals on a two-year contract, pending a physical. But the Bengals, wary of the damaged knee, backed out. With his NFL options exhausted, he landed with the Shreveport Pirates, a Canadian Football League team during the CFL's brief expansion into the United States. During his four-week stay with the team, a harsh reality set in. In the span of three years, he had gone from a promising NFL starter to a practice-squad quarterback in a second-tier professional league. He could no longer justify the pursuit of a football career.

"For two years, I really wasn't making much of a living," Dilweg says. "I almost felt invisible. I looked at myself physically. I'm not a big guy, I'm a skinny guy. I've got two reconstructed knees. I hadn't play a whole lot. I've got a good education. It's time to move on."

He quickly found his niche in the business world, working for a company that brokered leases for commercial properties. After learning the commercial real estate game from the ground up, he founded The Dilweg Companies in 1997. The private investment company in Durham, North Carolina raises money from individual investors to buy office buildings and shopping centers.

Today, Dilweg is satisfied with his role in the working world. But reaching a level of comfort did not come naturally. "I had to shift my self-worth from being a football player to just being who I am." he says. That meant more than just giving up the thrill of life in the high-stakes NFL. He had to come to terms with some unpleasant football memories and acknowledge their role in the demise of his career. As a result, he carries a keen sensitivity for other athletes whose careers never bloomed in full. "I'm always interested in the healing process. Very few of the athletes I know left on their terms."

There was a lot of quarterback left in Dilweg when he called it quits, but he has let himself off the hook for never getting a foothold in the NFL. "I was as close to being a fan as anybody," he says. "In my world, I saw the game as a spectator for 95 percent of my time as a backup quarterback. I never had a heavy dose of football in my life."

The 95-percent fan did surface once during an NFL game. While guiding the Packers offense against the Chicago Bears, Dilweg found himself side-by-side with Bears hall-of-fame linebacker Mike Singletary during a first-down measurement. "I remember going, 'I'm your biggest fan. I can't believe I'm talking to you.' He's like, 'Alright kid, back in the huddle.' He thought I was trying to distract him. I wanted to shake his hand and stuff like that. That's cool stuff."

It's a nice memory now, but it didn't feel that way heading back to the huddle. "I felt stupid," he says with a chuckle.

The lack of game experience was just one issue. He faced another simple truth beyond his control. "The reality is I was a scrapper. I wasn't that gifted. I just found a way to make things happen."

For Dilweg, inexperience and average talent are matter-of-fact truths, not excuses. If you want an explanation for the descent of his career, he points to his handling of three defining moments—losing his roster spot in Green Bay, brushing off the Arizona offensive coordinator, and listening to Al Davis's message about being an enigma. Those three instances had little to do with football. All of it was personal.

"The connections and the relationships at the pro level are critical with head coaches. There's a world beyond performance. It's called politics," he says. "You stay in front of the coach, you fight, you take a demotion to third string. I had hubris, I was young. I was very immature. And in games, I was not very successful. I didn't handle it very well. It was more, I don't need this, I've got a good education.

"When I look back, I should have lobbied a lot harder—whatever it takes to be on the third team. If I can't be the starter, I want to be the second-team guy. If you don't want me, then some other team will take me.

"I've learned that (football) is all you've got. You've got to find a way to stay in the league. I can see how guys stick around. Blair Kiel is a perfect example, with six years in the league. Who is this guy? He can barely hold a football. But he was very good at working the coaches and he understood his role. I didn't understand my role."

Today, it seems so clear. Whatever Dilweg lacked in talent and experience might have been overcome with simple people skills. "A lot of it comes down to relationships. I never played that card. I play it now like there is no tomorrow," he says. "I think I've learned a level of passion, commitment, dedication and politics. The dividend it's paid because of my NFL experience has been off the charts. I wouldn't replace that with anything."

The lessons serve as a silver lining now. They keep him from dwelling on a promising career that just seemed to vanish. "At one time, it felt like coming up short, and (later) I viewed it as success. I have transitioned from failure to success the longer I have lived. It feels a lot better than it did before. I think that's what I've learned from it, the bigger picture of how things work. There's a spiritual journey, a philosophical journey. I can go back and look at my experience and say I missed an opportunity. But I've been given the gift back."

Because Dilweg has made peace with his athletic career, his current life is a nice mix of the past and present. He stays directly involved with the game by serving as a sideline reporter for Duke radio broadcasts. He also owns and operates the Gus Purcell Quarterback Camps, where he and other retired NFL quarterbacks teach the game. "That's the best of any world to me," he says. "I can go and share what I've learned."

Some of Dilweg's best days are the ones when football and business work together. It took a while to find that balance. "I didn't want to be one of those players who tells all the stories. I wanted to have some substance to my life. Then I started thinking that I was proud to be a player. People enjoy that. And in business it's a great tool. I've totally under-utilized that because I didn't think it was appropriate or modest. I still don't use it that much, but it sure is fun when I do."

The weekly emotional swings of the NFL are behind him now. In the investment world, Dilweg rarely feels the exhilaration of a three-touchdown afternoon—or the letdown that follows a messy loss. But there is still plenty at stake each day. He has to prepare properly, make the right reads. Properties turn a profit or they don't. That's the win or the loss. "I try to re-create that on a healthy level. It sure is nice to cast the opportunity out there and pursue

it. Hopefully through the journey a lot happens, whether it's good, bad or ugly. When you get there, it's a special place. I like that."

That special place, like the red zone in football, keeps the adrenaline flowing—as long as no one gets sacked. "It feels like game time. I've created a platform that feels like you're playing for keeps. You may make $20 million, you may lose $20 million."

As he moves further away from his playing days, Dilweg is also coming full circle. "I don't want to say, 'Oh, that was my other life.' It's a lot of who I am today. The full healing process to me is to be able to write a thank you note to all my coaches. I feel pretty close to that point right now."

And when that time comes, it might stir up some old dreams. It reminds him of how he felt when his college coach, Steve Spurrier, was named head coach of the Washington Redskins in 2003. Dilweg was 37 at the time, 13 years removed from his last NFL game.

"I almost wanted to say, 'Hey, Steve, you need a backup?'"

He says this with complete sincerity, even though the idea sounds crazy.

"I'm serious," he insists, allowing just a little smile.

Maybe he could have pulled it off. Now more than ever, Dilweg is prepared for the job.

ANTHONY DILWEG

Pain and progress

Washington Redskins coach Joe
Gibbs had big plans for Tom Flick,
but a simple misunderstanding
between them changed
Flick's career forever.

Before **Tom Flick** ever set foot in an NFL locker room, he was handed the perfect game plan. The third quarterback taken in the 1981 draft, Flick was the handpicked selection of Washington Redskins rookie coach Joe Gibbs.

The former University of Washington star and the new coach would build their futures together. "I remember being picked up by coach Gibbs when I flew into the airport in D.C.," Flick says. "He pulled me aside and said, 'We believe you're the quarterback of the future.'"

Gibbs inherited a 6-10 team, and Flick gave him a potential alternative to veteran starter Joe Theismann, who remained a middling quarterback after seven seasons. Flick played sparingly as a rookie, but he had a good grasp of the offense. His confidence soared in the apprentice role, to the point that he could resort to a little teenage humor to earn some playing time. "Towards the end of the games, I remember standing behind coach Gibbs going, 'Put Flick in.' A lot of times I'd use a different voice so he didn't know if it was a different player. Then I'd move a couple steps over, and I'd be real attentive with my helmet in my hand, going, 'I'm ready to go.' I loved that first year in the NFL. It was just what I expected it to be."

When the season ended, Flick headed home to the Seattle area for the offseason. He was a homebody, one of seven children. More importantly, he felt the call of family duty. His father, a test pilot, had nearly died in a plane crash prior to Flick's senior year in college. So he spent the summer preparing for his second season and tending to his family's needs.

When he joined the Redskins for training camp the next summer, he discovered that something had changed. Gibbs was screaming at Flick every day during practice, noting each mistake the second-year quarterback made. Flick noticed he was the only player drawing the coach's wrath, and he grew miserable wondering why Gibbs was so angry at him.

Then one night as Flick readied for bed in his Dickinson College dorm room, he heard a knock on his door. There stood Gibbs at 11 p.m. The head coach doesn't do bed checks. "He says, 'Let's go for a drive,'" Flick says. "And we start to communicate for the first time. The issue was he was upset with me for not living back there in Washington D.C. in the offseason. For not showing leadership, for not being the guy the team could look up to as the first guy there and the last guy to leave. He was very mad. But it was a great conversation and very respectful. I had a chance to speak my piece."

Flick realized that Gibbs' side of the conversation was the only one that mattered. Everything was clear now. He should have spent the offseason in Washington D.C. While sitting in the coach's car, he told Gibbs straight out, "Maybe you said it clear enough, and I didn't want to hear it." Feeling humbled, Flick apologized and went back to his dorm room. Lesson learned, apology made. Clean slate tomorrow.

In Cleveland, he told coach Marty Schottenheimer, "Put me in the game, and if I don't play up to your standards, cut me. Don't even pay me for the game I played. I'm so sick and tired of sitting on the sidelines and not having a chance to play."

That lasted until breakfast. The equipment manager sent Flick to see the coach. "He (Gibbs) says, 'Tom, listen. We've traded you.' And about 28 teams went through my head at that moment. He said, 'We traded you to New England, and we traded you there because...' And as soon as he said 'because', I just cut him off. I didn't want to know why. Your pride jumps forth to protect yourself. It was devastating. It just sunk my ship.

"From that point forward, I was digging to gain confidence again. It was an uphill battle for the next four years. I was struggling to get my feet back underneath me."

Today, Tom Flick is a corporate motivational speaker. You might think that line of work would be the exclusive province of the great achievers and

champions. But when Flick takes the stage today, he has plenty of useful lessons to share with the folks at AT&T, Honeywell and 3M. Because his pro football career never got back on track, he cannot call on memories of classic playoff games or heroic comebacks. Instead, he relies on some of the real-world lessons he learned in pro football. He explains to audiences how people instinctively avoid pain and seek comfort. He lays out a blueprint for handling change successfully. He tells people how to "move to a future place of more value." What he lacks in uplifting platitudes from the fields of the NFL, he makes up for with dead ends, near misses and perspective. Those harsh football lessons, it turns out, just kept coming long after he left the Redskins.

For starters, the fresh start in New England never took root. He was haunted by the conflict he left behind in Washington. Why had Gibbs bothered to clear the air, only to trade him the next day? Could Flick have said anything in the car that night that would have made things right? The trade felt so extreme, and Flick took it hard. He had done more than lose his job. He had disappointed Gibbs.

"At New England, I had so many nightmares that on three different occasions I flew to D.C. and stayed at a hotel on Capitol Hill and just walked the city streets because I was so bothered. Like, what happened? I just really struggled. I left on such strange terms.

"Joe never did say outrightly, 'I expect you to live back here.' He must have thought he made it clear enough for me to understand. Apparently, I wasn't bright enough to catch what he was saying. I didn't read the tea leaves, and that's my mistake."

Flick's season in New England did not help the healing process. His introduction to his new teammates came during the Patriots' final preseason game in Dallas. "(Head coach) Ron Meyer, in all his wisdom, says, 'You're going in." I'm going, 'Hey coach, I don't know the snap count, and I don't know any plays.' He said, 'Here's a couple running plays and here's a pass play. Why don't you go down and meet your offensive line and introduce yourself because you're going in.' I literally went and said, 'Guys, hey, I'm Tom. I'm the new guy that was traded from Washington. You saw me stand up in the meeting last night. I'm your QB." That's how bizarre it was. I was shaking hands with the offensive line right before going out. New England was really strange. It was a bizarre place to play."

His first regular-season action was no better. In the second-to-last game of the year, the Patriots trailed Pittsburgh at the start of the second half. Meyer pulled starting quarterback Steve Grogan. But instead of turning to backup quarterback Matt Cavanaugh, he sent in Flick, the third stringer. Flick threw two incomplete passes before getting sacked on third down. He then came out of the game without explanation. "Afterwards, Meyer comes over and goes, 'Got a call from Mr. Sullivan (team owner Billy Sullivan). He wanted to see what you can do, so I put you in.' That was really a bummer."

Given the frustration of his first autumn in New England, the following season was a blessing in disguise. The Patriots had just two quarterbacks at the start of training camp, Flick and first-round draft pick Tony Eason. Forced to overwork his arm for the first few days, Flick soon lost feeling in his forearm and two fingers. He was diagnosed with ulnar neuritis, forcing him to miss the entire 1983 season.

By the start of the 1984 season, the arm was OK and Flick was in demand around the NFL. He signed with the Cleveland Browns, where Paul McDonald had taken over as the starter after four years of backup duty. Halfway through the season, Cleveland was floundering at 1-7, and McDonald was struggling badly at quarterback. Head coach Sam Rutigliano was fired and replaced by Marty Schottenheimer.

The situation was ripe for a quarterback change, and Schottenheimer pulled the trigger—demoting Flick from second string to third string behind rookie Terry Nugent. Having learned that his career was on life support two teams ago, Flick decided to make some noise. He could not force his way into the lineup, but he could force his way into Schottenheimer's office. "I blew right past his secretary, walked right in his office unannounced and closed the door firmly behind me, and I was ticked," Flick says, his voice welling with emotion.

"I should be the quarterback on this football team," he told his boss.

"Paul's been getting hammered, we've been losing games, and what we need is leadership. Here's the deal: Put me in the game, and if I don't play up to your standards, cut me. Don't pay my salary, just cut me. Don't even pay me for the game I played. I'm so sick and tired of sitting on the sidelines and not having a chance to play."

Schottenheimer never said a word. Flick told the coach he appreciated his time and walked out. He wondered what consequences he would face for his rant. "The next day, Schottenheimer comes up to me and says, 'You're my backup quarterback. As soon as there is a need, you will be in. I appreciate what you said to me yesterday. That's the kind of guy I want on my football team.'"

The move up the depth chart was nothing more than a moral victory. Flick appeared in one game with the Browns, throwing just one pass. His dream of becoming an NFL starter was fading. In 1985, it nearly slipped away for good. The Browns drafted Bernie Kosar and brought in Gary Danielson from Detroit. Flick was released by the Browns during the preseason and remained out of football all year.

In 1986, he finally recaptured some of the excitement of his first season. He won the backup job with the San Diego Chargers, where Dan Fouts was in the twilight of his hall-of-fame career. Flick had no illusions about winning the starting job, having thrown just six passes in the previous four seasons. Instead, he embraced the backup role and enjoyed working with the affable Fouts.

"Dan Fouts was one of the most generous guys because he was not threatened," says Flick. "Joe Theismann was threatened. I remember asking Joe things, and he'd go, 'Forget you. You go figure it out. Sonny Jugensen and Billy Kilmer never told me anything.' Joe got testy when you'd try to pick his brain. Fouts would tell you secrets and tricks of the trade."

In week eight against Philadelphia, Flick relieved Fouts after an injury. Although the Eagles cruised to a 23-7 win, Flick connected with Charlie Joiner for the first touchdown pass of his career. With Fouts still on the mend a week later, he earned his first NFL start. But after waiting six seasons for a game of his own, Flick fizzled. The Chargers lost to Kansas City, 24-23. He made no effort to deflect the blame. "I studied myself into this robotic mind-set. I was just so stiff. I tried to be so perfect. I really played a horrendous football game. I think I was 4-for-16 with four interceptions. All I could say when the reporters came to me after the game was, 'I owe everyone an apology. I stunk. And I apologize to you and my teammates and the city.'"

Flick was scheduled for one more start. After wandering so long in the NFL wilderness, he was determined to be remembered for something more than one rotten Sunday. He would not let his embarrassment paralyze him. He was going to learn from the Kansas City loss and do what he set out to do years earlier—lead an NFL team to a win. "You just talk yourself back into your go side," he says, recalling his mindset. "If I'm going down, I'm going down in flames, I'm going to play like I know I can play. I was 17-for-23 and I was player of the game and we upset Denver, 9-3."

Fouts returned to guide the Chargers over the final weeks of the season, but Flick had that elusive win under his belt. It bolstered his enthusiasm for another season. He promised San Diego head coach Al Saunders that his best was yet to come. But when Flick returned for the 1987 season, the Chargers had hired Roger Theder to coach the quarterbacks. Theder had come from the defunct USFL, and he brought San Antonio Gunslingers quarterback Rick Neuheisel with him.

"Meetings consisted of Rick and Roger telling USFL stories—like it was of interest to Dan Fouts. I liked Roger, but he was really thrilled to be in the NFL coaching. At the end of meetings at 10 o'clock at night on a couple of occasions, Rick would go, 'Coach and Roger—do you think Dan, Tom, Mark (Hermann) and I could stay afterwards and watch extra film?' Dan would say, 'Rick, you can stay here until midnight. I'm going to bed.' Roger and Rick had their relationship intact."

In the exhibition season, Theder made sure Neuheisel took plenty of snaps, leaving Flick on the sidelines for two weeks. The Chargers cut Flick after the final game of the preseason, leaving him with no hope of finding another team before the start of the season. After a few days of fly fishing

and trying to accept that his career was likely over, he received a call from the New York Jets. Flick signed, but he was third on the depth chart behind Ken O'Brien and Pat Ryan, making for an uneventful season.

As the 1988 season approached, Flick's interest in football was waning. He was cut by the Jets, but other teams remained interested. The Houston Oilers brought him to town to sign a contract, but when he arrived, the Oilers decided that Warren Moon was healing more quickly than expected. Flick went home without a deal.

On the flight home from Houston, Flick tried to sort out his fading relationship with the NFL. Soon, however, football became irrelevant. He learned his mother was in the late stages of pancreatic cancer. While caring for his mother and his pregnant wife over the next few months, Flick lost 22 pounds. "I had no interest, no desire. The flame had gone out. My job was to be a dad and to be a son to my father. That next year was kind of a lost year, wondering, Who am I? I was trying to bring stability to my life and my family."

With his family responsibilities taking over, Flick did not dwell much on the end of his career. He found some personal direction when he joined a speakers bureau, giving motivational talks to high school students. For a few years, it was a good fit. The next step was taking his message from the classroom to the boardroom. "I feel that's God's hand and plan on me. I feel that's what I'm called to do. And I think He gave me the skills and gifts to do that.

"I'm an encourager by nature, but I also challenge people. I bring the velvet hammer. Not in the sense that they feel their backs are against the wall, but where they can sit up and go, 'I can.' I love that role. I like leading the 10 other guys down the field as much as I like throwing the touchdown. I'm more fulfilled doing this than I was playing."

When you are billed as a former NFL quarterback, your audience expects a certain amount of bravado. But Flick isn't about to present his career in a glorified light.

"In my own head, I would not call it a success," he says quietly. "I really wouldn't. It was disappointing that I didn't start, and I wasn't consistent. I didn't play a good period as a starter in the National Football League. I know

I was good enough to be a starter. I just know I was. It just never panned out, for whatever reason. And I have no excuses to make, and a lot of that happens to be on my shoulders. You can tie it into youth, and bad breaks and tough luck. But in the final analysis, I would say no. It was not a success."

In five seasons, Flick threw just 106 passes with two touchdowns and 10 interceptions, numbers that are both sparse and unproductive. "That was very hard to swallow for a number of years. What I've done is just say, OK, that's a piece of my life, and it was an interesting phase of my life. I learned a lot of things from it. It's helped me to move on in what I'm presently doing."

In the years after the NFL, Flick felt he had drifted away from some of his personal values. Since childhood, he had been trading on the privileges that came with being a football player. "Ever since we were young kids, there was a sense of specialness about us—or we thought there was. Your name is in the paper, you can turn in your homework a bit later. You're just treated by people a little differently. I'm almost thankful that things did not work out in the NFL. It sounds really odd, but I don't know if I would have handled success successfully.

"I was raised by a wonderful set of parents with good values and those types of things. I played the humble game really well. I'd walk away and you'd think, That guy was a great guy. But inside, I had an ego and a pretty healthy one. I think God really likes a humble heart. He opposes the proud, but He gives grace to the humble. I am compensated very well for what I do. And I have humility hopefully."

Flick knows that his bittersweet memories will resurface from time to time. The one that still haunts him is his departure from the Redskins, the one that crippled his confidence and changed the course of his career. If only he had understood Gibbs' message about staying in D.C. and positioning himself as a leader. Maybe there would have been no trade, no nightmares, no backup roles with aimless teams.

"The void that I have to this day is Joe Gibbs is the one person I'd like to go back to in life and say, 'Let's talk about what happened.' Because I wanted badly to please him and play well. He was like a father figure. I still respect

him to this day. I was never bitter at him, never mad at him."

The Gibbs episode and other humbling circumstances are now just part of Flick's history. Hard times look different a couple decades later, but all the heartache had some staying power. "It was hard for quite some time," he says. "Was it easy? No. Was it fun? Never. Growing pains aren't fun."

Every so often, Flick has occasion to wrestle with his NFL memories. When he attended the 2005 Pro Bowl as a guest of a corporate sponsor, he shared the field and the Hawaiian sunshine with plenty of former NFL greats. As he sat in a golf cart watching the stars from yesteryear make their rounds, he noticed their body language. His contemporaries still had their swagger after all these years. "Some guys never had to grow up, and I don't mean that in a bad way," he says. "They made it through their careers and they had success, and it's easy to get locked in. There's a comfort zone right there. It's not a bad place to anchor yourself."

But it's not Tom Flick's place. What would he do with a swagger anyway?

"That's not where I want to be in my life," he says. "I'm really happy where I'm at right now."

TOM FLICK

Working it out

Odell Haggins played
sparingly in the NFL,
but he left the game
with no regrets.

With **Odell Haggins**, everything boils down to hard work. After earning all-America honors as a defensive tackle at Florida State, he was selected by the San Francisco 49ers in the ninth round of the 1990 NFL draft.

His small frame for an interior lineman—6 feet 2 inches, 260 pounds— might explain how he slipped to the late rounds. But that didn't matter.

"As hard as I worked, with my mentality, I thought I'd make the team," Haggins says from his office at Florida State, where he coaches defensive tackles on Bobby Bowden's staff. "But when you go in the ninth round and they have Jim Burt, Fred Smerlas and Michael Carter, it's tough. I thought I could outwork them. I'm going to do whatever I have to do on the football field, and I'm going to get a roster spot. But there's other things in the equation that affect making the team. They've got money in (the veterans). They don't care how hard you work."

The three veteran tackles had a combined 29 years experience, leaving little opportunity for Haggins to play in the preseason. That didn't stop him from believing he belonged on the 49ers roster. "The way I was raised, I was so driven. I thought I could outwork them and outprepare them. In my mind, I said I'm going to make it. My mother pushed me as a young man to work hard. The cream always rises to the top."

San Francisco waived Haggins before the start of the season, but he was offered a spot on the practice squad, the in-between world where players are part of the team six days a week—just not on Sundays. Missing the games was bad enough, but soon he learned that even the taxi squad was not a sure thing. San Francisco released him again in the middle of the season, only to bring him back for more taxi squad duty a couple weeks later. Despite the hard knocks, Haggins was up to the task. "It wasn't hard to be on the practice squad. I had that inner drive. It's not over until it's over," he says. "Jim Burt used to look at me and just shake his head, 'Man, you work hard. One day something is going to open up for you.' Something like that you never forget."

Haggins built his confidence by taking all the positive feedback to heart, knowing that most ninth-round draft picks get an early start on life after football. In a world where young players often squander their new-found riches, he felt lucky to draw the standard weekly paycheck for practice squad players. "To me, $4,000 was a lot of money," he says. "I saved my money."

And because he was in the good graces of the San Francisco organization, he made a little extra on the side. The 49ers often rounded up players to take part in charity basketball games against local high schools and civic groups. The team would never allow stars like Joe Montana, Jerry Rice or Ronnie Lott to risk a torn ACL playing hoops, but guys like Haggins were fair game. For each game he played, he earned $1,000 from the 49ers. By the end of the season, his nest egg had grown by $8,000. "That organization treated me with respect because they knew what I brought to the table, and they knew I worked hard," he says.

 **"At that time I had to realize –with my dream right there–it was time to get in the real world in another profession."**

He finished the year on the practice squad without ever being activated for a game. The 49ers wanted him back for the 1991 season, but Haggins also attracted the attention of the Buffalo Bills. Unlike the 49ers, the Bills were thin at defensive tackle. Buffalo was also offering more money. "I invested so much time with the 49ers and learned their system like the back of my hand," he says. "If I had stayed in San Francisco, they might have drafted another guy." The lure of more playing time finally convinced Haggins to take his chances with Buffalo.

Although he left the 49ers without playing a down of NFL football, he never doubted the value of his experience. "The lesson I learned was don't sit around like a knot on a log even though you're not playing. Learn!" says Hag-

gins. "Michael Carter, Jim Burt, Fred Smerlas, Charles Haley, Pierce Holt, Kevin Fagan. That's a world of experience. That's like making money right there. And I knew one day I wanted to coach. I thought, Let me gather this experience up and listen to you guys."

In Buffalo, Haggins assumed his familiar role on the practice squad. But when Pro-Bowl defensive lineman Bruce Smith went down with a knee injury, the Bills gave him a chance to suit up on game day. He anchored the middle of the defensive line on first and second down, playing mostly when opponents were in running situations. But if you want stories from the NFL trenches, you won't get many details from Haggins. "That's long, long ago," he says. "I can't even sit back and think about it. I cherished going out and help-ing the team win and playing as hard as I possibly could." While most young players are inclined to soak up their surroundings and file away a few mental images, Haggins was not so sentimental. "I was out there just playing, having fun. That was my goal, to get out there and play and prove myself."

In five games, the Buffalo Bills officially credit him with two tackles and one assist. Those numbers sound a bit low to Haggins, and he probably has a point. He surely had a hand in many more stops—slowing the ball carrier, making the first hit—without getting statistical credit. He remembers forcing a fumble against Chicago too, but those are among the details that don't mean much anymore. All he knows is he enjoyed the challenge. Playing in the middle of an NFL line felt good, just as it had in college. "It was no different for me. We always played elite teams in college, and the speed of the game at Florida State was fast."

At the halfway point in the season, he returned to Buffalo's practice squad, where he spent the rest of the regular season. "That's when I got a little frustrated," he says. "You think you're doing a better job than some of them, but that's when politics are tied up in it. Guys making a lot more money had to play, and they had been there before me. Loyalty, in other words."

Although he was a bystander for the balance of the 1991 season, he had a front-row seat on a team with championship hopes. After playoff wins over Kansas City and Denver, the Bills went to the Super Bowl for the second straight year. Buffalo's 37-24 loss to the Washington Redskins was heart-breaking for Haggins, who watched the game in street clothes on the Buffalo sidelines. "It hurt me. I'm a team person. That's my team. I wish I could have played. Maybe I could have done something to help them out."

After the Super Bowl, Haggins found himself facing the same dilemma as in the previous offseason. Once again, the 49ers and the Bills both made contract offers. But this time he had experience with both organizations, making the choice more difficult. He wanted to do more than take baby steps. He wanted to sign with the team that gave him the best chance to make the active roster and contribute. In need of some guidance, Haggins turned to Buffalo general manager Bill Polian, a man with a reputation for shooting straight with players.

"I knew both systems, the 49ers and the Bills. Buffalo wanted to keep me there. I started weighing my options. Some of the higher-paid San Francisco players went on to other places. So I talked to Mr. Polian, and he gave me advice. He said, 'We'd love to keep you here. But you've got to do what's best for you.' I will always respect that man for how he treated me as a person. That's why he's built the teams he has. Players respect people who can look in your eyes and tell you the truth."

Haggins took Polian's advice and put himself first. San Francisco looked like a better opportunity, so he signed with the 49ers. "I was having a great training camp. I was tearing it up. I was going to play a lot in the first pre-season game," he says. "And about four days before the first preseason game, we were in pads and somebody rolled up on my ankle."

At first, the injury appeared to be a small setback. After resting the ankle for three weeks, Haggins felt better and tried to practice. "It felt OK, but it was not 100 percent where it should have been to go out and try to win a job. In the NFL, everybody's out to get a job. They don't have time for a hurt person. I went out and re-injured it in practice." This time he had a serious problem. The ligaments in his ankle were torn. The 49ers suggested that he go on the injured list, but Haggins was already thinking about moving on to something other than football.

"It was hard. I had to pray about it," Haggins says. "I'd been playing for 17 or 18 years of my life, knowing (if I retired) that I wouldn't be able to do it again. It hurt. I talked to my mother and my brothers."

Then he called Bowden at Florida State. His old coach said, "You keep playing if you still feel you've got a burning desire."

"Coach, I do," Haggins told him, "but it seems like I keep going around in circles."

He had his answer. He had spun his wheels long enough. "I think God had something else in life for me. As bad as I wanted to play, I had to go on with my life."

At age 25, Haggins left the game with plenty of runway still ahead of him—but none of the thrust to get airborne. With just five games to his credit, Haggins was finished as a player but content with his experience.

"I didn't give up, now," he says forcefully. "Bad as I wanted to play, I wanted to go and do something else. At that time I had to realize—with my dream right there—it was time to get in the real world in another profession."

Having come to terms with football, he took a job working with juvenile offenders in the state attorney's office in Jacksonville, Florida. He performed assessments of preteens, hoping to steer them toward programs that limited their chances of becoming repeat offenders. Later in 1994, he joined the Florida State coaching staff.

Today, Haggins has fond memories of the camaraderie that he enjoyed as a player, but not much else. "I look back and it was a lifetime ago," he says. "I don't miss it now."

If any of the Florida State linemen want to chat about Haggins' NFL days, they will have to keep after him. He's not big on particulars. If his players ask, "I'll elaborate on it. I'm very humble about that," he says. More likely, Haggins will turn the subject to the big picture. He has plenty of messages that college players need to hear. "Get your education," says Haggins, who earned a degree in criminology at FSU. "The NFL is not what you think, it's a business."

You play the hand you are dealt, and certainly Haggins could have hoped for a better one where the NFL was concerned. The league is plenty tough without being an undersized, late-round pick. Add a bad injury to the mix and it becomes a recipe for disappointment. Not everyone would take all of it in stride, but Haggins knew no other way. And that brings up another bit of wisdom that he can pass along as a coach. "You take the good and the bad and go on," he says. "If you dwell on the bad stuff and the negative stuff, you're going to fall back into a hole. You've gotta take the negative and make it a positive and run on with it."

That is what Haggins has done. He is not indifferent to the opportunity he missed in the NFL. He just doesn't see the point in worrying about games and seasons that never came to pass. "Sometimes it would have been nice to have the money, and maybe put some of that money up. Maybe now I'd be a multi-millionaire," he says. "Hey, you can't miss what you never had. I got paid good money when I was in Buffalo. But how could I miss a quarter of a million dollars? I never had that before.

"But you know what? With my happiness and the opportunity to be in the NFL and doing something I loved, that was a million dollars to me. I'm always going to be positive. There's no need to be negative. What is that going to do?"

All it can do is stand in the way of some other dream. In Haggins' case, maybe that will be a college head coaching job down the road. But for now, he is happy with his current path. He has paved it proudly with hard work— which is its own reward.

"My mother taught me nothing comes easy in this world," he says. "If you work hard, you won't have to go back and pick up trails."

Kickin' around

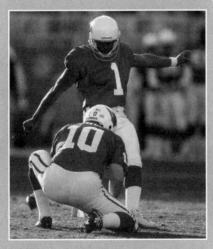

Cedric Oglesby's
dream didn't last long,
but his performance
was nearly perfect.

Like all kickers, **Cedric Oglesby** has played the waiting game. It was the fall of 2001, and Oglesby was coming off a strong performance at the NFL kicking combine, where teams browse for strong legs to bring to training camp.

Scouts from Arizona, Dallas and Kansas City had given him business cards, a sure sign of interest. He felt like he was right on the brink. "I saw what I could do compared to the other guys," says Oglesby. "Once I realized I could do it, I couldn't let go of it that easy."

So three times a week, Oglesby dragged a sack of footballs to a high school near his home in Atlanta. Each day he made 50 kicks. To pay the bills, he picked up substitute teaching jobs and gave private instructions for young kickers. But in his heart, he was a kicker. He just didn't have the job to prove it yet.

As the calendar turned to December, Oglesby's dream was nearly over for the season. Few teams replace their kickers in the final weeks. Then one Sunday afternoon while he was giving a kicking lesson, his cell phone rang. A buddy was calling to report one of the most foolish acts in the history of NFL kicking. Arizona's Bill Gramatica had torn the ligaments in his knee after leaping in the air to celebrate a field goal—an over-the-top reaction to a 42-yard kick in the first quarter.

Oglesby figured he would be on Arizona's short list of candidates to replace Gramatica. After all, he had their business card. He planned to get in touch with the team first thing Monday morning.

But with his dream job dangling in front of him, Oglesby was cut off from his normal lines of communication. He was substitute teaching in a kindergarten class, unable to get a signal on his cell phone. He couldn't walk out on the five-year-olds, and he also couldn't wait forever to find out if he was in the mix for the Cardinals job. His only hope was recess. When he finally got the kids outdoors, he checked his phone and breathed a sigh of relief. In his voice mail was a call from the Arizona Cardinals.

"I had to be on a flight at 7:30 that night, so I got the biggest suitcase I had. I was about to get on the plane, and the security guard saw the cleats and shoulder pads, and he asked what I was doing," says Oglesby, noting that the tryout came a few weeks after 9/11. "I said, 'I'm trying to get a job in Arizona.'"

It was not the first time Oglesby had come close to landing an NFL job. By the time he flew to his Arizona audition, he had already invested 18 months trying to crack one of the most exclusive positions in sports.

Just before his graduation from South Carolina State in 2000, he earned an invitation to the Dallas Cowboys mini-camp. Dallas looked like a perfect opportunity. At the very least, there seemed to be some good karma. Oglesby was familiar with the team's kicking coach, Steve Hoffman, having used the coach's instructional videos in the past.

Oglesby had three competitors for the Dallas job. Rian Lindell and Jon Hilbert were also free agent kickers with no NFL experience. The three were to challenge incumbent kicker Tim Seder, who had just one year of NFL experience. "I started to kick my set, and on my fifth kick, I pulled the quadriceps," says Oglesby, who had come to camp already nursing a strain in the muscle. "I was done for the rest of mini-camp. Rian Lindell said, 'I'm not going to lie that I'm sad you're injured. It's just one less man to compete against.'"

On the last day of mini-camp, Oglesby got a tap on his shoulder on the way into the locker room. He was sent to Stephen Jones, the son of team owner Jerry Jones. "He just said, 'I'm sorry, we're going to have to release you. You won't heal up in time, and we need the roster spot.'

"I said, 'You'll see me again somewhere down the road, with you or with someone else.' I was disappointed and upset. They had given me the impression they would wait until summer and give it time to heal up. That was my first experience with what the NFL was all about. They don't care. To coach in the NFL, you almost have to have a degree in lying with a straight face."

Oglesby left mini-camp with just a few assorted memories of playing for America's Team. He dressed in the locker next to Troy Aikman, an arrangement that did nothing for Oglesby's ego. Whenever he came out of the shower, he had to wait out the throng of reporters that took over his locker space to pursue the star quarterback. Even though he never played a game for Dallas, Oglesby will always be remembered as a true Cowboy—at least for a few fans. "When I was practicing, there were people touring the stadium. They wanted to take a picture with a Cowboys player. I wasn't even on the team, but they didn't know. They were Oriental."

By September, Oglesby landed another tryout, this time with Seattle. He was still having pain in his quadriceps and he was not able to train properly. "I was not at 100 percent," he says. "But I went ahead and took the workout. I figured maybe I could pull a rabbit out of the hat."

Instead of a rabbit, it was as though a black cat had crossed his path. Once again, he would have to compete with Lindell, who had literally added insult to Oglesby's injury in Dallas a few months earlier. As Oglesby anticipated, his leg was not up to par. His kickoffs lacked what kickers call explosion. They were coming up short of the end zone. Seattle's coach told Oglesby he didn't look like the same kicker he saw at the combine. "I wasn't disappointed because I wasn't 100 percent. Then the next Monday, I turned on Monday Night Football and Lindell was playing in the first game of his career. If I'd have been ready, it could have been me. It was a missed opportunity."

He found another interested team in the spring of 2001. The San Diego Chargers brought him in for mini-camp, and this time he had no lingering injuries. Everything checked out OK during his physical exam, but the medical staff nearly ruined Oglesby's opportunity by dilating his pupils. No one realized the coaching staff wanted the kicker on the practice field right away. "They told me, 'We want to sign you, but coach wants to see you kick a few first,'" he says. Right away, he realized the sunlight was blinding. "I put my cleats on and I went outside. I said, "I can't see, there's no way I'll be able to kick."

The Chargers sent Oglesby back to his hotel, promising to pick him up after his eyesight returned to normal. After a couple anxious hours of pacing the room, he got a call from the team. San Diego decided to go ahead and sign him, even without an audition.

Even with a deal in place, he knew he had little shot of winning the job. The Chargers had also signed former San Francisco kicker Wade Richey to a five-year deal worth nearly $6 million. Oglesby was just an extra leg in camp, someone to provide a little competition. At best, he hoped to impress another team during the preseason.

In his first exhibition game, Oglesby connected on his only attempt from 46 yards. The following week he made a 19-yard chip shot against Miami. Then when the game went to overtime, he had a chance to prove himself in the clutch. He delivered the game-winner from 33 yards. Expecting a few words of encouragement after sealing the overtime win, he was left cold. "Not one coach congratulated me after the winning field goal," he says. "I wasn't the guy they had invested money in."

Although he was keenly aware of the coaching staff's indifference, Oglesby was soothed a bit by the reaction of his teammates. Chargers quarterback Doug Flutie made a point of congratulating him on the kick. Other veteran players showed their approval by calling an audible on post-game shower privileges. "Normally the veteran players shower first in preseason. The rookies have to wait. But they were yelling, 'Come on in, you've earned it.' At least the players said congratulations. But you don't get pats on the back from coaches, you get your check."

The temporary nature of his role became more clear each day. Oglesby was told he would not get his usual one-third of the kicking reps in practice for the upcoming week. Instead, Richey got all the work. When Richey kicked the game-winner later in the week, the Chargers had seen enough. Oglesby was called to the front office, where he learned that an NFL exit interview could be conducted as quickly as a snap, hold and kick. "They said, 'Thanks, you did a great job. If you need any help, call us. Your plane is leaving at two o'clock.'"

Although disappointed, Oglesby returned home to Atlanta with improved credentials. His perfect 3-for-3 kicking in the preseason gave him hope of being picked up by another team. The San Diego special teams coach had made a point of telling him to stay ready. Even if they were just words of encouragement, Oglesby took them to heart. He decided to focus on kicking three days a week and make ends meet with substitute teaching jobs.

So when the Arizona Cardinals tracked him down in kindergarten, Oglesby was already a seasoned tryout kicker with Dallas, Seattle and San Diego. After a year and a half of close calls, he had a make-or-break chance. With a handful of decent kicks, he could be kicking in the NFL by the weekend. He flew to Phoenix, checked into his hotel room and turned on the news. The sportscaster was talking about Arizona's vacant kicking job. Oglesby learned that his competition at the tryout would be Vitaly Pitesky, a rookie from the University of Wisconsin. When he took the field the next morning, the pressure took hold right away. "It was just Pitesky and me stretching out on the field," he says. "Then the snapper and holder came out. The snapper was Trey Junkin. Halfway through, I was doing well. We finished kicking, and the coaching staff was off to the side. The coach said, 'We appreciate your coming out.' And I thought, This sounds familiar."

Prepared for another letdown, he could barely believe it when Arizona head coach Dave McGinnis said, "We're going with Cedric."

"I wanted to do a cartwheel," Oglesby says.

Having endured Gramatica's ill-fated celebration, McGinnis put a stop to whatever Oglesby had in mind.

"Whatever you do, don't jump," McGinnis told him.

The Arizona media took an immediate interest in Oglesby, if only because of his race. Black kickers were so rare in the NFL that his former San Diego teammates had nicknamed him "Igwe" after Donald Igwebuike, a black kicker for Tampa Bay in the 1980s. One of his Cardinals teammates made a point of telling Oglesby he had never seen a black kicker in his life. "I felt like I was doing it for a whole group of guys to come behind me," he says. "It's the last position in the NFL that's not integrated."

Oglesby had little time to worry about the sidebar stories that captured the attention of the media. His first NFL game was days away, and his debut would come against the Dallas Cowboys. His promise to meet them again someday had come sooner than he expected. He had never imagined the emotions that would be involved. "My first game was like a blur. To tell you

journeymen

the truth, I didn't enjoy the first game," he says. "I was so fine tuned after playing with San Diego. But with Arizona I went from kicking on a practice field to kicking on a field with a crowd and an offensive line and a snapper. You're out on the field with a bunch of guys you don't know."

At least he started in a friendly environment. In front of the Arizona home crowd, Oglesby converted one 35-yard field goal but missed another from the same distance. He also added two extra points in a 17-10 win.

The following week at Carolina, Oglesby showed consistency, the hallmark of successful NFL kickers. He made all three of his attempts, from 41, 19 and 26 yards. For good measure, he converted three more extra points. But Oglesby's performance did not generate much notice in a decisive 30-7 win over the Panthers. "I got nothing from the coaches," he says without any hint of frustration. "I had the media coming around, drawing a little bit of attention. It doesn't make you feel like you've arrived, but you feel a sense of accomplishment."

In the season finale at Washington, he was on target again, making his only attempt from 26 yards and converting two extra points. His final numbers for the season—5-for-6 on field goals, 7-for-7 on extra points—made him an ideal candidate to compete for an NFL job in 2002. At the very least, Oglesby felt certain Arizona would invite him to camp. They didn't. In fact, no NFL teams showed interest prior to training camp. Oglesby had no choice but to return to the annual cattle call of the kicking combine. That decision backfired. After a bad day kicking, Oglesby's stellar performance with the Cardinals was old news.

However, the Carolina Panthers had a long memory after being on the receiving end of Oglesby's kicks the previous season. After veteran kicker John Kasay was placed on the injured reserve list, the Panthers had called on Jon Hilbert, who had beaten Oglesby for the Dallas job a year earlier. But Hilbert missed both of his field goal tries in his first game with Carolina, so the team held another tryout. Oglesby, Shayne Graham and Tim Duncan challenged Hilbert in a mid-week competition.

The day after the tryout, Oglesby learned that Carolina had cut Hilbert.

CEDRIC OGLESBY

Oglesby called Graham to share the news. Graham had already heard. He had signed a contract with the Panthers a couple hours earlier.

It was the last time Oglesby would get close to a job. Four seasons after his brief stint with Arizona, he recognizes that his chances of making it back to the NFL are slim. With each passing year, his success in Arizona seems more like part of his personal history rather than his current resume. "I'm proud of it," he says, "but at the same time, I might have been one or two kicks from establishing a long career."

Even though a return to the NFL is unlikely, Oglesby knows that kicking is a unique job. If he were to resume kicking competitively—he still receives inquiries from arena football teams—he could put himself back in the mix one day. At 29 years old, he has plenty of leg left.

"I'm at a crossroads now," he says. "I don't think everyone understands what it takes to make it. A lot has to be in your favor. If you halfway do it, you won't make it."

Oglesby is keenly aware of that point. He now has a full-time job as a high school physical education teacher. Plus, he is married with a child on the way. Finding time for training is a challenge, but he keeps kicking. Just in case. "I do wrestle with that a lot," he says. "If I don't do it again, I wouldn't be hurt. No one can take that away."

More likely than another stint in the NFL is the possibility he will help someone follow in his footsteps. The Cedric Oglesby Kicking Academy is designed for young players with college and pro aspirations. Currently, Oglesby runs four summer camps in Georgia and South Carolina. In the future, he hopes to find corporate sponsors to foot the bill for kids from underprivileged backgrounds. "The kids I have are pretty well off. It leaves out some kids with ability who can't afford it."

Oglesby has moved on. His life is filled with other plans and responsibilities. Still, he thinks about the NFL occasionally, especially when he talks to his old buddies who are now making a living on Sundays. "It would be nice to make a lot of money," he says. "But it's not the only way to be successful in life. I've learned that."

A place to run

Coming from a
Division II school, Wilmont
Perry faced an uphill battle
to establish himself.

Wilmont Perry strolls into a downtown hotel bar at noon on Tuesday. The place is closed, but he takes a seat at a table and spreads out his lunch from Taco Bell. A woman working behind the bar notices him but says nothing.

The pub's operating hours do not really apply to Perry. For the past couple months, this hotel in Fayetteville, North Carolina has served as his home. "Fayetteville is a nice place to play football," he says casually, as if the military town were just another football stronghold like Green Bay or Denver.

It's as good a football home as any for Perry, and it's not because he's hoping to get noticed. He just enjoys the gig. He's a running back for the Fayetteville Guard of the National Indoor Football League. The NIFL is somewhere close to the bottom of the pro football food chain, even among arena leagues. The players make $200 per week. The league's website boasts, "Call now to own a team!"

It isn't much, but for Perry, it will do.

"People assume every player makes a million dollars," he says. "No, every football player doesn't make a million dollars. Don't assume a guy makes a lot of money because he's got a nice truck. That truck might be the only thing he owns."

His truck is a jumbo-size sport utility, an appropriate ride for a guy who is all muscle and brawn. He is here in Fayetteville because a friend phoned him a couple months earlier and said the Guard could use a couple more players. Perry had just finished a season in the more prestigious Arena Football League, and with nothing better to do, he loaded up the truck for an indoor encore. Now after eight weeks, Fayetteville's season is over, too. Like all good running backs, Perry is anticipating his next move. "I'm thinking about retiring. I might play one more year. I've been contemplating it for the last two years."

Not so long ago, he ran with a more accomplished class. He spent the 1998 and 1999 seasons in the NFL. Since then, his paychecks and his football

stature have been steadily shrinking. So while some of the retirement talk stems from wear and tear—"I'm getting older," he says. "Injuries don't heal as fast."—it's also a matter of dollars and common sense. He certainly did not come to Fayetteville for money. And make no mistake, he stopped thinking about the NFL years ago.

"The sooner you accept that what's done is done, the better," Perry declares. "I had a ball. That's all I can say about the NFL."

Perry took a roundabout path to the top. After high school in Franklinton, North Carolina, he was offered a scholarship to North Carolina A&T, but he failed to qualify academically. He eventually landed at Livingstone College in Salisbury, North Carolina, where he ran for 1,911 yards and 28 touchdowns as a senior and was named Division II player of the year. But statistics don't excite NFL scouts when you do your best work against second-tier college programs. As a result, Perry was lightly regarded. The New Orleans Saints selected him in the fifth round.

From the start, New Orleans felt like a good fit. Saints coach Mike Ditka had completed his first season with a 6-10 mark, and he was eager to upgrade a weak backfield. "I knew I brought something else to the table," Perry says. "I was bigger than most of the guys they had there, and I could dish out more punishment. The others were more scat backs, trying to run away from everybody. Ditka wanted everybody to be physical. So you just tried to dominate your opponent on every play."

But any advantage he enjoyed with his running style was quickly neutralized. His small college experience left him exposed to second guessing every time he made a mistake. "With Division II players, the first thing they say is, 'Oh, he can't comprehend the playbook.' But if a Division I player makes the same mistake, he just made a mistake. What is that? A lot of times, it's the coaches having confidence in you. You just play as hard as you can play and hope that they like what they see."

Perry had no illusions that he could become the franchise running back. Like most late-round NFL picks, Perry knew he would need to make the squad as a special teams player. "Special teams is still a journey for me sometimes," he says, letting out a deep laugh. "It wasn't one of my strong suits."

Despite a so-so performance on punt and kick coverage in preseason, he made the team and suited up for several games in the first half of the season. But he never saw the field, even on special teams. If Perry was going to keep his job, he would have to get some carries. Then in week nine against Carolina, he got into the game at running back. On third down and short, he broke through for seven yards. "Then I came out of the game and didn't play anymore," he says with a smile.

For the next four weeks, Perry waited his turn until Ditka called his number against Miami. This time, Perry ran twice for 22 yards. Good numbers, but Perry was barely working up a sweat. "Not long after the season started, I realized if I'm not going to play, I've gotta be smart and do whatever it takes to prepare," Perry says. "Do what I'm supposed to do, learn more and hopefully help convince the coach to put me back on the field. If they decide not to play me, I'm still getting paid."

"When your confidence leaves you, you start declining in the things you were good at. That really shows they're getting to you—when you're not strong enough in the mind."

His patience paid off when starting running back Lamar Smith came up hobbling before the next week's game against Dallas. Perry started the game and ran for 38 yards on 12 carries. The performance was adequate, but it lacked any impressive moments. "We had a decent offensive line, and everybody makes mistakes, so I'm not going to say the line wasn't good," he says, trying to be diplomatic. "I just know I ran as hard as I could every play. All you can do is exactly what got you there—play as hard as you can. When you're playing, just try to make up for whatever they do wrong."

After 15 games, he had 21 carries for 85 yards. The numbers showed some promise, so Ditka offered him a longer look in the season finale. Any yards Perry gained would be hard-earned against the Buffalo Bills, who boasted Pro Bowl defensive linemen Bruce Smith and Ted Washington. "Bruce Smith is the first guy you look at when you come out of the huddle," he says. "You're like, Alright, where's he at? That's automatic."

Perry ran nine times for 45 yards, finishing the season on a high note. His average of 4.1 yards per carry was the best among the five Saints running backs. But heading into the offseason, he felt no closer to becoming a fixture on the Saints roster.

"You always have to think you're on the bubble. Because if you're not the number one guy, there's pretty much not any room to make mistakes. Every time you make a mistake, you think it might be the one that gets you cut. Some coaches are sticklers like that."

At the NFL draft the following spring, his chances took a major hit. The Saints traded all their draft picks to the Washington Redskins for the chance to select University of Texas running back Ricky Williams fifth overall. Perry didn't need anyone to interpret the selection. "I'm now thinking I'm going to do all I can to be Ricky's backup. We already know who's going to be the starter because they gave up all their draft picks."

To many observers, trading away an entire year's picks was sheer madness on Ditka's part. Perry felt the Saints could have addressed their shortcomings with more traditional acquisitions. "Ditka did it for fan support," he says. "There was no reason to do that. A lot of the time, running the ball was one person breaking down on the offensive line. If they wanted to fix something, they should have fixed the line. But I'm not a coach."

Perry went about his business in training camp, staying out of the Ricky Williams hype. On a personal level, the two runners hit it off just fine. "We were alright. We were cool," he says. "We spoke a lot, but Ricky was always to himself, so I let him be him."

Perry was close enough to Williams to know an important secret about the Heisman Trophy winner. Early in training camp, the media had become impatient with Williams for his practice of conducting all interviews while wearing his helmet. Most of his face was hidden behind a dark shield, which led to a perception that he was aloof and uncooperative. Perry knew that nothing was further from the truth. "That was because of the acne on his face. He wasn't comfortable. He didn't want anybody to see his face like that. People made it out to be that it was depression or he was crazy," says Perry, before cracking up at the thought. "There was nothing wrong with that boy."

For much of the 1999 season, Perry was out of the backfield mix altogether. But after Williams was hurt in week 12, he got the starting call the next week against Atlanta. Instead of simplifying the play calling for a seldom used running back, New Orleans ran the same off-tackle plays designed for Williams. The strategy was ideal for Perry, who was most confident when he could run into cutback lanes. He finished the game with 93 yards on 16 carries, but his breakout day was overshadowed by a 35-12 loss.

Perry was set to start again the following week against St. Louis. He knew that he could raise his profile around the league if he could string together back-to-back performances near the 100-yard mark. But New Orleans did not call his number as often against the Rams. He settled for a respectable day of 54 yards on 14 attempts— well short of the plateau that creates a buzz around the league. He knew better than to dwell on it.

"You can't even think about that," Perry says. "The coaches are going to think what they want to think anyway. Like I always say, you just try to play as hard as you can play. If they like it, they like it." For Perry, it wasn't the yardage that mattered anyway. Playing well helped him maintain the confidence necessary to compete against the rest of the NFL. "When your confidence leaves you, you start declining in the things you were good at. That really shows that they're getting to you—when you're not strong enough in the mind."

Despite an unproductive day against Baltimore in week 15—he carried 11 times for 11 yards in a 31-8 loss—Perry finished the season with a respectable 3.8 yards per carry. His second-year numbers and his role were similar to those of his rookie season, but he detected one difference in how opponents viewed him. When he replaced Williams late in the season, defenses expected the Saints offense to shift gears. "When I went in the game, nobody expected us to be running the ball. That's no respect from the defense. They're so much

looking for Ricky that when they don't see him in the game, they're automatically thinking, If the backup is running the ball, then we're alright."

The Saints finished the season with a 3-13 mark, leading to Ditka's dismissal and the hiring of Jim Haslett. Right away, Perry caught a vibe that he was on the outs with the new coach. "When I would see him talk and interact with other players, he'd talk one way," he says. "Then he comes and talks to me, and he's totally different attitude-wise. Me and Ricky could make the same mistake. I'd get cussed out."

The Saints released Perry in the preseason, but he found another opportunity with Carolina. The Panthers had an undistinguished group of runners, which gave Perry some hope of making a quick impression. "I was just hoping to open some eyes," he says.

Instead, he was put on Carolina's practice squad. Meanwhile, the Panthers running game floundered. The team averaged 3.27 yards per carry, finishing 29th among 31 teams. Perry's career average of 3.9 yards offered the potential of an immediate upgrade, but the Panthers never activated him, leaving him as a forgotten fourth-stringer. "I was hoping they would look at what they had out on the field and realize they had a practice player who could come in the games and help them. But they never saw it that way. It was quiet all year."

In 2001, he found no takers in the NFL. He moved back to Franklinton, North Carolina, where he worked out and waited for another chance. He landed workouts with the New York Giants and Baltimore Ravens during the season, but neither team offered him a contract.

To fill his days, Perry pitched in at his cousin's clothing store. He drove round trips between North Carolina and New York, hauling the latest fashions back to the store. "I didn't have anything else to do," he says. "I was trying to figure out what else I was going to do. Football was getting further and further away from me. I needed a way to pay my bills. So I thought about coaching or going back to school. I had less than 30 hours to go (to graduate)."

There were still football jobs out there, but Perry had to adjust his thinking. Arena football was a decent showcase for former NFL players, but it was

not a fast track. "It was football, man. It was getting me doing something."
He joined the Fayetteville-based Cape Fear Wildcats in 2002, a franchise in
Arena Football 2. After starting out as a tight end and defensive end in the
indoor game, he took over running back duties when a teammate got hurt.
With the ball in his hands, Perry was back in his comfort zone. Of course, the
indoor game was a far cry from the NFL. He was playing both offense and
defense, getting slammed into walls on a miniature field. "I don't dwell on all
that. Once you start feeling sorry for yourself, you start making excuses. The
only thing you can control is what you're doing right now. It's football. It's
what you want to do. So you're gonna put your heart into it and learn everything that needs to be learned and make as many plays as you can make."

After two productive seasons with the Wildcats, Perry moved up in class
to join the Columbus Destroyers of the Arena Football League in 2004 and
2005. With the added visibility of playing in the premier indoor league, he
earned one last ironic flirtation with the NFL. The Miami Dolphins offered him
a workout before the 2004 season, but he was recovering from a knee injury
and was not healthy enough to practice. It proved to be a better opportunity than he could have imagined. Ricky Williams had moved on to become
the workhorse runner in Miami. But Williams would soon fail a drug test,
retire and disappear to study holistic medicine. Without their top runner, the
Dolphins spent the season desperate for help in the backfield. Again, no harm
done. Perry was happy in Columbus, where he spent two seasons earning a
$35,000 salary.

But after stringing together two indoor season in 2005, Perry is now feeling the pain of the constant hitting. He is 30 years old, the line of demarca-
tion for running backs. That is when the pounding really takes its toll. Both
elbows hurt, along with his left knee, left ankle, right wrist and back. Not only
do the injuries heal more slowly, but stamina becomes an issue. "When you're
young, you can pretty much wing it a lot," Perry says, polishing off his Taco
Bell. "When you're older, you still have energy, but you don't have the energy
you used to have."

Pro football has been a success by Perry's measure. He didn't light up

the NFL, but he did manage to brighten up his mother's world. "I bought her a modular home in Franklinton," he says. "She tells me every day, 'Boy, I'm so glad you gave me that money when you were in the league.'" Perry also bought himself a house in New Orleans when he played for the Saints. He sold it when he was released, knowing the $1,500 monthly payment would be a drain without the big paychecks. Talking about New Orleans makes the NFL seem like a long time ago. "It was fun while it lasted. I don't feel cheated. I feel like they got cheated."

Perry harbors no resentment over his NFL career. His two seasons with the Saints are good memories, plain and simple. But they are in the past. As far as he is concerned, the subject is off limits as a conversation starter. "My friends and cousins always do that," he says, rolling his eyes. "They say, 'This is my cousin who used to play in the NFL.' I'm like, This is your cousin Wilmont. Leave that alone. If they ask about football, then I talk about it."

Perry's time with the Fayetteville Guard is shaping up as his football swan song, a last lap as a high-level athlete. Along the way, he has made an effort to do more than just excel at football. He is proud of the person he has become. "I have a little girl (Dashua) who is 10 years old. So I've always want- ed to make sure I leave a good impression with the kids," he says. "Whether people know me because of the things I've done on the field, or just because of my personality off the field, they still know I'm a person they can talk to. That means more to me than any amount of money I could make in the NFL."

Perry would like to coach someday—maybe start out in high school and work his way up, perhaps to the NFL. But for now, he's still working on the plan and considering how to make ends meet. Getting started might be a challenge at first, but he will get his feet underneath him. That's what runners do.

"I saved a little bit of money, but I didn't save anywhere near what I wanted to save because I didn't expect my NFL career to end like it did," he says. "That helps me realize that I have to save the money I make now."

With that, Perry heads out into the bright afternoon sun and climbs into his truck. It has been a good ride.

HOCKEY

Character counts

What Dallas Eakins
lacked in talent,
he made up for
with big-league attitude.

Dallas Eakins is taking a quiz, trying to recall assorted details from his long professional hockey career. He is not doing very well.

Question: With which NHL team did you play the second-most games?

"I'll say Winnipeg," he says.

Sorry, it's Calgary.

How many professional teams did you play for, NHL and minor league combined? "Maybe 22?" he offers.

Too high. The correct answer is 17.

"As easy as those questions seem, they're so hard because it's a blur sometimes," Eakins says. "To last that long in the minor leagues or moving forward to the NHL, you're never looking back or remembering where you've been. You're always looking forward to where you're going next."

For 16 years, Eakins was always on the move. Here is what stands out most: For 10 straight seasons, he played in both the NHL and the minors—a streak unlikely to be duplicated. In his best season, he played 23 NHL games. One year he played a single NHL game with the Florida Panthers. Or so he is told. "I don't even remember the one game," he says. He pauses, searching for something to connect him with the 1993-94 team. "I think someone got hurt and they needed someone for one game. I cannot remember it at all."

NHL teams typically carry seven or eight defensemen, with six dressing for games. The guys at the bottom of that depth chart are often young players. Typically, they spend a year or two on the NHL bubble before blossoming into full-time NHL players or settling into minor league roles. Eakins was the exception, spending his entire career in a gray area on the blue line. In the process, he became what hockey people call a "character guy." That's an endearing term for a marginal player who possesses a strong work ethic and attitude. Sometimes that combination keeps you in the NHL, sometimes it means you're the class of the farm team.

"I think you know deep down inside," says Eakins, reflecting on his prospects. "As much as I tried to work at my skills and get better, I knew who I was on the ice, and I knew where I was going to fit in. There were never thoughts of grandeur, that I was going to win the Norris Trophy and score 25 goals. I knew I was going to be a defensive guy. I knew I was there to play good defense, to be a leader, to play tough, to work hard and to keep my mouth shut. By knowing that really early, I was able to keep moving on all the time."

 **"When you get sent down, you either get that sour taste out of your mouth really quickly and move on, or you get caught up in it. That's the worst thing a player can do. Because within two days, they're calling down there and saying, 'Was he pouting or was he ready to play?' You never want them to say you're still pouting because then you're done."**

Eakins sensed his limitations as a junior player in Peterborough, Ontario, but he fully understood the fragile nature of his career after his first pro season. A 10th-round selection by the Washington Capitals in 1988-89, he was released after one season with the American Hockey League's Baltimore Skipjacks. "I was really stunned by it," he says. "Obviously, a lot of other teams felt the same way because I couldn't even get a tryout anywhere."

With no teams showing interest, he made plans to go back to school. Then came one nibble. His defensive partner with the Skipjacks, Dave Farrish, had retired and accepted the head coaching job with the Moncton Hawks of the AHL. Farrish convinced the NHL's Winnipeg Jets to give Eakins a shot. After earning a roster spot, he developed slowly, finally earning a call-up to the Jets during his fourth season in Moncton. He joined Winnipeg for a game in San

Jose, where he was paired with veteran defenseman Mike Lolar. "Before the game, Mike comes over and says, 'How many games have you played in the NHL?' I looked at him and said, 'None, this is it.' He took off his glove, and he put out his hand and said, 'It's an honor for me to bring you into this league. Let's go have a good night.' We ended up losing the game. We didn't do anything spectacular, but we weren't in any trouble all night."

By the end of the season, he had 14 NHL games under his belt. He hoped to parlay that initial experience into a better opportunity, so he signed with the expansion Florida Panthers before the start of the 1993-94 season. He now regards that move as a mistake. Over the next two seasons, Eakins played just 18 games with Florida. He spent the rest of his time with the minor league Cincinnati Cyclones. But rather than be discouraged, he found plenty of reasons to enjoy life in the minors. "The crowds were unbelievable," he says. "They used to pull in 9,000 to 10,000. We'd go catch a beer every once in a while with (Cincinnati Reds reliever) Rob Dibble. That team caught on. We weren't the Reds or the Bengals, but we weren't too far behind them."

While Eakins thrived as a B-list athlete in Cincinnati, he also realized that his career was leveling off. "Once you get into your mid 20s, you can still improve on your speed and your puck handling and your feel for the game, but your advances aren't going to be leaps and bounds," Eakins says. "If I knew I could be the number six defenseman on an NHL team, that's what I was going for. I wanted to be the guy who was in the lineup every night. I knew I wasn't going to play 30 minutes every night, but if I could play my 12 to 15 minutes, then hey, giddy up!"

That approach served him well over the next two seasons, when he wore seven uniforms—four in the NHL, three in the minors. Prior to the 1995-96 season, Florida traded him to St. Louis, where he added 16 games to his resume. The Blues released him near the end of the season, and he caught on with Winnipeg for two games. When the Jets moved to Phoenix after the season, Eakins went with them. He believed he was a lock to make the opening-day roster for the 1996-97 season. "I knew I played myself into a spot during training camp. Then they called me in and said they were going a different way. It was the first time I ever got up, gave them the f-you, slammed the door and walked out. And as I walked down the hallway, I remember thinking, Should I have given them the f-you and should I have slammed the door?"

In Eakins' world, the door was merely revolving. After playing a half season in the minors—and four games with the Coyotes—he was dealt to the star-studded New York Rangers. After doing time in Binghamton, he skated in three NHL games alongside Wayne Gretzky, Mark Messier and Brian Leetch as the Rangers wrapped up the regular season.

When the playoffs began, Eakins was a healthy scratch from the New York lineup. He watched from the press box as the Rangers dispatched Florida and New Jersey in the first two rounds. Then, without warning, he took center stage in the Eastern Conference finals. New York had lost the series opener to the Philadelphia Flyers, prompting Rangers coach Colin Campbell to change his strategy for the second game. Campbell needed someone to shut down Flyers star Eric Lindros, who had dominated the first game. He handed the assignment to Eakins with simple directions: Play wing, go on the ice every time Lindros is out there, and keep him off the scoreboard.

It worked. The Rangers won, 3-1, with Eakins logging more than 20 minutes of ice time in his first playoff appearance. Right away, the media wanted a piece of this Eakins guy, who came out of nowhere to put the brakes on Lindros. "It was such a surreal thing. It's almost like it didn't happen," he says. "After the game, I had my own little press conference, which was crazy to me. I just thought it was really funny to be right in the middle of it. Things just slow down. And as much as you're talking, you're looking around. It's like, What's going on here? Am I dreaming?"

The Rangers quickly fell to earth, losing the next three games and the series to the Flyers. But Eakins shadowed Lindros until the end, making for an unexpected career highlight.

By summer, he was back home in Scottsdale, Arizona, moving among hockey mortals. He was hanging out with Rangers teammate David Oliver, another part-time contributor during New York's playoff run, when the phone rang. It was Gretzky.

"I was flabbergasted—why was he calling me at home?" he wondered. "He's your teammate, but he's still Wayne Gretzky." Normally, a spare part like Eakins does not move in the same circles as a legend, but he had built a bit of a rapport with Gretzky in New York. Eakins' roommate on the road was Russ Courtnall, who happened to be Gretzky's closest friend on the team. The two buddies often invited Eakins to join them for dinner. It had been a nice perk for Eakins, but he was not expecting a summertime courtesy call. After a bit of small talk, Gretzky made an offer Eakins couldn't refuse: Come out to Los Angeles for a couple days of golf. Bring Ollie along. Stay at the house with me and Janet.

The decision was a no-brainer. Eakins and Oliver hopped on a plane and were on the first tee at Gretzky's club the next morning. The Great One took care of finding a fourth, Olympic figure skating champion Scott Hamilton. There was even a little bit of Hollywood flair. On the back nine, someone began waving and calling to Gretzky from the next fairway. It was actor Will Smith. Eakins tried to convince himself that he belonged in the midst of the excitement, but it felt more like he had won a contest. "Here is the best player to ever play the game, and he had the heart and goodwill to pick up the phone in the middle of the summer and call the 23rd guy on the team to see if he wants to spend a couple days golfing. That says volumes about him."

But the deluxe tour of Wayne's world was just beginning. Finally, he and Oliver gave up trying to keep their cool.

"The night that we stayed over, we slept in the boys' room. There were two single beds in there. We had been out to dinner, and we'd had our fair share of wine. And I'm laying in bed trying to get comfortable, and Ollie's in the other one. I said, 'Hey Ollie, we're staying over at Wayne Gretzky's house!' And Ollie let out the biggest cheer I've ever heard."

By autumn, reality had set back in. Gone were the intoxicating days as a central figure in the playoffs. No more hobnobbing with Gretzky. Eakins signed with the Florida Panthers for the 1997-98 season, this time playing 23 games in the NHL and just four in the minors with New Haven. The following year, he played 18 games for the Toronto Maple Leafs and 20 with their farm team in St. John's, Newfoundland.

In 1999-2000, the New York Islanders tested his level-headed outlook on hockey. At the end of training camp, Eakins thought he had earned a spot on the Islanders roster, only to be ticketed for the minor league Chicago Wolves. By December, he earned a call-up to Long Island, where the Islanders were winless in their previous eight games. No one expected Eakins' arrival to set the Islanders straight. Instead, head coach Butch Goring used the veteran minor leaguer to send a message to the rest of the team: If you don't want to play hard, I can find players who will. In his first game against Buffalo, Eakins led all New York defensemen with a hefty 25 minutes of ice time, even taking a regular shift on the power play. New York earned a 2-2 tie. The following night, Eakins posted a +3 plus/minus rating and assisted on a goal in a 5-3 win against New Jersey.

Goring's strategy had worked. Allowing a guy from the farm team to anchor the defense for two nights woke the team from its three-week slumber. New York rewarded Eakins by throwing him back to the Wolves. "The team was out of the funk and they sent me back. And once again it was a total joke," he says, a bit agitated at the memory. "I think I deserved a little more reward or a little more respect. That just wasn't fair. It left a sour taste in my mouth."

Instead of jeopardizing his reputation as a reliable, no-fuss insurance player, Eakins swallowed his pride and headed back to Chicago. "When you get sent down, you either get that sour taste out of your mouth really quickly and move on, or you get caught up in it. That's the worst thing a player can do. If you want to sulk, sulk on the plane and get it out of you. When you walk in that (dressing) room, you better be upbeat and ready to go. Because within two days, they're calling down there and saying, 'How was Eakins when he came in there? Was he pouting or was he ready to play?' You never want them to say you're still pouting because then you're done.

"I never moaned and complained. I just went to work. It's the old lunch pail hockey deal. That's the only way if you're going to be a journeyman guy. I've seen so many guys with way more talent pack it in before I ever did. I think they got caught up in thinking, That team didn't want me. And that manifested into something else."

In the homestretch of his career, he became a fixture in Chicago. He played four straight seasons with the Wolves, winning an AHL championship and playing 20 more NHL games with Calgary. In 2002-03, Eakins saw his streak of consecutive NHL seasons come to an end, spending the entire year with the Wolves. Ironically, he was under contract to the Atlanta Thrashers, who led the NHL in goals allowed. If ever a team needed defensive help, it was the Thrashers. But Atlanta was content to take its lumps and leave Eakins blowing in the Windy City.

Eakins' career crossed the finish line in Vancouver's farm system. He played a full season with the Manitoba Moose in Winnipeg, finishing his professional career in the same city where he made his NHL debut 11 seasons earlier. In another bit of symbolic closure, Eakins played his 1,000th professional game in the final week of the season. With NHL labor trouble looming in the fall of 2004, the decision to retire came easily.

He spent the next year with his wife, Ingrid, looking after their investment properties in Arizona. But as he soon learned, a funny thing happens to character guys. They become ideal coaching candidates. When he cold-called the Toronto Maple Leafs about an opening for a minor league assistant, word spread around the league that he was ready to try his hand behind the bench. Four teams expressed interest in hiring him. Eakins took the job in the Maple Leafs organization, serving as an assistant coach to Paul Maurice with the AHL's Toronto Marlies. "It's really weird. I don't miss putting on the equipment," says Eakins, just a few days into the job. "But I like throwing on the sweat suit, and I've got my skates, my gloves and my sticks. That's enough for me. I don't miss running into each other."

As a coach, Eakins will have a chance to connect with the newest members of the character guy brotherhood. In one short pep talk, he can prepare his successors for life on the NHL bubble. "If you're a minor league guy, every day you have to be prepared to be called up," he begins. "That means you have to be eating right, working on your fitness level, your skill. If the day comes that they call you up and you're out of shape and you don't play well, that was your chance. At first, it is stressful. Then it turns into habit. You just bring it every day."

"The one thing I did find is I was a different player in the minors because I was the guy walking the tightrope. When you're in the minors, you're one of the better players. You're the guy playing 30 minutes a night. You're able to relax on the ice a little bit and maybe try to make plays and maybe be a bit more creative. If you make a mistake, you know they are going to put you right back out there the next shift. There were things I did in the American Hockey League that I just wouldn't try at the NHL level. There's just more at stake. There's that whole perception that, this is a guy who was just called up, he just made a really risky play, it got picked off and it's in his own net. So sit him on the bench and don't put him back out there. I guess there's not the trust in you yet. You have to build the trust."

Eakins can dispense wisdom on a variety of hockey topics, but you will never hear him lecture on how to celebrate a goal. Always a defensive defenseman, Eakins never found the net in his 120 NHL games. "It's almost kind of fitting. As much as it would have been nice to have one puck that you scored, I think, What's one going to do?" he says, adopting a mocking tone. "Oh, way to go! You scored one goal! What's the big difference? It just goes back to knowing who you are. I know that no team ever put me on the ice to score goals."

He may not have a first-goal puck to display in his family room, but Dallas Eakins has 1,000 games of everything else.

"I think I came away with so many lessons. I'm extremely resilient. There's not much now that you can tell me I can't do. Just little things, like maybe looking for a job. What can they do? They can only say no. It's not like I haven't heard no a thousand times before."

Best of the rest

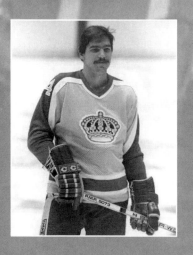

Minor league scoring legend Scott Gruhl also left his calling card in the NHL.

Scott Gruhl has a personal highlight reel from his three seasons with the minor league Fort Wayne Komets. If you ask, he is happy to pop the tape in the VCR. For eight solid minutes, you get a montage of booming slap shots and fancy top-shelf goals.

Then the scoring action abruptly gives way to video of a fight behind the net. Gruhl's greatest hits collection has taken a turn for the literal—and he is absorbing most of them.

"Here he feeds me lunch," says Gruhl, providing his own play-by-play. After a few seconds watching in disbelief, he adds, "What was I thinking? Thirty-some years old."

Gruhl could handle the physical rigors of the minors, but his game was putting pucks in the net. For 17 years, he left his calling card in minor league arenas across the United States and Canada. Most of his output came at the highest level of the minors, playing alongside former NHL players and top prospects. "I didn't dwell on it all that much because I was getting paid to play something that I'd done since I was two years old," says the 45-year-old Gruhl. "I never thought when I was a kid that I would get to that level, even when I was 10 years old and playing on the pond and Bobby Orr was coming into the league. I never sat down when I was 14 or 15 and said, 'Here's my five year plan.' No one ever does that. It's all just circumstances. All the way along, I lived in the present. I was happy."

Near the end of his career, Gruhl became the leading goal scorer in International Hockey League history. Surprisingly, his dominance in the minors did not translate into much NHL action. Instead, he spent several years as the best North American hockey player not making a living in the NHL.

He honed his scoring touch during two seasons at Northeastern University, followed by a year of junior hockey. The Los Angeles Kings were intrigued enough to select him in a supplemental draft in 1979. He topped the 50-goal plateau in each of his first two minor league seasons in Saginaw, Michigan

before earning a promotion to New Haven of the American Hockey League. Then in December of 1981, the Kings decided to take a closer look, calling Gruhl to the NHL. But with the famed Triple Crown line—Marcel Dionne, Charlie Simmer and Dave Taylor—filling the nets in Los Angeles, he was an unlikely candidate to play on a scoring line. "When you go up, you're just a fourth-line guy," Gruhl says. "You're not going to play a regular shift. They had the Triple Crown line. They were carrying the team."

To his surprise, he was treated to an immediate upgrade. With Taylor out of the lineup, Gruhl took the open spot on the right wing of the Triple Crown line for a game at Colorado. Although he was a natural left winger, he skated his off wing, waiting for his chance. It didn't take long. Dionne took a centering pass from behind the net and fired a shot on Rockies goalie Chico Resch. The rebound came to Gruhl, waiting on the doorstep. "I had a wide open net," he remembers. "I'm thinking, I gotta get this up. It hits the shaft right at the heel of my stick and the puck stays on the ice. It's going about five miles per hour. So as Resch dives, the puck goes under him and into the net."

It was no thing of beauty, but he had his first NHL goal—with an assist from a superstar. Before he could bank the goal in his memory, he had to answer for the not-so-pretty tally. "After the game, I'm walking down the corridor and I see a Colorado player coming at me. It's Chico Resch. He says, 'Hey, you were trying to get that puck up in the air, weren't you?' I said, 'No, I wanted to shoot underneath you because I knew you were coming across.' He goes, 'Yeah, right kid.' And he walked away. I thought that was awesome."

The Kings met the Rockies again the next night in Los Angeles and Gruhl was on his game again. When he drilled a slap shot over veteran goalie Phil Myre from just inside the blue line, he had his second goal—one with some artistic merit. But after a couple weeks, the Kings needed Gruhl's roster spot and they sent him back to New Haven. His first trip through the NHL was a solid one, with two goals and an assist in seven games.

In March, Los Angeles sent word that Gruhl would be returning to the NHL for the final weeks of the regular season. He got the news the same day that he and his wife, Barbara, were planning to host a theme party at their apartment. Instantly, they had a real reason to celebrate. "Now it turned into a call-up party. I packed two dozen sticks and all my gear. Then at nine o'clock at night, the phone rang. It was George Maguire, the Kings general manager. And he said, 'We decided not to call you up. We're going to call up Darrell Evans.' I was so disappointed. I thought that was my big chance."

In 1982-83, Gruhl played seven more games with the Kings, but the circumstances were nothing like the previous season. Rather than getting his feet wet with a long stretch, he was often called up for just one game to fill in for an injured player. In the eyes of the Kings, he had gone from an NHL prospect to a minor league insurance player, even though he maintained an impressive scoring pace in the AHL. With just one assist to his credit in Los Angeles that season, he could see the writing on the wall. His contract was not renewed. "I knew the business side of it by that point, so I didn't worry too much about it. I just thought I'd get another (NHL) contract somewhere else, but I never did. That's what hurt."

"I never felt I didn't belong in the NHL. There were guys I know I could compete with. But there were certainly guys at a level I could never dream of attaining."

So Gruhl joined the IHL team in Muskegon, Michigan, where he became a dominant player. Over the next four years, he won two IHL goal-scoring titles and an MVP award. The Muskegon Lumberjacks won the Turner Cup twice. Still, the NHL yawned. Since Muskegon was an unaffiliated team, Gruhl was rarely under the watchful eye of NHL scouts.

But the Pittsburgh Penguins made the Lumberjacks their top minor league affiliate in 1987-88, and soon their NHL roster was depleted by injuries. Pittsburgh needed a farm hand to fill in for a few games, and the general manager asked Muskegon coach Rick Ley to name his best player. He recommended Gruhl. There was just one problem: Gruhl was not under contract to

Pittsburgh. So the Penguins signed him to an NHL deal and called him up.

As soon as he arrived, the team made it clear that he would be sent back to Muskegon when the Penguins got healthy. If this was to be his last trip to the NHL, he was going to enjoy the ride. "I was 28," he says. "That's kind of old for a call-up. I was a little bit more comfortable because I thought, If I just get a chance to score a few goals, who knows what could happen."

Having spent the previous five seasons in the minor leagues, he wondered how he would be treated in the Pittsburgh dressing room, where 22-year-old Mario Lemieux was the established leader and resident superstar. "He spoke to me like I'd been there all year," Gruhl says with satisfaction. "He knew how well I'd done at Muskegon. I have the utmost respect for him because he is a genuine person. There was a presence about him in the locker room that gave him instant respect."

Not all of Gruhl's new teammates were so grounded. One day, as the equipment manager handed out the players' paychecks, Gruhl realized that rookie winger Kevin Stevens was a work in progress. "He says, 'Paycheck? I didn't even spend the last paycheck.' He pulls his jacket out, and there's his last one. He hasn't even opened it yet. He says, 'I can't spend all this money.' One guy grabs it and holds it up to the light. It's $45,000. That's more than I made that year."

When Gruhl cracked the lineup, his playing time was limited. But on the day after Christmas—his fourth game—he made the team take notice. With the Penguins clinging to a 4-3 lead at home against Detroit, the puck came free in the defensive zone. Gruhl corralled the puck at the Pittsburgh blue line and saw nothing but open ice all the way to Red Wings goaltender Greg Stefan. "I have never skated any faster. I just didn't want to get caught from behind. I never really thought of what I was going to do. I just wanted to get to the net as fast as a could. I'm thinking, Don't get caught, don't lose the puck. I'm skating with my head down all the way, making sure I don't lose it. I see the red line, the blue line. And I look up, and I see no net. All I see is goalie. I went to my right and back to my left, and when I did that, I got the puck right up under the cross bar and it stuck up under there. The water bottle flipped off. It was all instinct."

Gruhl had himself a goal-scorer's goal, one that is equal parts skill and beauty. But two games later, he took the memory back to the minors for good. His six games with the Penguins marked the end of his NHL career. The minor leagues were his destiny and he knew it.

He spent one more season in Muskegon before a three-year stint with the IHL team in Fort Wayne. He helped the Komets win the Turner Cup in his first season, then led the team in goal scoring for two seasons. As always, none of his accomplishments seemed to impress the NHL. After splitting the 1993-94 season between Milwaukee and Kalamazoo in the IHL, Gruhl knew it was time to think about the future. Friends in hockey offered advice about the right time to call it quits. One player suggested he quit while he was still on top. Another told him to play until he can't play anymore.

Gruhl found his own way. He signed a two-year deal with the Richmond Renegades of the East Coast Hockey League, serving as a player-coach. The ECHL was a clear step down on the hockey ladder, but he wanted to play on a team where he had a large role. In his first year, he led the team in scoring and delivered a league championship to Richmond. After a second season as the Renegades leading scorer in 1995-96, Gruhl was ready to retire—but not without a quick farewell on his own terms. Richmond had missed out on the playoffs, and a handful of Gruhl's teammates were moving up to IHL and AHL teams as extra players for the postseason. Gruhl itched for one last shot at the high minors. He went to Richmond's general manager and said, "Call and ask if I can be one."

Fittingly, Fort Wayne welcomed him back for one last spin on IHL ice. "I was 36. I thought I played respectably," Gruhl says. "It was certainly not how I would have played 10 years before that. I had an assist in two games. I just felt good about how it ended. After I flew back from Fort Wayne, Barbie said, 'Have you got it out of your system?' I said, 'Yeah, I'm done.' I was tired. Not physically. It just got to be a grind. I just knew."

Gruhl left the game with no regrets. He remained in Richmond to make the transition out of hockey, serving two years as the Richmond Renegades head coach immediately after his retirement. He then spent several years as a

self-employed contractor, doing home maintenance and renovations. Now he is a field operations manager for a painting contractor. He spends most of his days on job sites, supervising painting and wallpapering crews. When he's in the office, he handles scheduling and payroll. It is the right kind of work for a guy who spent his hockey offseasons working in construction. "The transition was easy for me," he says.

To this day, Gruhl's name appears near the top of most minor league scoring lists. He is second all time in IHL goals, as well as goals scored in the IHL and AHL combined. In both categories, he trails only Dave Michayluk, his former teammate in Muskegon. All of which makes you think something does not add up about his lengthy career. How does a guy with 663 minor league goals play just 20 NHL games? For a three-year stretch, he averaged 50 goals in the IHL. His teams won five championships. Surely there were NHL teams who were curious about a guy with that kind of track record.

Gruhl has been asked the question before. If you press him, there is an explanation. Back when his career was still on the rise, he figures he may have been undermined by Muskegon owner Larry Gordon. "I had heard that Larry had interfered and told a couple of NHL clubs that I didn't want to move or play anywhere else," he says. "I heard from an NHL coach some years later after I left Muskegon, 'Oh, we called about you, and Larry said you didn't want to go anywhere else, that you just wanted to stay there.'"

Because he did not have an agent, NHL teams were likely to follow the unwritten protocol of contacting the minor league team's owner or general manager to express interest. If Gordon had rebuffed even a couple NHL inquiries, word may have traveled through the league that Gruhl was happy being a big fish in a small pond.

That encounter with the former NHL coach came late in Gruhl's career. By then, his NHL window of opportunity had long since passed. "At first, I didn't want to believe it, but it was all water under the bridge, so what's the point in going back and confronting (Gordon) about it?" he says. "If things were different, would I have chosen to go somewhere else? Probably. I would have been a little more proactive contacting NHL clubs. But I was young and I trusted the wrong people in that regard. On the flip side of that coin, I had a great career. I'm very proud of it. I can go to bed at night without worrying about my integrity."

Plus, there is no guarantee that his NHL career would have flourished with one more opportunity. Gruhl is realistic about that. Yes, he could score 50 goals and win championships in the minors, but he had no illusions about giving Mark Messier a run for his money. "I was in that 25 percent where I could have been (in the NHL) with the right timing or with certain clubs. I wasn't in the other 50 percent that absolutely belonged in the National Hockey League, and I certainly wasn't in the 25 percent of the elite," he says. "I never felt that I didn't belong. There were guys there that I know I could compete with. But there were certainly guys at a level I could never dream of attaining.

"I felt I made the most of my chances," says Gruhl, who now gets his fill of sports watching his sons, Tyler and Logan, play hockey and baseball. "The time I spent on the ice in those 20 games, I was a happy camper. It was all a blur. I think I did OK. I'm not saying had I done any better I could have stayed. You don't just get there and have the puck follow you. It either happens or it doesn't. Every shift I was out there I was extremely proud."

The same goes for the minors, from Saginaw to Richmond. Hoisting trophies can make a guy want to play forever. Or at least into his mid 30s.

"Every year you play for championships. If you haven't won one, you haven't experienced euphoria like that," he insists. "You've won your last games and you are with 20 other guys, and that's something you'll share forever. You've got the ring to prove it. The party afterwards invariably lasts for a couple days. It's the whole package. You can call anybody you know on those teams, and it's a bond."

That's why Gruhl never worried much about the missed opportunities. His career was always about what he had—not what was just beyond his reach.

"I lived in the present the whole time. I enjoyed every minute of it. That's why I played so long—the people you meet, the places you go. The average person doesn't get to enjoy any of that. And they were paying me to do it. I hope all athletes would have that in the back of their mind."

Here Today, gone Tomorrow

Darren Jensen earned
his NHL break
when tragedy struck
his organization.

 When **Darren Jensen** packed his goalie equipment for his first Hartford Whalers training camp in 1983, he believed his timing was perfect. He was fresh off two national championships at the University of North Dakota, and he was about to join an NHL team that had given up the most goals in the league the previous season.

Jensen had been drafted after his freshman year, but because he stayed in college, the Whalers did not contact him until the end of his senior year. But once he arrived in Hartford, he learned the ropes of camp, taking his turns in practice and playing in intrasquad games. Then he noticed he was not scheduled to play in any of the team's exhibition games. No one was communicating with him.

Then came the first clue. On a Wednesday afternoon, with roster cuts scheduled for the following Monday, a team official passed out the next week's meal allowance. "Usually the per diem is one week at a time," Jensen says. "My per diem wasn't as much as everybody else. Mine went to Monday. It didn't matter what I did, I was gone."

Although Hartford let the meal money do the talking, Whalers general manager Emile Francis made sure there was a live voice to deliver the news to Jensen on Monday. "He told me they were going to let me go," he says. "So I asked if they could send me anywhere (in the minors). And he said they didn't have anywhere to send me. They had too many goalies under contract. I was pretty devastated that I didn't go somewhere. I just wanted to play. I didn't care about the NHL. I just wanted to continue playing hockey."

With no immediate prospects in hockey and nothing waiting back home in Creston, British Columbia, he headed back to North Dakota. "I had nowhere to go now," says Jensen, his voice conveying the same shock he felt back in 1983. "I was just about done with hockey. Then my agent called, saying he got me a tryout with Fort Wayne."

The Komets, an independent team in the high-level International Hockey

League, looked like a dead end too. The team had eight goalies in training camp. When Jensen told Fort Wayne coach Ron Ullyot he was leaving to play for a team in the low-level East Coast Hockey League, Ullyot told him to hold off. A couple days later, most of Fort Wayne's tryout goalies were gone. Exactly why Jensen was chosen to stay was never clear.

"Ron Ullyot told me, 'You're going to be the lowest-paid player in the league.' I said, 'I don't care.' I made $9,000 dollars—$275 a week." The salary dropped to $8,500 after Jensen's agent got his take. "I didn't care about any of that. I was happier than any time in my entire life."

Jensen claimed the starting job and strung together 17 games in a row. "Coach came up and said, 'Darren, are you tired?' And I had nothing in the tank. I said, 'I feel great.' There was no way I was going to let the other goalie in. The other guy never talked to me the rest of the year. He was mad at me."

No team ever got more for its money than Fort Wayne. Jensen posted a 40-12-3 record for the Komets, and he won the IHL's most valuable player and rookie of the year awards.

With a spectacular year under his belt, Jensen was in demand around the NHL. He sifted through offers from Washington, New Jersey, Los Angeles and Philadelphia. He chose the Flyers, despite their solid NHL goaltending duo of young Swedish star Pelle Lindbergh and veteran Bob Froese. But when he arrived in Flyers camp, Jensen was on his own once again. "There was no goalie instruction, absolutely none. I think the most Bernie Parent did was go on the ice once and show one move that he did. The rest of the time he just came in the locker room and shook your hand," Jensen says. "Basically, if you stopped the pucks, you stayed. If you didn't, you were gone."

As Jensen expected, the Flyers assigned him to the Hershey Bears. "I didn't mind going to the American Hockey League. It was very first class. I have no regrets about the team I selected or the direction I went. I was happy."

Early in the season, he was summoned to Philadelphia after an injury to Froese. Although he was wearing an NHL sweater, Jensen had no illusions about challenging Lindbergh, who was marked for stardom in his fourth NHL season. Jensen rode the bench for several weeks while Lindbergh shut down

Philadelphia's opponents. "After the second game, I was bored. I tried not to let (Flyers coach) Mike Keenan see, but I'd be oiling my pads on the bench. I found it boring. When you work so hard to get there and you're sitting, sitting, sitting, it's not good enough."

The only player he had anything in common with was Lindbergh, but the Swede was busy running the show in goal. "We didn't socialize together. It's a highly-competitive position. But he was always very nice to me. It was more or less a lot of small talk. He was the established guy and I wasn't."

When Lindbergh finally faltered, losing three of four, Jensen got his chance. He was given a start against the New York Islanders, a team still riding the wave of four straight Stanley Cups in the early 1980s. He would have to face the likes of Mike Bossy, Brian Trottier and Dennis Potvin. "I got killed," says Jensen, recalling the 7-5 loss. "I was really, really nervous. It's quite intimidating when you watch these guys on TV for a number of years. Now all of a sudden you're going against them. I wish I would have fared a little better, but what do you do? Bossy got his 40th and 41st goals. I don't know why I remember that 20 years later." Soon Froese returned to the lineup, and Jensen went back to the Hershey Bears for the balance of the season.

The Lindbergh-Froese tandem was back in place at the start of the 1985-86 season, leaving Jensen to play in Hershey again. As the team's starter, he lost only once over the first month of the season. The Bears were riding high in early November when they visited Sherbrooke, Quebec for a weekend game. That's when Jensen and his teammates received shocking news: Pelle Lindbergh had crashed his Porsche into a retaining wall after a night of drinking. He was dead.

"I was just in shock," Jensen remembers. "We weren't really close, but I knew his impact in the NHL and what he was like. So it was pretty upsetting." As the Hershey players prepared for their game, Bears coach John Paddock went to Jensen and delivered a message.

"Jens, you're going up to Philadelphia," he said.

"Really?" Jensen responded. "Don't they play the Oilers tomorrow night?"

"Yeah," Paddock said. "You're playing."

The Edmonton Oilers were the two-time defending Stanley Cup champions.
Their offense was among the greatest ever assembled in the NHL. Jensen
gathered his gear, got some sleep and went to the airport before dawn. The
Flyers had a private plane waiting. "I got to the airport in Philadelphia, and
(general manager) Bobby Clarke and Mike Keenan were there waiting for me.
They wouldn't even let me go to the pregame skate in the morning. They sent
me straight to the hotel. I remember so clearly that I ordered a huge spaghetti
dinner. And I didn't eat one thing. I was so nervous.

"I knew quite a few of the guys because I was up the year before, so I felt
some comfort. But when we got on the ice, everybody had to line up on the
blue line. I was looking out at my guys, and they were all crying. Then I'm
looking over at Wayne Gretzky and Mark Messier. I was so scared."

The anxiety he felt during his debut against the powerful Islanders was
nothing compared to what he faced now. Jensen had to wait out an emotional tribute to Lindbergh prior to the game, as well as the steady flow of tears
from his teammates. Making matters worse, his second chance in the NHL
was coming against a juggernaut.

"Have you ever been in a situation you couldn't get out of?" he asks ear-
nestly. "I couldn't get out of it. I literally would have given anything to get
that microphone and say, 'Does anybody have any goaltending experience?
Please come down to ice level immediately!' Once again, it was all fear. I
didn't play a very good game. It was pure adrenaline. I just played great from
the gut."

When it was over, Jensen and the Flyers had a 5-3 win. "I remember
Messier scoring. I remember stopping Gretzky on a point-blank slap shot. That
was huge for me. The nice thing about it is it happened very fast. Just, bam! I
got thrown into it."

With a critical win under his belt, Jensen was assured a role with the Flyers
for the short term. But his opportunity was tempered by the heartache that
gripped the team. "They were all continuing to mourn," he says. "I didn't have
time to mourn. I was too busy trying to figure out how I was going to stop
the next puck."

Although Froese carried the load for the Flyers, Jensen was a major contributor. His best game was a 48-save, 2-0 win over St. Louis, one of two shutouts. He also earned a measure of revenge with a win at Hartford, where he was drafted.

Jensen was holding up his end of the bargain for the Flyers, who were on their way to the second-best record in the NHL in 1985-86. Like many goaltenders, he felt the enormous pressure of knowing he could single-handedly affect the outcome a game. "As a goaltender, 99 percent of it is confidence," he says. "If you are missing some confidence, you're done."

For Jensen, confidence was the most fragile of qualities. When he had it, he was golden. But in Jensen's head, confidence always had to face off against a dreaded force. "I literally played on fear," he says. "Fear of letting in a goal. And that's where I needed to be to even play at that level. You're focused, you're concentrating. You're whole game is concentration. If I didn't have that, there's no way I would have been successful."

The anxiety did not subside after a good night in the net. Each day Jensen had to contend with Keenan, who was already notorious for making players uncomfortable. "Once I was going in for the second period," Jensen recalls, "and in front of the other coaches, he said, 'You f--- up this time and you're gone."

While Keenan's threats may have raised Jensen's blood pressure, they also helped the goalie fine-tune his focus. "I don't think I've ever said this to anybody," Jensen says, before pausing to sort out the logic of his point. "As much as Keenan was the way he was, I think he was absolutely the best thing for my game. I think I needed someone to scare the living daylights out of me to make me realize where I was—and that if I don't do well, I could go down."

As the season wore on, he grew accustomed to his emotional tightrope. The horrifying fear he felt against the Oilers eventually gave way to a game-day routine more mundane than the traditional hockey nap. "There was no way I could take that nap," he says. "I'd always watch PBA bowling on Saturday before the game. Why bowling? I don't know."

By the time Jensen arrived at the arena before each game, he was giving

off a unique vibe. And it wasn't just the mind-numbing effects of too much televised bowling. "I'm an early bird guy. When game time came around, guys would ask me if I was playing. And as I was saying yes, I was yawning. I was very tired mentally from all the thinking. They'd say, 'Are you sure you're OK?' And I'd say, 'Yeah, I'm just beat. I could literally go to sleep right now.'" Game after game, his teammates walked away in confusion, wondering why their starting goalie was doing head bobs in the locker room. "But I could go out and have a good game," he insists. "I don't know how."

Through the holidays and into the stretch run of the season, the routine worked. But in the blink of eye, Jensen found himself on the outs with the Flyers. In early March, he was in goal for a 2-1 overtime loss at Edmonton. To the best of his recollection, the game-winning score was not a mistake on his part. But it left the Flyers second-guessing Jensen's readiness to back up Froese in the playoffs. "The coaching staff and management were so down on me," he remembers. "I just remember that they weren't happy, whether it was verbal or I read it in the paper. I just had the vibe."

Jensen's early success in Philadelphia had leveled off, giving way to several losses in the second half of the season. Still, his 15-9-1 record was impressive for a rookie. But nine days after the loss in Edmonton, Philadelphia acquired veteran goalie Chico Resch from the New Jersey Devils. Jensen was assigned to Hershey.

"I never got over it," he says.

At the same time, the return to the minors was a relief. "I had fun down there. I enjoyed playing in the American League. I had way more fun. You're not playing on the fear as much, but you're still on the edge." Although the Bears reached the Calder Cup finals that season, he quickly learned that his previous dominance in the AHL was yesterday's news. During Jensen's NHL stint, Ron Hextall had emerged as Hershey's go-to goalie, eventually playing the majority of the playoff games. The next season, Hextall claimed the starting job with the Flyers. Jensen's days in Philly were over. He spent the entire 1986-87 season in Hershey.

Jensen was traded to Vancouver before the 1987-88 season. The Canucks assigned him to Fredericton, New Brunswick. For the second year in a row, Jensen reached the Calder Cup finals, this time earning most of the playoff starts. In a cruel twist, Fredericton was swept by Hershey, 4-0.

The following season, Vancouver sent Jensen, Troy Gamble and Frank Caprice to the IHL's Milwaukee Admirals, where head coach Rick Ley set up an unusual competition. Jensen recalls Ley saying, "I want each goalie to play three games, and I'm going to go with two goalies. The third guy is not going to play."

Ley remained undecided after three starts each, so he extended the competition through the first couple months of the season. Ley settled on Gamble and Caprice, despite Jensen's 7-2-1 record. In reality, the competition may have been a sham. Gamble was a 21-year-old prospect, a second-round draft pick of the Canucks. Caprice had divided the previous six seasons between the Canucks and their top minor league team. Having invested in both goalies, Vancouver probably preferred to develop two home-grown players instead of an outsider like Jensen.

Once the reigns were handed to the other goaltenders, Jensen sat in the stands for nearly every game. Vancouver was content to pay him a $150,000 NHL salary to do nothing but practice. When Ley offered Jensen a chance to play an exhibition game against a Russian all-star team in December, he simply said no. On one of the rare occasions when Ley dressed Jensen as the backup goalie, his teammates tried to lighten the mood. "The guys took out my jersey and put baby powder in it," he says. "So when I opened it up it looked like dust. You have to laugh at that. They didn't understand why I wasn't playing."

The comic relief could not mask the hurt. After starting the season believing he was Milwaukee's best, Jensen's mindset took a season-long beating. He was still in his prime at 29, but he felt his only option was to call it quits. "I didn't really want to retire. But when you're not playing and you have no confidence...it was just kind of the time, eh?"

Jensen moved into the working world, turning his focus from forward lines to hairlines. He teamed up with an acquaintance from his Philadelphia days

to open hair replacement clinics in Vancouver. "I went a million miles an hour with my head chopped off," he says. "I made a lot of money but I lost a lot. We had television shows. We were getting tons of clients." But when he fell into a dispute with his business partner, Jensen started his own company. "It was a terrible experience. It was a nightmare. I ended up getting into a legal battle, and that guy took me down. He had a lot of money. Live and learn and move on."

Today, Jensen and his wife, Angel, live in Kelowna, British Columbia with their two daughters. He continues to operate a hair replacement clinic with 400 clients, but most of his attention is back on hockey. He coaches goaltenders at the prestigious Okanagan Academy, which operates junior teams and summer camps. He also serves as a sales rep for a goalie mask manufacturer, which allows him to travel through Eastern Canada. But the work with the teenage goaltenders gives him the most satisfaction. "Each year as I get older and I'm watching guys struggle to get to the next level, I realize I did pretty good. Today I'm much more appreciative and proud of what I did when I was playing."

As a result, he is less inclined to think about the hard knocks he faced as a player. Take Jensen's first training camp with Hartford, where the Whalers had too many goalie prospects to give their own draft pick a minor league job. Four netminders played for Hartford's farm team in Binghamton that season. They combined to allow the second-most goals in the AHL. Within a year, all four had retired. Had the Whalers done a better job evaluating talent, Jensen might have become a rising star in the organization, instead of being left to climb out of Fort Wayne as a minor league free agent. As he learned, the difference was night and day. In the AHL, players were in constant view of NHL scouts. In the IHL, where he won three individual trophies as rookie, Jensen created almost no buzz. "I didn't even know I won them," he says. "I think my parents told me in the summer. There was no banquet or acknowledgment."

Not all the breaks worked against him, of course. He was handed a golden opportunity after Lindbergh's death. Jensen's 3.68 goals-against average was not particularly impressive, but he showed flashes of major league form.

Yet he never earned another shot in the NHL. Many players would say they deserved a better chance to realize their potential. Not Jensen.

"Absolutely not!" he says emphatically. "I played with guys who played 12 or 13 years and never had the opportunity to put an NHL jersey on, not even for an exhibition game. Can I be mad? Hey, I had an opportunity. I got to play in games. I could have run with it."

More to the point, NHL hockey was not what Jensen expected.

"There was no enjoyment. I didn't enjoy that time. There was a lot of pressure. If you lost, ownership and the general manager were in the dressing room. When you add that element, I had a hard time having fun. But it was neat to actually be there and see how everything works at the highest level, to play in front of 18,000 people. I knew I was not going to get that feeling again."

Most one-year careers quickly fade into obscurity, but Jensen's 29-game season is noted prominently in NHL history. He and Froese combined to win the Jennings Trophy, awarded to the goaltenders on the team that allows the fewest goals. Unlike the imaginary honors he earned in the IHL, the NHL award is an actual trophy. Jensen even received a small piece of hardware for himself. "It's just a little, wee cup. It's small, about a foot. I probably could have bought it down at the store."

A wee cup for a brief career in the NHL. In the end, that's just about right, he figures.

"It was one hell of a ride. I got opportunities, so I have absolutely no regrets. I wouldn't change a thing."

Jensen glances again at the Jennings Trophy in his den. OK, there's one thing.

"Something I would change is the death of Pelle."

A legend in one Town

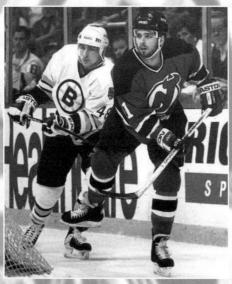

Fred Knipscheer
is a hero in Boston,
despite a wandering
minor league career.

Fred Knipscheer always had semi-big dreams.
"I grew up watching the Fort Wayne Komets," he says.
"That was a goal that I thought was realistic, to possibly
someday play in the minors for them."
Who could blame him for being practical?

For starters, Fort Wayne, Indiana does not launch many professional hockey careers. And at the age of 17, Knipscheer was 5 feet 6 inches. So when he landed a spot with a junior team in Omaha, Nebraska, he was happy just to continue his career. A year later, he earned a scholarship to St. Cloud State University in Minnesota.

For the next two and half years, Knipscheer was a steady but unspectacular player. But something happened when he returned to campus after Christmas break of the 1992-93 season. Knipscheer had morphed into Mario Lemieux. "I had about three straight weekends in January where—I don't know what happened—all of a sudden, everything came easy," he says, still marveling at his transformation. "I had a five-goal game, and the next weekend I had a hat trick. I had 14 goals in six games."

Knipscheer led all of college hockey with 34 goals during his junior season. Having grown to 5 feet 11 inches, he was attracting plenty of attention from the NHL. "At the end of January, all the agents started calling. That's when it finally hit me that I might be good enough to play in the NHL. When you're a kid, or even in college watching the NHL, you put those players on such a high pedestal that sometimes it's not a goal that seems fathomable."

At 23 years old, Knipscheer was five years older than most top prospects, so he had to respond quickly to the NHL's overtures. He left St. Cloud State after his junior year and signed with Boston, where he had lived until he was eight years old. But because he played his college hockey far away from the elite programs in the Northeast, his arrival at training camp created no buzz among the fans and media. "When I got to camp in Boston, there were

no external expectations. The Bruins had only sent one scout to see me play in college."

Being anonymous had its advantages. With no pressure to perform, Knipscheer made the Boston roster for the 1993-94 season. But after playing on the penalty-killing unit on opening night against the Quebec Nordiques, he was sent to Boston's American Hockey League farm team in Providence. "I think they saw that I was more of an offensive player than a fourth-line checker," he says. "But I was pissed. It took me a good three weeks probably to get over it. I didn't think I deserved to be there. Quite frankly, I thought I was better than three or four of the rookies the Bruins kept."

Knipscheer's reaction was hardly unexpected. Providence head coach Mike O'Connell pulled him aside and said, "Fred, you're so close to being in the NHL, you don't even understand. You need to go out and play and have fun. You need to work your butt off and show them that you deserve to be up there."

"That changed my outlook on everything," he says. "That made me feel like I'm down here for one reason—to get playing time. I had never been cut from any team I played for. I was always one of the better players. I had never dealt with that before."

Knipscheer scored 26 goals in 62 games for Providence and was rewarded with a call-up to Boston in March. In his first game back in the NHL, he took a pass from Brent Hughes and drilled a one-timer past Anaheim goalie Guy Hebert. Two nights later, he beat Montreal's Patrick Roy. Knipscheer's game looked ready-made for the NHL. It didn't hurt that he was playing on a line with future hall-of-fame forwards Adam Oates and Cam Neely. "I was more of a goal scorer, and they tried to use me in that capacity. That's why I think I did succeed."

With three goals in 11 games, he earned a spot in the lineup heading into the postseason. For the first two games of Boston's opening-round series against Montreal, he played a limited role. Then Bruins coach Brian Sutter put Knipscheer on the third line, where he skated a regular shift with Ted Donato and Steve Heinze. Knipscheer responded with a goal as Boston won Game 3.

The Bruins and Canadiens battled to a decisive seventh game with Knipscheer skating a regular shift.

For Game 7, he was paired on the fourth line with Cam Stewart and Mariusz Czerkawski, forming an all-rookie trio. "I was as nervous as you could ever imagine. I couldn't sleep the night before or pregame. By 5:30, I had all my equipment on. I was ready to go. I was thinking in Game 7 our line would see the ice maybe three times." But the line played well in the first period, so Sutter kept putting them on the ice. "As soon as that game started, I wasn't nervous anymore. I felt more comfortable in that game than I had in any other game. I expected just the opposite in that setting. It was weird."

 **"The thing I find funny is people automatically assume a couple things about former pro athletes. One, they think we're multi-millionaires. And, two, they think we've never had to work for a thing in our lives."**

Then came the moment every athlete dreams about. With the Bruins leading 3-1, Knipscheer deflected a pass toward the boards in the Bruins defensive zone. Stewart took the puck the length of the ice and skated wide as he approached the Montreal net. He made a drop pass to the high slot, where Knipscheer blasted a shot over Roy's right shoulder. For an encore, Knipscheer made a perfect pass to legendary defenseman Ray Bourque, who scored the final goal. The Bruins won the game, 5-3, and the details played out like a pond hockey fantasy: Knipscheer had the game-winning goal on home ice, eliminating the defending Stanley Cup champions in Game 7. Regardless of what he would accomplish the rest of his career, he would forever hold an honored position in Boston's playoff history.

Boston's playoff run ended in the second round against New Jersey Devils. Although Knipscheer was held scoreless against the Devils, he had shown

the Bruins he could deliver in the clutch. That gave him the inside track on winning a job in training camp before the 1994-95 season. But with NHL players and owners on the brink of a work stoppage at the start of the season, the Bruins sent him to the minors. He had no problem with the assignment, figuring he would be in top form when an abbreviated NHL season began. But when the two sides reached a deal in January, Knipscheer was left in Providence.

"It kind of hurt. I dealt with it by saying, 'Well, I'll show you' instead of pouting about it," he says. "Part of it was I loved the teammates I had the second year in Providence." By the time the minor league season hit the homestretch, Knipscheer had appeared in the AHL all-star game and was averaging nearly a point per game. He had nothing to prove in the minors and Boston knew it.

When he finally earned a call-up in late March, the Bruins must have wondered why they left him toiling in the minors. In his season debut, Knipscheer scored an unassisted goal at Quebec. He followed up with an overtime goal at Tampa Bay in his next game. Two games, two goals. But his triumphant return was soon interrupted by a dislocated shoulder, knocking him out of action for five games. When he returned to the lineup wearing a sling, his mobility was severely limited. "Obviously, I wasn't 100 percent," he says.

When the playoffs began, the Bruins could not find their offense. New Jersey beat Boston in five games, posting three shutouts. Knipscheer played four games without registering a point. "I didn't think we had a chance to beat New Jersey. During the series, you say you're going to win, blah, blah, blah. But we were outplayed every game and really didn't have a chance. It wasn't just me, it was our whole team."

The Bruins fired Sutter and replaced him with Providence coach Steve Kasper. Knipscheer was thrilled. He had served as Kasper's captain in the minors. "I was never more excited," he says. "I worked my butt off that summer. I truly believed when I got to Boston I was going to be in the lineup."

At the start of training camp, word began to circulate that the Bruins were in the market for a defenseman, although none of the rumors involved

Knipscheer as trade bait. So when he was called to Kasper's office before a preseason game, he was stunned to learn he had been dealt to St. Louis for veteran defenseman Rick Zombo. In an instant, his fledgling career with his dream team was over. "I was shocked. Stunned. Upset. Really everything. I took it harder than somebody else might because Boston was where I wanted to play. It's the only team I ever wanted to play for."

But Knipscheer soon began looking on the bright side. Maybe the Blues would give him a chance to be an everyday NHL player. After all, St. Louis had traded a major leaguer for him, "so they're not going to trade for me and not give me a chance to play in the NHL." He returned home and waited for a call from his new team. When the phone rang, it was Jimmy Roberts on the line, the coach of the Worcester IceCats—the AHL farm team for St. Louis. Knipscheer was going to the minors.

When he arrived in Worcester, the trade scenario became clear. The Blues were never high on him in the first place. Roberts told him straight out, "I was a big reason why they traded for you." With that, Knipscheer was no longer a prospect. He was a big fish in a small pond, the prize acquisition of a minor league coach. Making matters worse, Roberts immediately bestowed an honor on Knipscheer that felt like the kiss of death—the assistant captaincy. "I was sitting there thinking, This isn't good. That means most likely I'm not going anywhere."

Considering that Roberts—not the St. Louis Blues—wanted Knipscheer, it is easy to question the coach's motivation. He had previously served as the head coach of the Buffalo Sabres and Hartford Whalers. By acquiring a bona fide NHL prospect to bolster his team, Roberts had improved his chances of landing another NHL coaching job. Although Knipscheer's career had drifted into the slow lane, he managed to produce the best statistical season of his career. "Coach Roberts was one of my favorite coaches I ever played for," he says.

St. Louis did call Knipscheer to the NHL, but his hopes were modest from the start. He joined the Blues in time for a game-day meeting. Afterwards, he introduced himself to Blues coach Mike Keenan, who responded with an indifferent how-ya-doin. "That was it. Coach Keenan didn't say another word

to me. None of the other coaches said a word. I got dressed, and I went out and played two shifts on the fourth line. After the game, I got called in coach Keenan's office and he said, 'We're going to send you back to Worcester.' I said OK. I was just dumbfounded about this guy. Then he said, 'You need to be in better shape.'"

Of course, Knipscheer's conditioning had nothing to do with his return to the minors—he was playing every night and leading Worcester in scoring. But Keenan's parting shot was indicative of his rink side manner. Knipscheer returned to the minors for the rest of the season, eager to move on to another organization.

Before the 1996-97 season, he signed with the Chicago Blackhawks, a team in need of scoring punch. Despite a hat trick in the exhibition season, he was farmed out to the Indianapolis Ice of the International Hockey League. It was Knipscheer's first experience in the IHL, and he struggled to get in sync with the rhythm of a different league. Because Indianapolis was the hometown of his wife, Nicole, hockey was not always front and center. "I didn't play well. When I was at home I had a lot of distractions. I really didn't deserve to get called up."

After an unproductive first half of the season, he was shipped off to the IHL's Phoenix Roadrunners for a minor league player to be named later. If that were not deflating enough, Phoenix sent him back to Indianapolis for the final two weeks of the season to complete the deal. Fred Knipscheer traded for Fred Knipscheer.

The more minor league stops a young player makes, the more difficult it becomes to get back to the NHL. Having shuffled among three AHL and IHL teams in two seasons, he knew he was no longer trading on his Boston Bruins magic. "I still held out hope that someone would give me a chance," says Knipscheer, who was 29 at the start of the 1997-98 season. "But you start realizing that something better happen pretty soon."

Knipscheer found a promising situation in the New York Islanders farm system. Butch Goring, the coach of the IHL's Utah Grizzlies, pushed the parent club to bring him on board. It was an ideal fit. Utah was dominant, and

Knipscheer was among the team's top scorers. But in the stretch drive of the season, he was traded to the Kentucky Thoroughblades of the AHL. At first he was angry about the trade, but there were a couple perks. For starters, the Grizzlies had to pay him $50,000 for violating his no-trade clause. He also arranged to return to Utah for the IHL playoffs once Kentucky's AHL season ended. "I was trying to play well and help Kentucky, but it was a weird time personally," he says. "I was talking to my buddies in Utah at least twice a week."

He returned to Utah for two playoff games, but the team bowed out in the first round. Undaunted by the temporary trade, Knipscheer returned to the Grizzlies for the 1998-99 season. But once again, the good feelings ended abruptly. In December, Utah traded him to the AHL's Cincinnati Cyclones. "That trade was a lot harder on me personally than anything else that had happened in my career. I flew home to Indy and drove to Cincinnati, and I thought about retiring at that point," he says, pointing out that his wife was eight months pregnant at the time. For the first time in his career, she stayed behind in Indianapolis.

Knipscheer could accept that he had slipped off the NHL radar, but he was worn down by the capricious notions of minor league management. "I was sick of being a pawn. I had done everything anyone had ever told me to do. I was pissed because we had a first-place team in Utah. I was second in scoring. I got along with every guy on the team. That put a sour taste in my mouth about everything."

Well, almost everything. "The only satisfaction is they had to write another $50,000 check," he says.

In Cincinnati, Knipscheer faced more turmoil. "I didn't see eye-to-eye with coach (Ron) Smith. I didn't like the way he interacted with the players. I didn't feel like he was in it for us guys to help our careers. I was fine with being in Cincinnati. I got along with the guys really well. We had great crowds. The hockey part of it was great." The following season, Knipscheer says Smith buried him on the bench. After two months, the Cyclones released him.

He joined the IHL's Milwaukee Admirals in December, his sixth minor league

team in four seasons. Soon he began to suffer concussions. The first two were mild, but the third one kept him out of the lineup for a month. The fourth concussion knocked him out cold. Against his doctor's wishes, he returned for the playoffs. "Part of it was I had so much fun in Milwaukee that year. I was always smiling in practice. I had lost that for a couple years. And I knew in the back of my head that I wasn't going to play many more years."

The four concussions were a sign, and Knipscheer knew it. By then, he estimates he had suffered 10 as a professional player. When he saw a specialist after the season, the doctor would not clear him to play.

Still, he was determined to get back on the ice. He had an invitation to attend NHL training camp with the Nashville Predators, so he began his summer training regimen. Right away, the doctor's orders made sense. Knipscheer began throwing up and having dizzy spells—lingering symptoms from the concussions. The decision to retire was now easy. Becoming a former hockey player was not.

"It took me at least two years," he says. "The hardest part the first year was that all the friends I had made in hockey were still playing, and I would talk to them every week. And you listen to all the stories about going on the road with the guys, playing, winning."

Today, Knipscheer lives in Indianapolis and makes his living in real estate. In addition to handling traditional home listings as a Century 21 agent, he builds spec homes in golf course communities. Now that he is firmly rooted in the 9-to-5 world, he is bemused by the reaction he gets from colleagues and clients who learn that he is a former professional athlete. "The thing I find funny is people automatically assume a couple things about former pro athletes. One, they all think we're multi-millionaires. And two, they think we've never had to work for a thing in our lives.

"Working isn't hard. Having a job isn't hard. It's a routine. You want hard? How about working out every day, four hours a day, and then playing 120 games a year. And you're away from your family. It's a different type of hard. The reason why there aren't more pro athletes is because it's not an easy thing. It's not all the best players who are the pro athletes. They are not always the most athletic or the most talented. It's the guys that have heart and desire and push themselves."

But living outside of the hockey bubble did require some adjustments. Knipscheer had become accustomed to making decisions for his own benefit. "When you're in the moment as a pro athlete, everything is about you. You're selfish in a way: I can't eat this, I can't go here, I can't do that. I can't go to the bar and get drunk. You're so into yourself that when you do retire, you have to learn how to put other people first. That's a big adjustment."

But he has taken to it well, immersing himself in the daily routines of his two children. His son, Jack, plays hockey and his daughter, Kylie, is on a travel soccer team. "It's more fun worrying about them than it is worrying about anything I have going on," he says.

Knipscheer maintains close ties with hockey. After coaching Carmel High School to three state championships, he became an assistant coach for the Indiana Ice of the United States Hockey League, the same junior league where he got his start. The position fills an important need for him. "Aside from the head injuries, I could easily still be playing," says Knipscheer, who is 36. "I still miss it. Playing in front of people was a drug for me—being the guy that everybody counted on. In the minors, I was always one of the better players, and I loved it."

And yes, he does still think about what might have been with the Bruins. "If I would have played a whole season, there's no doubt in my mind I would have scored 20 goals in my rookie year in Boston. The game is not that much different at the NHL level than it is at the AHL level.

"When you're in the NHL, and you're playing every game and things are going well, everything becomes easier. You're not looking over your shoulder. But when you get called up at the end of the year, you know that if you make a lot of mistakes, you're probably not going to be in the next game."

Knipscheer will always view his 44 NHL games as something more than just a quick view of life at the top of his sport. "There are times when things are going bad, I know I was able to do something not a lot of people are able to do. If I could get to where I got hockey-wise coming out of Fort Wayne, I feel

like I can do anything. That has helped me with my real estate.

"When athletes get out of their respective sports, it amazes me that more guys don't say, 'I can do anything because I made it to the major leagues.' If you can be a major league athlete, there's really nothing you shouldn't be able to accomplish in your daily life."

When Knipscheer needs to draw on his past for inspiration, he has an advantage. His best hockey memory is a classic. How many people can call up a magic moment like the winning goal in Game 7 against the greatest goaltender ever? That's not your run-of-the-mill reverie.

"It crosses my mind at least a couple times a week," he says. "I've never been in a building louder in my life. The bench was literally shaking. I remember most of my shifts, I remember all the goals. That night was so much fun. It was such a great memory, you almost can't help but think about it. It's almost like when my kids were born or my wedding.

"I remember it like it was yesterday. I think those are things you should reminisce about. They give you strength."

FRED KNIPSCHEER

PETER LeBOUTILLIER

A fighting chance

Peter LeBoutillier paid
his dues with his fists,
then wrestled
with his emotions.

Peter LeBoutillier was 16 years old when his

career path began to take shape. He was the new kid, a forward playing junior hockey in Manitoba. "It was an exhibition game, and I had never fought in my life," he says. "I got challenged by a 20 year old. He was beating me up. He was abusing me."

When LeBoutillier returned to the bench, he wanted nothing more to do with his tormentor. But his own coach was planning a rematch, holding his rookie off the ice until the older kid was winded at the end of his next shift.

"I'm sitting on the bench hoping a puck hits me in the head and I don't have to go out there," he laughs. "It got to a point where it was either fight back or just take it for the rest of my life, so I went up to the guy and said, 'Let's do this.' And he just laughed at me because I was this lanky 16-year-old kid, probably 170 pounds. I ended up cutting him for stitches. I must have caught him with a lucky punch. I never felt anything like that. My adrenaline was pumping and I was fairly good at it. It was a good feeling."

In that moment, a hockey enforcer was born. From that day forward, LeBoutillier would head down hockey's pugilistic path.

A year later, he joined the Red Deer Rebels of the Western Hockey League. The day after the season opener, Rebels coach Peter Anholt cornered him and asked if he had noticed Prince Albert forward Shayne Toporowski the night before. "I told him I thought he was a pretty good player, but he runs around a little bit," LeBoutillier recalls, using hockey speak to describe someone who dishes out punishment, legal or otherwise.

"Why don't you take care of that?" Anholt shot back.

LeBoutillier got the drift. Two coaches, two green lights. He fought Toporowski on the first shift of the next game. "After that, I just knew my role. That was how I was going to play."

Fighting is a time-honored hockey tradition. The players who handle those chores are known as tough guys and enforcers when they play for your team.

Less-polite terms apply when they play for the opponent. The purpose behind the designated fighter, hockey people will tell you, is to police the other team.

When an opponent takes liberties against your smaller, skillful players, the coach sends out a tough guy to throw his weight around, starting a fight if necessary. Despite the dangers of the role, many players are happy to embrace it. For those not blessed with elite skills, learning to throw a punch on skates is the only way to earn NHL ice time, short of driving the Zamboni.

That is how LeBoutillier was slotted in professional hockey. He showed enough promise among the brawling set to be selected by the Anaheim Mighty Ducks in the sixth round in 1995. His first NHL training camp got off to a bad start. Someone in Anaheim's front office decided LeBoutillier should wear a visor, a piece of protective equipment that was incompatible with the tough guy code. He might as well have carried a purse. "They were making me look like a fool," he says, still getting worked up over the personal affront. "I don't know if that was part of their strategy. You can't make a tough guy wear a visor."

"Fighting isn't fun. It's straight fear. I had fear every day that I would get knocked out. Fear is good. If you're not scared, you're stupid."

So LeBoutillier waited for his chance to ditch his windshield. In the first scrimmage, he watched a player run into the goaltender, an objectionable offense that called for intervention. He was on it. "I figured I'm going to get rid of this visor one way or the other. I'm going to keep fighting until they take it off. We had our fight, and I came off the ice. Then I went out there and tried challenging people again. Finally after the first scrimmage, the assistant GM came down and said I could take it off."

Despite the embarrassment—and because of his feisty play in camp—
LeBoutillier earned a spot with the Baltimore Bandits of the American Hockey
League. Like his previous coaches, Bandits boss Walt Kyle immediately made
his expectations clear. He was not about to tolerate any hockey.

"One night Jeremy Stevenson and I were playing on a line, and we made
a pretty nice play. There was a toe drag and a cut and a nice drop pass, and
we got a shot on net and almost scored. We were pretty proud of ourselves,"
LeBoutillier says, before delivering a raspy impersonation of his coach. "We
came off the ice and Walt comes down the bench and starts yelling at us, just
screaming, 'Your job is to kill time, not make plays!'"

After a season and a half of tune-up bouts in Baltimore, the Mighty Ducks
were ready to turn LeBoutillier loose on the NHL. But when the call came, he
found himself strangely conflicted. His girlfriend, Alison, had moved to San
Diego a week earlier to take a job as a college lacrosse coach. Now he was
on the move and concerned about his future with her. And as long as he was
worrying about his personal life, he wondered if he had any business playing
in the NHL. "I didn't see myself as an NHL guy. Maybe that was my downfall.
I always thought of NHL players as so good. What the hell do they see in me?
At the same time, I was confident. I knew I could play."

From the time he was a kid, LeBoutillier had made lists of his goals—his
aspirations, not the kind he was now discouraged from scoring. At the top
of his list was playing just one NHL game. His time had arrived, and he was
not about to let a little bit of self-doubt interfere now. He joined the Mighty
Ducks on the road in St. Louis.

In the hours leading up to his debut against the Blues, he reminded himself
that the fighters would be bigger and stronger. And just as a newcomer had
something to prove, the veterans wanted to teach a lesson. Making matters
worse, the Mighty Ducks had embellished LeBoutillier's height and weight on
the game roster, listing him at 6 feet, 2 inches and 215 pounds. In reality, he
was an inch shorter and fifteen pounds lighter. "They were making it sound
like I was some big heavyweight," he says. "So I'm thinking someone's going
to take a run at me."

Thankfully, Ken Baumgartner, his teammate and fellow puncher, pulled LeBoutillier aside before the game to offer a few pointers. The veteran rattled off several Blues players who could turn a guy's lights out: Kelly Chase will grab your arms, do swim moves and try to uppercut you. Mike Peluso will try to spin you and hit you with a left. Then Baumgartner mentioned Tony Twist. "This guy will hurt you," he warned.

"But that's like a green light to a young kid," LeBoutillier says. "He'll hurt you? That's who I want."

As game time neared, he took in his surroundings, remembering that this could be his one and only NHL game. "The first time my skate hit the ice," he says, "I looked at the way the lights hit the rink and the big crowd. I'm skating around the rink thinking, I'm in the National Hockey League and it's pretty cool."

When LeBoutillier climbed over the boards for his first shift, all his worries about upper cuts and swim moves vanished. St. Louis had all skill players on the ice. His first shift was shaping up as a skate in the park. "Then I see a big leg come over the boards, and sure enough, it was Twist. He came out for one reason. He was going to teach this young kid from the minors a lesson. We lined up and he put his stick between my legs. I wasn't going to look at him because I might have second thoughts. As soon as the puck dropped, the gloves came off. It was a pretty good go."

When he watched a tape of the fight afterwards, he saw that Twist nearly landed a haymaker to the jaw. But Twist did leave a souvenir. "I remember on the bus going to the airport, thinking, What the hell happened to my back? I had a big bruise in the middle of my back from his fist."

With his first fight behind him, LeBoutillier earned the more traditional rite of passage in his second game. He scored his first goal on his first shot, beating Dallas Stars goaltender Andy Moog. It was not pretty. "Ted Drury came across the line and passed one to me and I snapped it. I swear to God it skipped by Andy Moog—like when you're skipping rocks—but it went in five hole (between the legs)."

Even as he scored his first NHL goal, he could not escape reminders that

his offensive skills were intended for emergency use only. This time, his lecture came from Anaheim superstar Paul Kariya. "It was late in the game, and Kariya came off the ice all mad because the Stars were running him, and I guess I hadn't done my job or something. And he was yippin'. He was the captain. I took it personal."

After his flirtation with goal scoring, he grew accustomed to fighting hockey's best. The NHL paychecks helped soften a few bruises, but leading with his chin caused side effects. After falling asleep each night, he would slip into a recurring nightmare of trading punches in a game. On game days, he felt sick to his stomach. "Fighting isn't fun. It's straight fear," he says, without hesitation. "I had fear every day that I would get knocked out. Fear is good. If you're not scared, you're stupid. I always fought better in fear because I knew I had to get it done, mad or not mad. To survive, you have to be fearful."

Considering that many of the NHL heavyweights were three inches taller and 25 pounds heavier than LeBoutillier, working up a little anxiety was never an issue. "You get beat up every night trying to learn your way in the NHL. Unless you're a real heavyweight, you're not going to beat these guys, and I knew it. I didn't go into every game thinking, I'm going to beat the hell out of this guy. I was a guy who would stick up for my teammates. Win or lose, I was going to take a licking."

From a professional standpoint, LeBoutillier was always immersed in survival mode. At the same time, he tried to remember that he was living his dream. The fight strategies, the dread, the sickness—it was the price he had to pay for a tour of the NHL. "I didn't know how long I was going to be up there," he says. "You've got to have something to tell your kids."

He stayed with Anaheim for the final 23 games of the 1996-97 season, taking part in 11 fights. Among his memorable moments was a game against the Hartford Whalers. Mighty Ducks coach Ron Wilson assigned him the task of making life miserable for Whalers defenseman Kevin Haller, who had taken liberties against Kariya in a previous game. LeBoutillier did his job, spearing and sticking his opponent every time he touched the puck. Soon, however, LeBoutillier's antics got the attention of Hartford's Stu Grimson, whose fighting skills were on a par with his nickname, the Grim Reaper. "Stu saw what was going on. So he's threatening my life from the bench, yelling, 'I'm going to kill you.' I went by the bench and I said, 'I'm not going to fight you tonight.' And that made him madder. I said, 'I'll fight him, and I'll fight him and I'll fight him,' right down the bench. I ended up fighting Keith Primeau that night."

At the start of the 1997-98 season, LeBoutillier was assigned to the Cincinnati Mighty Ducks, Anaheim's new AHL affiliate. Although he earned a February call-up for 12 NHL games, he was sent back to the minors a few weeks later. He was confident that Anaheim would bring him back after the NHL trade deadline, but he spent the rest of the season in Cincinnati.

In the offseason, the Ducks traded for Grimson, leaving little opportunity for LeBoutillier. He was stuck fighting opponents on the undercard in Cincinnati, and he struggled to accept that his career had stalled. "When I was 21 or 22, I never thought I deserved to play in the NHL. And now when I'm back in the minors, I'm thinking, Why in the hell am I not playing in the NHL? How could I play at 22 and not at 24? What's going on? And you get this bitter feeling. That's the thing I regret the most about playing hockey.

"I remember driving to the rink one night in Cincinnati, and I didn't want to go to the game. I was like, I'm done. It didn't matter if I got in a fight or I didn't."

But he still had to show up and go through the motions. The job description was the same, whether he dropped his gloves for Anaheim or Cincinnati. And just because there was less at stake in the minors didn't mean the punches hurt any less or the fear went away. "I still didn't sleep the night before. I didn't feel better until I got in a fight because then I knew it was over."

As far as LeBoutillier was concerned, a fighter's life had its rewards in the NHL. But if he was going to face a steady diet of fear, sickness and sleepless nights, he did not want to do it for $70,000 in the AHL. Suddenly, hockey didn't feel so good. With each passing day in the minors, his chances of getting back to the NHL faded. When he thought about life after hockey, a new set of fears set in. "I don't have any education. What else can I do?" he asked himself.

"I was terrified. I was thinking, I've got to play hockey, but I'm not going to make it. And if I stop playing, now I have a wife I have to take care of. There's so many things you think about."

The season unraveled quickly. A knee injury put him on the shelf after just 12 games. When he wasn't worrying about his future, he was battling the team's training staff. Six months of rehab had not produced good results, and he didn't like the way the organization responded. "I wasn't getting any respect. They thought I was faking it. I couldn't cross over when I skated, and in hockey you have to. So I'd be fighting with the trainer. I wasn't the nicest person because I was frustrated. I thought the organization was giving up on me."

When the season ended, Anaheim let him go. Over the summer, LeBoutillier met up with Los Angeles Kings coach Andy Murray, who was looking to sign an enforcer for the farm team. "I remember Andy interviewing me and I was bull----ing him," LeBoutillier admits. "I had no other choice. He said, 'Can you still do the job?' I said, 'Yeah, I can still do the job.' In my head I'm thinking, There's no way I can do the job. I don't want to do the job. But I didn't have a choice. It was play hockey or do nothing. I was scared. I have a tough time talking to him today because I feel like I let him down."

LeBoutillier spent the entire season playing in Lowell, Massachusetts. He fought the good fights and chipped in with a little offense, just as he had done in previous years. But as the season went on, his role diminished. By the end, he played on the seldom-used fourth line. His frustration finally spilled over when his coach, Bruce Boudreau, sent him out to challenge an opponent to a fight in the final seconds of a 5-1 win—an assignment LeBoutillier regarded as unnecessary and demeaning. As he readied to drop the gloves, he shot a look toward Boudreau on the bench. Then he made sure his coach got the message. "I threw my helmet into our box at him. I knew I would miss him, but I wanted to show him this wasn't acceptable."

Los Angeles did not pick up the second-year option on LeBoutillier's contract. "I was in shock. I was almost in tears. I knew no one else would take a chance on me." His agent poked around, looking for that one team—just an AHL team—with one open roster spot. But the only feedback he received came from an AHL coach who said LeBoutillier was not tough enough. He felt like the entire hockey world had turned on him. "Not only is your career over," he says, "but now you have people degrading you."

One last hockey opportunity awaited on the furthest fringe of the game. LeBoutillier was offered a tax-free, $35,000 contract to play in Sheffield, England. It did not matter that hockey ranks in England about same place as cricket in the United States. It was a paycheck that held the real world at bay. With a roster full of former North American professionals, the Sheffield Steelers won the league championship. Best of all, LeBoutillier kept the fisticuffs to a minimum while skating a regular shift at center. It was just the experience he needed to restore his love for the game before moving on with the rest of his life.

Back when LeBoutillier was 20 years old, he met Gord Lane, a financial planner and a retired defenseman who won four Stanley Cups with the New York Islanders. LeBoutillier was starting his professional career in Baltimore, armed with a $35,000 signing bonus and lofty hopes that the hockey paychecks were just beginning. As their friendship grew, LeBoutillier realized that Lane was putting a damper on his dreams.

"You may play in the NHL, you may not," Lane told him. "You may make some money, you may not. You're going to find a girl in Baltimore. You're going to marry her. You're going to wait to figure things out, and when you're done with hockey, you're going to be scrambling."

As it turned out, Lane's crystal ball was crystal clear.

"And I hate that he was right," LeBoutillier says, his respect showing through.

Though he dismissed Lane's predictions at the time, he made a wise decision. He handed over the bonus check to Lane, who invested the money. Today, LeBoutillier is the director of business development for Lane's company, Next Shift Enterprises. Several dozen current and former pro hockey players hold investments through the company, including restaurants, real estate, and hockey camps.

LeBoutillier got off to a sluggish start in his first days with Next Shift.

When he accompanied Lane on car trips to check on investment properties, he would nod off in the passenger seat. It took a while to separate himself from the pace of a hockey player's life, where a typical day was very orderly: practice, workout, lunch, nap, movie, dinner, sleep.

Those days are behind him now. At 30, LeBoutillier no longer pencils in a snooze. He is comfortable and confident wearing business casual, spending the day at one of the company's Bennigan's restaurants in Cary, North Carolina. Sensing that the restaurant employees view him as a higher-up, he is careful to be respectful and polite. As he sits in a booth drinking coffee, he is focused on spelling out the lessons of his hockey career.

"People hold professional athletes in such high regard. And they shouldn't. Granted, it's great for us, because people will talk to us. But it almost hurts us in the long run because athletes really start to believe they are something special. It affects your psyche."

And that explains, in part, why his slide from the NHL hurt so much. After 35 NHL games and 176 penalty minutes, LeBoutillier had become a believer. "Did I deserve to be in the NHL in the first place? I don't know," he says. "To this day, I'm disappointed in myself. I'm disappointed I didn't play 10 years. When I was 15, I only wanted one game. So now I think, What the hell is my problem here?"

Part of the problem is his age. Deep down, he knows it. He is still young enough to be out patrolling the NHL ice and standing up for his teammates. He hopes the bitterness—like those fight dreams that still surface occasionally—disappears soon.

"I hope so, I really do," he insists.

Until then, he reminds himself how lucky he is. Thanks to Lane's guidance, LeBoutillier is further along than he could have imagined just a few years earlier. He knows his hockey journey has given him far more than 35 games in the NHL.

"Everything I have is due to hockey."

A defining moment

Long after
his playing career,
David Littman
virtually controls the NHL.

David Littman is 38 years old and he plays video games all day long. Sometimes 10 hours a day. For months at a time. "Since I was seven years old, I've been a video game fanatic," he says with obvious pride. "Ever since my parents bought me my first Atari."

Most thirty-somethings would be reluctant to spell out the details of their gaming obsession. Not Littman. Sometimes he doesn't even break for lunch. Joy stick in one hand, turkey and swiss in the other. It all sounds like an intervention waiting to happen. Until you learn one key fact—he's getting paid.

Littman works for EA Sports, the popular video game maker. He works in the hockey division, making sure the annual edition of the NHL game is the next best thing to the game on ice. And he would know. Before his gig as a virtual hockey player, he was a real, live one.

Beginning with his pee-wee days on Oyster Bay, Long Island, he realized he had a knack for playing in the net. His parents were New York Islanders season-ticket holders, which afforded little David the chance to sit near the goal and become inspired by the goalie tandem of Billy Smith and Chico Resch.

Littman joined the Buffalo Sabres in 1989 after a successful career at Boston College. But as an 11th-round pick, he was not in the club's immediate plans. The Sabres assigned him to Phoenix of the International Hockey League. "It was 100 degrees and we were playing hockey," he says. "We had no defense, but it was a lot of fun."

As the holidays neared, Littman made plans for a visit from his fiancée. Her first trip to Phoenix was scheduled to coincide with a Roadrunners home stand. He spotted her for the first time as he came off the ice at the end of a game. "Just as I'm giving her a hug, the coach calls me in his office and says, 'You're going to Rochester in the morning.' Poor Brenda. Not only was I leaving, but Rochester was on a 12-day road trip. Her whole vacation was ruined. That's when I realized this was a tough business. Family is not taken into account. You come to work, and they have the right to do with you whatever they want. That's the first lesson I learned."

The move to Rochester put a damper on his love life, but it was a promotion to Buffalo's top affiliate. Littman played 14 games for the Americans before watching starting goalie Darcy Wakaluk lead the team to the Calder Cup finals.

When Wakaluk joined the Sabres the following season, Littman took center stage in Rochester. He made the most of the starting role, earning a spot on the AHL all-star team. "More than anything it was the confidence of being the number one goalie," he says, offering an explanation for his play. "When you play all the time and the coach has confidence in you, that's everything. You stop thinking and go into cruise control. And when you stop thinking, you play way better."

As Rochester's starter, Littman was first in line for a call-up to Buffalo. When the big moment finally arrived, it was nothing like he imagined. The call came six hours prior to a Sabres game. Buffalo's starting goalie had injured his back during the team's morning skate, leaving the team without a second goaltender. But Rochester was in Newmarket, Ontario, and there were no direct flights to Buffalo. So Rochester's general manager resorted to hitchhiking in front of the team's hotel. "Our GM was offering people in the streets free tickets to a Buffalo Sabres game if they would take me and my equipment to the Sabres game," he says. "We found two people, and I drove down in their van with my equipment. It was seven o'clock and we were at the U.S. border. They wouldn't let us through at first. I was an American and they were Canadian. I showed them the equipment, and I called the GM using the phone in their booth."

Finally convinced that Littman and his goalie gear posed no threat, the border patrol allowed the van to enter the country. By the time he arrived at the arena, the game was in the second period. There was no big welcome, no time to take in the atmosphere. He simply took his seat at the end of the bench. "It was awesome. I wasn't nervous because I wasn't playing. It was a wild beginning to what you think is going to be so glamorous."

In late January, Buffalo summoned Littman from Rochester again, this time for a game in St. Louis. When the Blues took a 5-2 lead early in the second period, the Sabres gave Littman his first taste of NHL action. Right away, St. Louis went on the power play. As Blues center Adam Oates closed in, Littman came out of his crease to challenge him. Oates countered with a pass to Paul Cavallini, who ripped a one-timer for a goal. Before the puck came out of the net, Littman realized he could have stopped the shot. "If I would have been in the minors, I would have stayed back in my crease and used my quickness."

In the third period, he left the crease again to pressure Geoff Courtnall, who cut to the net and put one in off the post. "It wasn't the play I usually make," he says. "If I would have just played my game, it was an easy save."

Instead of stopping pucks, Littman was trying to make the right impression on the Buffalo front office. He knew the coaches and scouts preferred goaltenders who relied on proper positioning and getting square to the shooter. The trouble was, Littman played a butterfly style, dropping to the ice to protect the lower part of the net. "No matter how good I played in the minors, the scouts and the Buffalo brass thought I went down too much—that I was too much butterfly, that I was a flopper. And that never carried well with them back then. I just got it in my mind that when you're in the NHL, you have to stay up more. It wasn't the right thing, and it was my own fault." In 36 minutes of action, he gave up three goals on 15 shots. It was an acceptable NHL debut, but not one that wowed the Sabres. After the game, he returned to Rochester, where he finished the year with a 33-13-5 record.

Littman led the way for Rochester again in 1991-92, playing 60 games. In March, the Sabres called him up for his first NHL start. He was going to face the team of his childhood, the Islanders—on Long Island.

With a full day's notice, he hurried to line up tickets for family and friends. His parents had moved away from Long Island seven years earlier, but they put everything on hold to travel to their son's first NHL start. As they walked into Nassau Coliseum, Roy and Muriel Littman felt the past and present come together in a whirl of emotions. During warmups, they returned to their season-ticket section to renew acquaintances with their old crowd. One by one, their hockey pals asked, "Where's little David?" Roy and Muriel pointed to the net at the near end of the ice.

Whatever the game meant to Littman's career, he knew it meant just as much to his family. He thought of his sister, Debbie, who died of heart failure. She had traveled to so many of his childhood games. He laughed at his uncle's long-standing proclamation: If David ever plays at the Coliseum, he has to give me a hug and a kiss at the red line. With the dream suddenly unfolding, Littman found the middle ground between nostalgia and common sense. He blew a kiss to his uncle before the game.

When the puck dropped, Littman focused on playing his own style. He was beaten early on a low shot by star center Pierre Turgeon, but he was holding his own and playing with confidence. In the third period, Islanders forward Steve Thomas scored to give his team a 3-1 lead. "Here's where there is no doubt there is a difference between the NHL and the AHL," he says. "Thomas went from his forehand to his backhand and roofed it in a quarter of a second. Because I was in the zone, I saw it come off his stick as clear as day. It was like it was in slow motion. But it was such a great move, I couldn't get to it." Littman finished with a respectable 25-save performance in Buffalo's 4-1 loss.

After three years in the Buffalo organization, he had just a game and a half of NHL experience. For some people, that would amount to an exercise in futility. Littman viewed it differently. "People don't think about the minors being a place that people want to be. They think, Oh, you're not in the NHL—you must be unhappy. They couldn't be further from the truth. You're on an awesome team, you're getting paid. You're doing what you love to do. I can't see it any other way. I'm proud of my years in Rochester. I don't think I ever thought, I should be in the NHL."

Littman became a free agent before the 1992-93 season and signed with the expansion Tampa Bay Lightning. But the Lightning had veterans Wendell Young and Pat Jablonski signed to guaranteed NHL contracts. Littman, who had a two-way contract, earned the top job with the IHL's Atlanta Knights.

Just one month into the season, Littman returned to the NHL when an

injury knocked Young out of the lineup for a couple weeks. And because Tampa Bay coach Terry Crisp liked to change goaltenders after each loss, Littman figured he would get at least one turn in goal. But with Jablonski in the net, the Lightning reeled off five wins and a tie over the next two weeks, a surprising unbeaten streak for an expansion team. When the Lightning finally lost, Young was ready to come off the injured list. Littman headed back to Atlanta. "I had so much confidence because it was the beginning of the year, and I knew they liked me as a goalie," he says. "I really think if I would have played when I had all my confidence, I would have done well."

But he had no complaints. Atlanta was an enjoyable place to play hockey, and the bustling night life made the city ideal for celebrating wins. That's what he was doing one night in late March. While he and his teammates knocked back a few drinks at a sports bar, Littman kept one eye on Tampa Bay's game in Chicago. He could not believe what was taking place. As Young was being pulled from the game, he swung his stick against the glass in frustration. It was clear that he had injured his shoulder during the outburst. It was also obvious that Young's misfortune would lead to an opportunity for Littman in Tampa Bay—but thankfully not until after a good night's sleep. "I was drunk by this point," he says, "I stopped drinking once I realized I might be going up the next day." Indeed, Littman was on a plane the next day. He was scheduled to start the next game at New Jersey.

It was a disaster.

"By the end of the first period, I had let in three goals. I knew it just wasn't there. The harder you try to get out of it sometimes, the worse it gets because you're trying too hard. I was thinking too much every time they came down on me. I just sucked. Again, I didn't play my game. We just got killed by New Jersey. I got pulled. It was probably the worst moment of my hockey career. It was just awful. I let in seven goals."

The Devils won, 9-3. Littman returned to the minors after the game, knowing that the terrible performance would alter his career. "There's no doubt that playing well against the Devils in that game would have helped my career. They would have kept me for the next year. Basically I was done in

Tampa. They watched it. They were there. They wanted to beat the Devils."

He signed with the Boston Bruins in 1993-94, but the organization had more goalies than it could accommodate. After playing 25 games for Boston's AHL team in Providence, Littman was traded to Montreal. The Canadiens assigned him to Fredericton, where the team missed out on the AHL playoffs, "I kind of got discouraged," he says. "The attitude in the locker room was terrible. It was like your family was in turmoil."

Littman did not receive any promising offers for the 1994-95 season. "And I didn't have the passion," he says. "It was the low point of my hockey career by far. I was living in Atlanta. I bought a roller hockey rink and ran it with a few other guys. There wasn't much to do there."

Then came an unusual inquiry late in the season. The Richmond Renegades of the East Coast Hockey League were looking for a goalie. All Littman had to do to become playoff-eligible was play in one game. At first the offer seemed ridiculous, but the team seemed poised for a championship run and Littman was intrigued. So he flew to Richmond, started a game and came out after the first whistle. Then he flew back to Atlanta.

The meaningless minute of hockey rekindled his passion. He returned to Richmond for the end of the regular season, determined to make the most of his chance. It was not the quality of competition he was accustomed to, but that didn't matter—especially when the Renegades won the championship. "It was awesome. It wasn't that hard to just have fun. The best part about it was it got me positive about my play and my team and hockey."

Littman's conquest of the ECHL was the springboard to the final chapter of his pro career. In the mid 1990s, the IHL was expanding. Unaffiliated teams were popping up in new cities, giving veteran pros a chance to make a decent paycheck and extend their careers. He jumped on board with the expansion Los Angeles Ice Dogs and signed an incentive-based contract. The deal called for a $50,000 base salary, plus an additional $1,500 for Littman's first 15 wins in goal. After that, his victories paid $2,000 each. So when he reached 15 wins early in the season, he looked forward to upping the ante.

Then the plan hit a snag. The Ice Dogs were having financial problems, and

soon the team began selling off its expensive players. Littman's base salary was not a drain, but the $2,000 bonus checks were a problem. The team could no longer afford to have him win. So Los Angeles acquired veteran goalie Kay Whitmore, whose contract was being paid by the Vancouver Canucks, and installed him as the starter. Littman earned just two more victories the rest of the season.

After a season with the IHL's San Antonio Dragons, he joined the Orlando Solar Bears. For two seasons, Littman led the Solar Bears deep into the play-offs as the starting goalie. The money was good too. He earned more than $100,000 in salary and bonuses in his first season. "By that time, most of us knew we weren't going to the NHL. But you're still doing what you love and getting paid well."

But by the start of the 1999-2000 season, Littman's body was failing him. He had already endured a half dozen knee surgeries in his career when he tore cartilage in his right knee during Orlando's training camp. He played two games, but he knew the knee would not stand up to the rigors of a full season. With retirement on the horizon, he received one more call from the NHL. His former coach in Orlando, Curt Fraser, had taken over the expansion Atlanta Thrashers. Fraser's NHL goaltenders were hurt, and he needed his former minor league starter. Littman's heart said yes, but his knees said no. "I wonder how I would have played," he says. "It would have been fun to get called up there that late in my career."

Instead of going to the NHL, he went home. "This wasn't something I could fix or make better. So I could easily accept it. It was just a sign that it was about time to move on."

Immediately, Littman found himself asking, "Now what?" For the next year, he stayed connected to his familiar world by providing color commentary for Solar Bears games on TV. But the job occupied just 20 nights and the work load was light. "It's the easiest job ever," he admits. "I basically took a year off."

That's when it occurred to Littman that he could indulge his other passion. Orlando was home to the EA Sports studio that makes the Madden NFL video game. He took a job as a game tester, spending his summer alongside a bunch of college kids who thought they had it made. "I'm kind of proud of that moment in my life," he says. "I was making seven dollars an hour as a tester at 33 years old. That's what happens when your career is over. All my friends out of Boston College were stock brokers or somewhere in money. It was like graduating again." After five months of video football, he landed an interview with EA's hockey division. He was offered a job at hockey headquarters in Vancouver, and he has never looked back.

As an associate producer, Littman has a hand in most aspects of product development, from designing the game to controlling the players. Thanks to his first career, his strength is his keen eye for details. "If the defenseman backs up too far into the goalie, that has to be fixed," he says. "If a goalie lets in too many goals, it could be that his attributes aren't high enough."

Every now and then, he has a chance to blur the line between the real NHL and the virtual one. When NHL teams are in town to play the Vancouver Canucks, he picks the brains of veteran coaches like Joel Quenneville, Bob Hartley and Mark Crawford. Like a mad scientist, Littman gathers power-play strategies and nuances of individual players. Then in the months prior to the annual release of the NHL video game, he spends 10 hours a day wearing out his thumbs. If you don't feel sorry for him, he understands. He knows he has had a pretty good run when it comes to making a living. "First it was hockey and now it's video games," he says. "And it's a hockey video game—it's both!"

By keeping hockey front and center after his playing career, Littman stayed within his comfort zone. But he was not prepared for other aspects of the working world. He had spent his entire life surrounded by hockey players and coaches. His colleagues at EA Sports were nothing like the people he knew from the rink.

"I had to realize that these aren't a bunch of hockey players sitting in the locker room ragging on each other, where you can say anything you want and no one is going to get upset. You come in the real world, and all of a sudden you have to be aware of people's feelings," he says with a soft laugh. "You don't have to do that on a hockey team. At first I think I was a little too hard

on people. It took a year to learn how to deal with people in professions I had no idea about.

"Every friend I ever had in my life was a hockey player. It was really eye opening to realize there is a whole world out there besides the hockey world. I didn't like it at first because I couldn't be myself. But it has helped me become a better person overall. Being a hockey player is a great way to live and it's a great part of my life, but it isn't everything in the end."

There is still a bit of hockey player left in David Littman, but the goaltender has left the crease for good. When there is a game at the local rink and his knees are up to the task, he plays forward. "When you've lived your whole life stopping pucks," he explains simply, "you want to score some goals."

But in Littman's world, hockey will always be about goaltending. For three nights spread over three years, he had the honor of standing between the pipes in the National Hockey League. Ideally, he would have played one stretch of five or six NHL games, just long enough to find his confidence and establish some credentials. But it didn't work out that way, and Littman knows why. "When I got my chances, I didn't make the most of them. I have no regrets except that I didn't play my best."

Sometimes it is not the duration of your memories, but the depth of them. The essence of Littman's career came down to just one night on Long Island. Saturday, March 14, 1992. His parents swelled with pride, while their season-ticket-holder friends cheered like never before. His uncle got his kiss, his sister was his angel. And Littman stood there in goal while his beloved Islanders, like his emotions, swirled all around him.

"Out of any moment in my career, that was the defining one," he says. "That made everything worthwhile."

BASKET
ball

LES JEPSEN

Whatever you say, coach

Les Jepsen never put his personal ambition ahead of his team, sometimes to his disadvantage.

Meet **Les Jepsen**, NBA stereotype.
We're not talking about the over-hyped superstar. Not the
flashy phenom with a combative personality. That's the other end
of the NBA spectrum.

Jepsen was the 7-footer at the end of the bench. The big backup center
from you-can't-remember-where. One of the guys who stands during time
outs, forming a human shield around the starters while they take a seat. The
player who makes a full night's work out of a few high fives.

For two years, Les Jepsen was just happy to be there.

"I was never disappointed. I'm kind of unique," he says cheerfully. "A lot
of players are selfish. They're worried about themselves. But I've always had
my best experiences with teams that did well."

Jepsen played two seasons in the NBA, beginning in 1990. That sounds
like a decent helping of NBA basketball, but in reality, he played just 192 minutes in 52 games. Every three games or so, Jepsen would shed his warm ups
and do his thing for three or four minutes at the end of the game. "I'm a very
good 11th or 12th man. I don't have an ego and I never did," he says.

Jepsen's selfless approach to professional basketball was cultivated far
away from the traditional setting of inner-city playgrounds and gymnasiums.
He grew up in Bowbells, North Dakota, where the lives of the 500 residents
revolve around farms and oil wells. No one gave much thought to basketball.
So when he reached 6 feet 9 inches by the end of his sophomore year in high
school, he was getting by on instincts. His coach at Bowbells High School was
only 23 years old.

"When I was growing up in northwest North Dakota, I couldn't go talk to
Alonzo Mourning. There were no other 7-footers up there," he says. "I couldn't
go to a playground and play against great talent. I literally learned how to
play by watching CBS on Sunday. Artis Gilmore and the Chicago Bulls were on
every week. I had a book called NBA Stars of 1975, and I read that like 500
times. That's all I had."

The lack of quality coaching and competition was just one hurdle. Despite averaging 27 points, 20 rebounds and six blocks per game, Jepsen had a tough time making a name for himself outside of Bowbells. "I put up stats, but there were no newspapers there. The nearest paper was 100 miles away. The *Minot Daily News* never covered us."

Eventually, word got out. Longtime Louisiana State coach Dale Brown, who owned farm land nearby, dropped in to watch Jepsen play. Then Gonzaga University assistant coach Bruce Wilson heard about him. After pursuing a recruit in South Dakota, Wilson drove 500 miles and put the full-court press on Jepsen. "They recruited me hard," he recalls. "He literally stayed in the Bowbells Motor Inn for two weeks."

But Jepsen wanted to be closer to home, so he chose the University of Iowa. He red-shirted as a freshman, working to reach the skill level of his more accomplished classmates. After two seasons of limited play, he made his way into the Hawkeyes rotation every night as a junior, earning a reputation for strong rebounding and a scoring touch. Best of all, under the direction of coach Tom Davis and his staff, he was getting the instruction he needed to refine his game. Assistant coaches Gary Close and Bruce Pearl helped him become an elite college player.

"Bruce was super," says Jepsen about Pearl, the current head coach at the University of Tennessee. "He told me if I wanted to make (Iowa's) top eight, this is what I had to do. Every day he pushed me. He's had unbelievable success as a coach. It's because of his energy and his enthusiasm and because of his honesty. I can't give enough credit to those guys. They never told me anything that wasn't true. They kept me working."

While Pearl and Close helped with the fundamentals, Davis was responsible for the big picture. Before Jepsen's senior season, Davis told him exactly what it would take to become an NBA draft pick. "If you can average 15 points and 10 rebounds," he said, "you can make $500,000."

Jepsen tracked his coach's theory, calculating statistics after each game. He finished the season with an average of 14.9 points and 10 rebounds for the Hawkeyes. "And I signed a contract for $500,000 a year down to the dol-

lar," he says, still sounding amazed at the accuracy of his coach's prediction. "He set the goals right. He knew the limits. He knew me better than I knew myself."

The contract was with the Golden State Warriors, who selected him with the first pick in the second round. Golden State's coaches told Jepsen they simply wanted him to fit in with the team and develop his game over the coming years. The goals were practical and reassuring but not the advice he needed to hear.

"Looking back, I wish they would have told me, 'You need to work your butt off, day in and day out, and take no breaks for the next two years.' If they would have said that, I would have done it. But to be honest, I relaxed a little bit. I should have been working on my game night in and night out."

From the start, his accommodating personality and athletic disposition were not a great fit for the NBA. Shortly after the draft, head coach Don Nelson sent Jepsen for a private two-week tutorial with University of Utah coach Rick Majerus. "That was one of the highlights of my life," he says. "He taught me a lot about the game." A week after the workouts, Majerus followed up with a letter, reminding Jepsen that he was already a good shooter and rebounder. He simply needed to gain weight and strength. "I have faith in you," Majerus wrote. "You can be a player."

Jepsen took the coach's kind words as encouragement, but he failed to see the message in a larger context. He did not realize that the two weeks of drills and teaching were just an outline for success. "I thought when I was done with Rick Majerus, I was OK," he says. "I should have continued that work for a year and a half."

Instead, he played a limited role with Golden State. The Warriors were led by the high-scoring trio of Chris Mullin, Mitch Richmond and Tim Hardaway. The team also had plenty of depth at center, leaving Jepsen on the bench for 61 of 82 regular season games. "Paul Mokeski, Jim Peterson, Alton Lister, Tom Tolbert—I could compete with those guys, but they were better," he says, referring to Golden State's go-to forwards and centers.

Because Jepsen recognized his limitations, he embraced decisions that

LES JEPSEN

gave his teammates a leg up on game days. "Don Nelson told me, 'We're close to making the playoffs, and I'm not going to sacrifice three or four games for your development.' And it made sense. Put the team first."

Not only did he sit quietly as the regular season wound down, Jepsen made no waves when he was exiled to the injured reserve list for the playoffs, making him ineligible to play. He wasn't really hurt, but that didn't matter. "When coach said they were going to put me on the IR, I said, 'Coach, you've gotta do what you've gotta do. And I want to do what's best for the team.' I literally said that a couple times. That's what it's truly all about. It's about the team. I could have fought it, but that's hurting the team."

The Warriors beat San Antonio in the first round before losing to the Los Angeles Lakers. For Jepsen, watching his team play two rounds made the season complete. "We overachieved. That's the memory I take from my experience at Golden State. We did have a good year. I didn't look at it and say, Man I didn't get any minutes. I have never thought that. Maybe I should have done that more, but no one ever told me to do that. I just figured it was the right thing to do. One of my faults, I think, is I was too nice."

At the end of the season, Golden State traded Jepsen and Richmond to the Sacramento Kings. More accurately, it was Richmond and a backup something-or-other. "Obviously, they wanted Mitch. When I went to the first players meeting, it was, Where's Mitch at? There's Mitch! Nice to meet you Mitch! I thought, OK, I'm a pedestrian here. I got the picture."

It was not a pretty one. Jepsen rarely played in the first half of the season, and the Kings were out of the playoff hunt by January. He made most of his appearances late in the season, but his playing time was never substantial. The Kings trudged on with their regulars, sinking to a 29-53 record. Jepsen played 31 games, averaging less than three minutes per appearance.

"When I played, I played minutes that didn't mean much. But they meant a lot to me. I expected to perform the best I could. I got a little bit discouraged. I wasn't used to being on a team that didn't win. We didn't have the cohesiveness we had at Golden State. We weren't expected to make the playoffs. The players didn't expect to make the playoffs. It just wasn't the same.

I don't know what they wanted. I never got any feedback from anyone."

The Kings released Jepsen in training camp before the 1992-93 season, but he welcomed the change. He caught on with the Rockford Lightning of the minor league Continental Basketball Association. His game thrived. "I made $1,200 a week, but I got a chance to start. It was a super experience. The CBA is nothing like the NBA. We had to jump on planes at five in the morning and stay in hotels that were not very nice. But it was a great group of guys. I had games where I had 24 rebounds and 15 points."

The CBA quickly became his comfort zone. He was flourishing in a world of Midwestern bus rides and too-short hotel beds. But as Jepsen renewed his love for the game, he began to lose his competitive edge.

After a game in which Jepsen scored 20 points and hauled down 24 rebounds, he learned that he was back in demand in the NBA. The Detroit Pistons had been scouting him and were considering offering a contract. But when he began thinking about returning to the NBA, it did not look so inviting.

"I didn't really have the mindset of wanting to get called up. I was having fun. I was playing the best basketball of my life. The trouble is I was playing in front of 800 people in Rockford. I was a little bit worried. I roughly failed in the NBA the first time. If I got called up again, what's going to happen?" Detroit never came through with an offer, but Jepsen had already worked through his ambivalence and self doubt. The NBA was no longer his central concern.

Jepsen took one more shot at the NBA the next fall, joining the Minnesota Timberwolves for a "decent but not great" training camp. When he was cut, he returned to the CBA once again for a season with the Fargo Fever. This time, the league held less charm. "I kind of lost my drive to play basketball, and I didn't want to go overseas. I just decided to shift directions."

Wanting to make a clean break from basketball, Jepsen returned to the University of Iowa to pursue an MBA. At first, the transition to the academic world was difficult. "It was very uncomfortable. It kind of scared me. When I got to school, I was out of my element. I was only out of it for four years. I knew I was smart and I knew I was a good person. But it took a while to get used to it."

Once his brain shifted back to the books, Jepsen felt at home on campus. Without much of an athletic ego, cutting ties with professional basketball was a lay up. "I've been in situations where I wasn't a superstar," he says. "I was a pedestrian before basketball, and I knew I was going to be a pedestrian afterwards. I knew there was going to be 50 years of life after basketball, and I was going to have to be happy with myself being anonymous.

"I'm a planner. I'm a goal setter. I didn't want to be that guy who just toiled and held on to that mindset—I'm a basketball player, look at me. My goal was to be of service to society. I wanted to be successful at other things."

At age 30, he left Iowa City with his MBA in hand. Not wanting to be remembered by Iowa fans as a guy who hung around his college town, he headed to Minneapolis and started Jepsen Consulting, a financial planning business. "I had no clients. I had a three-year goal, a five-year goal and a ten-year goal. I just grew it slowly," says Jepsen, who is also a realtor. "I just wanted to do it the right way. Now it's 10 years later and I have happy clients. I have 125 families I work with."

Many of those clients know that their financial planner once played in the NBA, but not because Jepsen ever calls attention to the fact. "It has opened doors for me in business and personally. I don't go around saying I played in the NBA. If you tell people you played in the NBA, you're an easy target. People automatically treat you differently. I don't want to be known as a basketball player. I want people to know I'm a real estate guy or an invest-ment person or a friend."

Many retired athletes have the luxury of slipping quietly into the work-ing world. But when you're the tallest guy in town, you might as well walk around dribbling. "People ask me all time if I played basketball because I'm seven feet. I don't want to share my story three times a day with strangers. If you tell them you played in the NBA, they will ask you 15 questions. All of a sudden, it's a 15-minute conversation."

In fifteen minutes, Jepsen could cover quite a bit of his NBA career. And if anyone were to walk away unimpressed, that's fine. "Anybody who looks at my career and my numbers, they'd say, 'That guy failed.' But it doesn't matter

to me," he says. "When I was a kid, I could have said, 'I'm a skinny white kid from North Dakota. I'm not going to play in the NBA.' But I made it.

"I wish I could have played at least three years. I think you get that full experience. It would have been nice to play in the Boston Garden three or four times. It would have been fun to play in the playoffs more than once."

But in the end, Jepsen settled for two NBA seasons that yielded 53 points. It may not sound like much, but he created some nice memories for himself. He guarded Michael Jordan a couple times. He banged bodies with Larry Bird and Hakeem Olajuwon. When he looks back at the NBA now, it feels a bit out of balance. "It was such a big part of my life trying to get there. I wanted to play since I was eight. Then you're 23. That's 15 years of preparation. All of a sudden it lasts two years."

But he admits, that's just nitpicking. The rest of his life includes plenty of basketball. Jepsen volunteers with a high school team and an AAU team. "I literally love the game," he says, emphasizing his words. "I should be coaching. That's my passion. Giving back is where you get your happiness."

Several years after he retired, Jepsen had one last memorable NBA experience. He was visiting Brad Lohaus, his former teammate at Iowa. Lohaus was playing for the San Antonio Spurs, and he took Jepsen into the locker room after practice. Soon Spurs star David Robinson came over and asked how Jepsen was doing, and the two centers continued to chat for a few minutes. Having squared off on the court a couple times, they had some history.

"I don't know if he knew me or not," Jepsen says.

Years later, he delights in the mystery. He didn't need the recognition when he played in the league, and he didn't need any validation later. So Jepsen stood there and made small talk with Robinson.

"I just said I was in town visiting a friend," he says. "Basketball never came up."

Knowing your limits

The NBA showed no interest in Rusty LaRue. Luckily, LaRue saw something that scouts missed.

As a senior in college, **Rusty LaRue** knew he was not NBA material. He was the starting point guard at Wake Forest University in 1995-96, averaging a modest 10 points per game and his skills were not flashy.

He was not surprised when the NBA ignored him on draft day. But the indifference did not stop there. When the minor league Continental Basketball Association began choosing from the college leftovers, the Sioux Falls Skyforce waited until the seventh and final round to call his name.

When South Dakota is ambivalent about you, it's a bad a sign.

Move ahead nearly a dozen years, and you will find LaRue at Greensboro College in North Carolina. He is the head basketball coach at the Division III school. If you knew nothing of what transpired between the end of his college days and this small-college coaching gig, you might do a double take when you walk into his office. On the wall behind his desk is a framed poster of a Chicago Bulls NBA championship team. Michael Jordan, Scottie Pippen and the rest are shooting and slashing in various action shots. And you would swear the guy right in the center of the poster is LaRue—perhaps courtesy of a friend who knows how to tinker with Photoshop.

But the poster is authentic. Just like LaRue's game.

Just about everyone with a basketball opinion thought LaRue's NBA dream was absurd. He didn't listen. He has a 1998 NBA championship ring to prove it. "I knew I had a lot more talent in basketball than people were seeing because I never had any prep time for basketball," he says. "I would go straight into it after football season. I knew I had potential there, and I knew I could play if I concentrated on it."

Most observers believed LaRue had a brighter future as an NFL quarterback than an NBA point guard. On the football field, he set a handful of NCAA single-game passing records. But he was just a complementary player in basketball on an Atlantic Coast Conference team that featured standout center Tim Duncan. "No one was knocking on my door for me to play basketball," he says, "So if I got an opportunity, I told people I would try out in football. I thought that would be my best chance."

LaRue worked out for the Cincinnati Bengals, and scouts from Carolina, Philadelphia and New Orleans expressed some interest. But the NFL passed on draft day. It was just as well. Deep down, LaRue was ready to make a clean break from football anyway. "I was on some really bad teams at Wake," he says. "You have a little bit of a bitter taste about football when you do that."

So he decided to pursue basketball, even though basketball had not pursued him. He performed well at the Portsmouth Invitational Tournament, a showcase for draft-eligible players, and earned a spot in the NBA's summer league. The Chicago Bulls were impressed enough to invite him to training camp. But because the Bulls were the defending NBA champions, LaRue figured he had little chance to make the team. He declined the invitation and accepted a one-month contract from a professional team in France.

"Was I an NBA player? Probably not. I was realistic and knew my limitations. I think that's one of the reasons I had an NBA career when nobody thought I would."

When he returned home in November, he found his market value in the United States was still at rock bottom. "I sat around for two and a half months waiting for a job," says LaRue, who already had the responsibility of providing for a wife and child. "At the end of January, I was going to quit. I had already called the Bulls scout and told him I was going to get a job. And the day I interviewed with Andersen Consulting and they offered me a job, I got a call from a (minor league) team in Connecticut." The decision was easy, even though he took a major financial hit. The job at Andersen would have provided a $40,000 salary for his young family. Instead, he made $15,000 while playing for the CBA's Connecticut Pride.

With a year of professional basketball on his resume, LaRue was again invited to Chicago's training camp before the 1997-98 season. This time he jumped at the chance. When the exhibition season ended, he was on the brink of fulfilling his dream. Everything hinged on whether injured guard Steve Kerr had medical clearance to return to the lineup. Three hours before the team was to leave for the season opener in Boston, Kerr was given the green light to play. LaRue was cut.

He took his family back to the minors, this time joining the Idaho Stampede. But after one game in the CBA, Chicago general manager Jerry Krause was on the phone. Kerr had gone down with another injury, and the GM wanted LaRue to be ready at a moment's notice. "He was supposed to call me that afternoon, and I had to go to my game," he recalls. "I told my wife, Tammy, to stay home until he called. I was in warm-ups when she gave me the thumbs up that they were calling me up. I still played that night, which I probably shouldn't have done. I could have gotten hurt."

LaRue made his NBA debut in Phoenix when Chicago coach Phil Jackson turned him loose in the fourth quarter. He finished with seven points, connecting on three of his five shots in a win over the Suns. The following night, he was 4-for-6 from the field in a 31-minute audition against the Los Angeles Clippers. If nothing else, LaRue had shown the Bulls that he could handle spot duty off the bench.

Still, there was a potential trap for a rookie like LaRue on a team like the Bulls. Chicago had already won five championships in the 1990s. Jordan, Pippen and Dennis Rodman were treated like rock stars wherever the Bulls played. Even Jackson was regarded as an intellectual giant among NBA coaches. For an undrafted, untested player, it would have been easy to get comfortable and enjoy the ride. LaRue knew better. "You don't really get caught up in that. I played with Tim Duncan. I played in the ACC against great competition. You just come in and try to do your job. You're really thinking more about the opportunity you have and thinking about what you can do to show that you can stay around. You're not worrying about getting autographs."

Most of the time, LaRue kept a low profile, a long-standing sports tradition among rookies. When the Bulls flew to road games, he never dared to poke his nose where it didn't belong—namely into Jordan's legendary poker games. "I wasn't in the back playing cards with MJ. I was getting beers for the guys because I was a rookie. That was my job," he says with an amusing sort of pride. "I put bags on the plane and took them off of the plane. If anyone wanted something on the plane, I would be happy to get it for them. I figured it was the least I could do."

If Jordan and company were the rock stars, Chicago's remaining players were the roadies. LaRue found his social level with Kerr, Jud Buechler, Bill Wennington and Luc Longley. But he did lean on Jordan once when he needed a favor. LaRue had invited four of his college friends to a Bulls game at Madison Square Garden, but because he was not on the active roster for the game, he did not receive complimentary tickets. Knowing that Jordan had already secured a large block of seats, he asked MJ for a few spares. "He gave me four great seats for the game and never asked me to pay a dime. My friends were sitting 50 yard line with great seats. He didn't have to do that."

As Chicago's season moved toward the holidays, LaRue experienced a surreal moment with the Bulls. The team's Christmas party featured a Secret Santa gift exchange, and LaRue drew the name of Dennis Rodman, the most mercurial and eccentric man in sports. "I'm the rookie on the team, and I'm thinking, What do I get Dennis Rodman? I knew he had a daughter that he really loved. So I got him a silver money clip with his daughter's name engraved on it. I did some research to make sure I spelled her name right.

"Dennis doesn't talk a lot, believe it or not. Away from his persona, he's a quiet guy. He said thank you, obviously. He said he really liked it."

As LaRue finishes the story, a goofy smile creeps across his face. After all, how many men have a tender-moment Dennis Rodman story to share? Finally he blurts out the most tasteful thing he can think of: "We're pretty much exact opposites."

After passing along the money clip, it was LaRue's turn to be on the receiving end. He had high hopes after learning that Jordan once gave Pippen

a Ferrari for Christmas. But LaRue's Kris Kringle turned out to be Scott Burrell, Jordan's backup. Burrell put the brakes on the sports car dream, presenting the pro athlete's version of socks and underwear—a $300 gift certificate to Nordstrom, a department store. "That went to get me some clothes, so I looked good on the bench," he says with a laugh.

Just as well, LaRue figured. He didn't need a high-performance import. He needed to keep his eye on the ball. From the start, he was at peace with his ancillary role in the Bulls dynasty. Even the coach had no reason to draw LaRue into the team's inner circle. "I was not integral to the success of the team. It's not like Phil Jackson was calling me into his office and having sit-downs with me. I had to do my role. And my role was to come in and shoot the ball when I was open and play basketball. I think one of the reasons I fit in with that team is the same reason everyone else did. They were guys who just knew their roles."

LaRue's role was a limited one. He played just 14 games with the Bulls in 1997-98, mostly when Kerr was out of the lineup. His best night was a nine-point effort at Washington in 15 minutes of playing time. But when the play-offs arrived, LaRue was left off the active roster. The decision was a reminder of his place on the team, but he was not about to feel sorry for himself. "Not when you're playing for a team that's going to win the NBA championship. I knew I wasn't as good as the guys who were playing. I was just happy to be there."

The Bulls won their sixth title, putting LaRue's name in the history books. While he is proud to say he was part of the team, his satisfaction is proportionate to the amount of time he played. "Obviously, it means more to you if you play and you're a big contributor. But would I trade it for anything? No. It's the NBA championship. But I cherish my ACC championship as much if not more because I played 35 minutes a game and I was a big part of that."

Before the 1998-99 season, the Bulls dismantled their dynasty. Jordan retired for the second time, Pippen signed with Houston, and Rodman went to the Los Angeles Lakers. Even Jackson stepped down as coach. The team was left with veterans Toni Kukoc and Ron Harper and a variety of spare parts, including LaRue.

The bottom-feeding Bulls were a letdown to Chicago fans, but the roster remake provided LaRue with a chance to prove he could handle a larger workload. Every now and then, he showed flashes. He went 5-for-5 in a February game against Charlotte, making all three of his three-point shots. But with the team going through a complete overhaul under new coach Tim Floyd, LaRue's fortunes did not improve much. "It was pretty much a disaster from the get-go. You had a coach coming from college who had never coached professionally. It was frustrating. They were rotating us in off the injured list. It didn't matter whether you were hurt or not, didn't matter how well you were playing. Two days after I had my 5-for-5 game against Charlotte, I was put on the injured list. I think I had tendinitis of the toe or something crazy.

"I had played the year before and was one of the few guys left from that team. I thought I was good enough to make it with those guys and play on that team, but I was getting shuffled around. And that's frustrating. I had games where I felt like I showed what I could do. It just really didn't develop."

The Bulls finished 13-37 in the strike-shortened season. LaRue averaged 4.7 points over 43 games. Even though his numbers were an improvement over the previous year, he could not overcome the stigma of playing for a woeful team. "It's hard to look good on a losing team. It was a hodgepodge of guys. You look at that team and look at how many guys are left in the NBA—there's not many."

The Bulls had seen enough of LaRue, releasing him in training camp prior to the 1999-2000 season. His roster spot was filled by Dedric Willoughby, who had played for Floyd at Iowa State. Willoughby's NBA career lasted 25 games.

LaRue headed back to Idaho for another tour of the minors. Then in December, Chicago came calling one last time. The Bulls had three injured guards, and they needed a replacement the same night. LaRue hopped on a plane in Grand Rapids, where Idaho was playing, and suited up in Chicago. For three games, he steadied the Bulls backcourt, posting 13 points against Seattle, 13 against Minnesota and 10 against New Jersey. His performance was on par with the other Chicago guards.

But when LaRue threw in a clunker against Indiana in his fourth game—0-for-5 shooting in 16 minutes—Chicago waived him. He knew not to take it personally. With a 2-23 record, Chicago needed impact players. Right or wrong, the Chicago front office viewed him as nothing more than a stopgap solution. So on the same day they dumped LaRue, the Bulls signed a player with a deeper resume. Khalid Reeves was a former first-round draft pick who had played for five NBA teams in five seasons. Reeves lasted three games in Chicago and never played in the NBA again.

In the meantime, LaRue returned to Idaho. In his first game back in the minors, he shattered his pinky finger and missed two months, ruining any chance of returning to the NBA for the rest of the season.

Wanting the stability of a guaranteed paycheck, he accepted a $280,000 offer to play a season in Russia in 2000-01. But the next season, he set out to return to the NBA. LaRue went to training camp with the Utah Jazz, but when he failed to win a backup job, he went to Asheville, North Carolina to play in the National Basketball Development League. The NBDL provided a pipeline to the NBA, but LaRue had to settle for a salary of just $18,000.

By mid season, the Jazz needed help at guard. LaRue completed a pair of 10-day contracts with Utah before signing for the remainder of the season. He averaged 5.8 points per game in 33 appearances. The Jazz called on him during the playoffs too. He chipped in five points per game in Utah's first-round loss to Sacramento.

LaRue's career was coming to a crossroads. Without a regular dose of substantial playing time, he could not prove that he could thrive in a larger role. He was typecast as a role player. In the eyes of the NBA, he had reached his maximum potential. "I got tired of hearing the word 'potential'. One guy has got more potential than somebody else. I was never a guy who was seen to have potential. Because they said I was an over-achiever, they always thought I was doing the best I could possibly do at that moment. That's just the lot I had as an athlete. And that was fine. I understood that. But I knew that, given the opportunity, I could show what I could do."

With no guaranteed NBA offers for the 2002-03 season, LaRue went overseas again, this time to Italy. By then, he and Tammy had three children. Accepting a $170,000 tax-free contract was an easy choice for the good of the family.

But big dreams die hard. LaRue took one last shot at the NBA in 2003-04, signing with the Boston Celtics. But a wrist injury cut short his bid to make the team. After surgery and another minor league stint with the Asheville Altitude, LaRue earned another look in the NBA in March. The Golden State Warriors, in the midst of a seven-game losing streak, signed him to a 10-day contract. He played just 22 minutes over four games before being released. The Warriors thanked him and explained that they had found another player they wanted to sign. "They were not a good team, and they were still looking for a player with potential," he says. "And I was just a guy who was serviceable who could do what they asked."

It was the same scenario LaRue endured during his final four-game stint in Chicago, serving as a placeholder until an intriguing name showed up on the waiver wire. For the Warriors, that player was J.R. Bremer, a castoff from Cleveland. Bremer shot a woeful 19 percent for Golden State and got the ax after five games.

LaRue noticed a similarity in the performances of Bremer and Khalid Reeves, his successor in Chicago. Reeves had an 0-for-7 shooting night during his brief time in Chicago, while Bremer was 2-for-16 over his first two games with Golden State. As poorly as his replacements played, at least they went down firing. "I'm not a selfish player, and I think that's what was frustrating to me about the NBA," he says. "It's a me, me, me league. A lot of times guys who aren't me, me, me don't fit in or don't get an opportunity."

LaRue returned to Asheville for the final weeks of the season and helped the team win the 2004 NBDL championship. He had the chance to leave the game on a high note. There was nothing more he could do to enhance his reputation in the NBA, and he was no longer content to prove himself 10 days at a time. "In the NBA, you're making money, the living is great, the hotels... You're on top of the world. But the competitor inside you wants to play. It got to the point where I realized I was not going to play day in and day out in the

NBA. It's easier to move on knowing I got that opportunity."

LaRue retired with 98 NBA games to his credit, averaging five points per game. It may not sound like a lot, but his career lasted 98 games longer that most people expected.

"Was I an NBA player? Probably not. I was realistic and knew my limitations. I think that's one of the reasons I had an NBA career when nobody thought I would. I could play for the Bulls and the Jazz. I could shoot and set screens for people, make the right pass, know who the open man is—that type of point guard. But there were a lot of NBA teams I couldn't play for. I was not a point guard who could beat people off the dribble and draw two defenders."

Now in his first year at Greensboro College, LaRue is satisfied to start on the lower rungs of the coaching ladder. When you have apprenticed as Michael Jordan's bellhop and flight attendant, you know all about humble beginnings. And no matter where he coaches in the future, chances are good that people will always connect him with those dynasty days in Chicago. They will want to hear about winning a championship with Jordan, Pippen and the entire Bulls circus. And they will wonder how LaRue managed to land right in the middle of the championship picture.

"I cherish the fact that I have the championship, and I cherish the fact that I got to play with Michael Jordan. But that's not who I am. I don't get my self worth from the fact that I played for that team. I get much more self worth from the fact that I busted my butt to get there when nobody else thought I could."

MIKE PEPLOWSKI

The real me

With other career ambitions,
Mike Peplowski grew weary
of NBA life both on
and off the court

Because **Mike Peplowski** is 6 feet 11 inches, he knows the basketball questions are coming. So if you're already aware that he played at Michigan State and in the NBA, do yourself a favor. Don't start gushing about the glory days. It might end badly.

"I had to tell that to someone at the country club I belong to," says Peplowski, who lives among the Spartan faithful in Lansing, Michigan. "And I had to say it the only way he would ever understand it, which is, 'If you come up to me one more time drunk off your ass and say how great I was and tell me how much you loved me when I played at Michigan State, I'm going to knock all your teeth down your throat.'"

That sort of warning may seem like overkill, especially to an intoxicated Michigan State fan trying to pay a sloppy compliment. But Peplowski has weathered years of chatter about his athletic career and it's getting old. "My wife asked me, 'Why do you always not want to talk about it?' I said, 'Because everybody else wants to talk about it, and that's not me.'

"What I end up saying is, 'That's who I was. Who I am now is totally different.' And if all people can see is that, then they don't see me. They don't understand how hard I've worked up to this point to get where I am right now, which I'm proud of. I'm not a professional athlete. I'm not a Michigan State basketball player. That's long since over. I never think about it. The only time I ever think about it is when somebody else brings it up."

Peplowski's Michigan State teams reached the NCAA Tournament three times in four seasons in the early 1990s. But after averaging double digits in points and rebounds as a senior, Peplowski was still a marginal NBA prospect. ACL surgery in high school left him a step slower than the elite college centers.

Sacramento drafted him in the second round in 1993. He quickly made his mark with the Kings, earning a guaranteed contract worth the rookie minimum of $150,000. With the ineffective duo of Duane Causwell and Randy Breuer at center, Kings coach Garry St. Jean moved Peplowski into the

starting lineup. In the fifth game of the season, he broke through with 14
points in just 18 minutes against New Jersey. He made the majority of starts
at center for the first two months of the season, averaging nearly 20 minutes
per night.

But the Kings never expected Peplowski to fill the starting role in his
first year. In February, they traded Causwell to Detroit in exchange for Olden
Polynice, upgrading the center position and taking the heat off their rookie.
"They thought they could do better in the center position, and truth be told,
they could, given the talent pool that was out there," he says. "Perfect.
I won't have the pressure on me to be a starting center in the NBA. I can
learn more and get 15 minutes a game and start to build a resume instead
of sink or swim."

 **"The only place to go after being a professional
athlete, professionally speaking, is down. And once you're there
and you're on even footing with everybody else, that little thing
that differentiated you from the rest of the populace...is gone."**

It would have been an ideal arrangement, but Causwell failed his physical with Detroit and was returned to the Kings, who sent another player to
complete the trade. Now Sacramento had Polynice as their starter, Causwell
coming off the bench and Peplowski gathering dust. "When Causwell came
back, I was literally the last guy on the bench," he says. "They wanted to deal
Causwell, so they had to play him to show that he had some marketable skills,
and it never materialized. Did I accept it? Yeah, I had to. I didn't control the
minutes. But I can tell you this: It was the only time I ever went to a coach to
talk about how much I was playing. (St. Jean) said, 'This is a business, you're
doing fine, we're happy with you.'"

Although his playing time tapered off, Peplowski appeared in 55 games
for the Kings, who registered a 28-54 record. He may not have had a high-

light reel, but at least he had a few months of solid NBA work. "It was nice to put up some numbers to show that I wasn't just this ham-and-egg type of guy, that I wasn't just a role player, that I could contribute to the team. That's what felt good."

At the start of the 1994-95 season, the Kings were still saddled with Polynice and Causwell, but they did pick up Peplowski's contract option. This time, a different mess was brewing. The new Sacramento general manager, Geoff Petrie, brought in Alaa Abdelnaby, a backup center who had played for the GM in Portland. "Every time they brought him in to work him out, I kicked his ass from end to end," Peplowski says. "But every GM and coach has his favorite player, and one of Geoff Petrie's favorite players from Portland was Alaa Abdelnaby. And I got caught in that shuffle. That kind of sounds like sour grapes."

The Kings kept Abdelnaby and cut Peplowski at the end of training camp. With no immediate offers, he packed his car and drove back to Michigan by himself. Along the way, he came to terms with a fundamental truth about major league sports. "You know you're good enough, you've proved to be good enough," he says, "but for whatever reason, the team has fallen out of love with you."

After working out with the Michigan State team for a few weeks, Peplowski got a call from the the Detroit Pistons in December. The team needed short-term help during a run of injuries. He joined the team for a pair of 10-day contracts, but he played just 21 minutes in six games. With the Pistons then obligated to sign him for the rest of the season or release him, they cut him loose. Peplowski began to see where his career was headed. "I kind of accepted that I was going to be bopping around the league for quite some time. It wasn't negative, it was just frustrating. I was happy to be working. The best thing about Detroit was that I was close to my family and friends. Playing for my hometown team was kind of cool."

After riding the bench with the Pistons, Peplowski focused on finding a job that offered meaningful playing time. Within a few days, he got his wish from a team in Spain. "Easy decision," he says. "I'm still getting paid from

Sacramento, I got a nice chunk of change from Detroit, and now Barcelona is going to pay me $100,000 to come over for the rest of the year. I'm having a good year financially."

Within 24 hours, he was alone in a world that looked nothing like the NBA. A team representative informed Peplowski that the team, FC Barcelona, was on a road trip. He was sent to a hotel and told to wait until his team-mates returned. "I'm not talking to anybody, nobody has contacted me. I haven't signed my contract, nothing. It was very much like living in a vacuum and it was tough. That was one of the hardest things I ever did up to that point in my life. I basically sat in a hotel room and walked around the city and tried to make the best of it. No one speaks English over there. It was pretty interesting." When the team finally returned, he helped FC Barcelona to the Spanish Cup. With a fatter wallet and more professional experience, he turned his attention to the NBA once again.

Peplowski signed with the Milwaukee Bucks for 1995-96, but he was traded to the Washington Bullets in the final days of the exhibition season. Before he even packed his bags, he suspected the trade was not in his best interests. Washington's starting center, Chris Webber, had a shoulder injury. Peplowski figured to be nothing more than a stopgap.

"So by this point, I'm so long in the tooth for everything that I just ended up saying to (Washington general manager) John Nash, 'I've been around the block a few times. Don't bull---- me. I have a feeling I'm only here until Chris gets healthy.' He said, 'Well, yeah, that's the plan.'

"I said, 'That's fine, I appreciate you telling me that. However, if Chris is fine, do not make me practice—and then after practice release me right after I get out of the shower.'"

Nash did observe that courtesy when the Bullets cut him six weeks later, but little else went right in Washington. Despite spending a month and a half on the team, he played a total of five minutes in two games. "I shook everybody's hands and said, 'Thanks, guys.' I went back to the place I was staying, packed up all my stuff, and I was back in my own bed that night."

Once again, Peplowski spent the drive home trying to make sense of the

NBA and his place in the league. He began thinking about options that looked more sensible than wandering around the NBA: "What the hell am I doing with my life? I haven't lived in one place more than six months since I moved out of my parents' house. I'm living out of a suitcase. I'm alone. What would be so bad about me stopping this, coming home, and taking the job at General Motors or Lehman Brothers that I was offered coming out of college?"

His third professional season was falling apart, so he decided to buy a house in Lansing and begin preparing for life after basketball. But after the holidays, another NBA offer came his way. It was Milwaukee again. Peplowski was willing to take another crack at the NBA, but he wanted nothing to do with the team that traded him before he ever reached the regular season. Taking the direct approach, Peplowski told his agent, "You can tell (Milwaukee general manager) Mike Dunleavy if he wants to sign me for a 10-day, he can shove it up his ass. He can sign me for the rest of the year."

Dunleavy made good, signing Peplowski for the rest of the season. But once again, he remained anchored at the end of the bench, playing 12 minutes over five games. "It was very discouraging because it was a terrible team," says Peplowski of the 25-57 Bucks. "That team had a lot of talent. The reason the Chicago Bulls were so successful was because they played as a team. You would think, Isn't that what you're supposed to do? Yes. Does it happen? No!"

Peplowski found the NBA to be full of individual agendas. The environment was especially discouraging after playing at Michigan State, where he took pride in playing for his school and his teammates. "I always yearned for that teammate atmosphere, that camaraderie, where you were going to war every night with the guys around you. But the selfishness that was displayed in the locker room by the teams I was on—I'm the franchise player, I've gotta shoot the ball 20 times a night—that's what made it frustrating."

At the start of the 1996-97 season, he took one more shot at the NBA. He signed with Golden State, another down-and-out franchise. The Warriors were thin at center, and Peplowski quickly earned a contract. Then in the last preseason game, Peplowski blew out his ACL.

"I knew as soon as I came down, it's over. Done. I went back in the training room. The trainer said, 'Don't think your career's over.' I said, 'Spare me the bull----. Get the beer out, put some ice on my knee and come toast my retirement.' In a way, I was upset that I was hurt and that it ended that way. But it was a sense of relief. Finally! I can stop! I can get on with my life."

In an instant and without hesitation, Peplowski became a former NBA player. The injury freed him of his basketball identity, but it did nothing to pave the way for the rest of his life.

"The only place to go after being a professional athlete, professionally speaking, is down. And once you're there and you're on even footing with everybody else, that little thing that differentiated you from the rest of the populace...is gone. Even in college, you were a cut above. It's a really interesting mental and emotional evolution that takes a lot of guys by surprise. And you either accept it or you fight against it."

Peplowski accepted it. Today at 35, he is the chief operating officer of the Boji Group, a company that purchases and manages commercial real estate in Michigan. "My life after basketball is far more rewarding than it ever was when I played," he says. "The things I've accomplished now are far more difficult to accomplish than what I did in the NBA. You've got years of training, years of ass kissing. You've got interpersonal skills that have to be refined and developed."

And as for the years shuffling around the NBA? "I wouldn't trade what I did for the world. I'm glad I did it. That has allowed me to enjoy what I do now."

For Peplowski, life after basketball is more interesting, full of opportunities to grow and be challenged. That's what the drunk guy at the country club doesn't understand.

"I think it's an intelligence thing," says Peplowski, who earned academic all-Big Ten honors. "I just didn't have a whole lot in common with everybody. You can only talk about basketball so much, or the things that everybody talks about—broads, money, cars. After a while, at least for me, I was yearning for some semblance of an intelligent conversation.

"And I think, at the end of the day, you were treated in accordance with the amount of money you made. I was the minimum-salary guy, and I was treated like the minimum-salary guy. That kind of deducts your opinion a little bit. It casts you in the light to where you're just the happy-to-be-here guy. And I've never been that type of person."

If you want to know the kind of person Peplowski is, just ask. He serves on the Sparrow Hospital board of directors, where he helped raise enough money to build a pediatric emergency room. He's the kind of guy who is comfortable putting on work boots and mopping up a building where a pipe has burst. "I will not ask anybody to do anything I would not be willing to do myself," he says.

These are the topics he likes to talk about today. If you start with the present and ease your way into hoops, that's fine. He won't bite your head off. In fact, he has a few nuggets to share about some of the greatest players in the game.

"By far, Hakeem Olajuwon was the best post player I've ever played against—and he proved it. Shaq, on the other hand, all I tried to do was keep him 10 feet away from the basket. It was more like a wrestling match than it was a basketball game. David Robinson, he's a frickin' small forward masquerading as a center. He's that quick. He's an absolute physical freak."

And did Peplowski hold his own against any of them?

"They took me to the cleaners. That's what they're supposed to do. Those are three of the best centers ever to have played the game. After the years pile up, you just say to yourself, You know what? You couldn't have done anything better than what you did."

Peplowski lets out a laugh and says, "They were that good."

For the moment, he is comfortable sharing a few basketball tales. At the same time, you wonder if he is just doing a little housekeeping, clearing out a few leftover items from that other era.

Mike Peplowski is not a basketball player. Got it?

"You know who I am? I'm a father to my children. I'm a husband to my wife. All I'm really interested in is my own personal things. That's it. *That's it.*"

A man of his word

Wayne Robinson
kept his promises,
even at the expense
of potential stardom.

There is a presence about **Wayne Robinson**. He's an imposing figure at 6 feet 8 inches, his voice is deep and smooth. If you didn't know he was a minister, you might suggest that he would make a fine prototype for a man of the cloth.

He's towering, strong, comforting—all helpful traits for a pastor. A blessing, you might say. But Robinson is more commonly typecast as a basketball player. And when people ask about playing hoops, he's got it covered. He made a pretty good splash in the NBA 25 years ago. Together, the two careers work magic. The mere mention of the NBA gets the attention of the young people Robinson tries to reach.

"It's a neat way to get a hook into kids," says Robinson, who is married with two children. "I have to say I've gotten more mileage out of that than anything outside of sharing the gospel of Jesus Christ."

Robinson knows his religious message can be a tough sell. But spreading the word of God is his life's work, and he is determined to help others make the most of their lives—just as he has always done for himself. Even as a young adult, he respected his God-given abilities. But there is irony in the details.

By the end of his senior year at Virginia Tech in 1980, Robinson had caught the attention of the NBA. He averaged 15 points and eight rebounds per game, and he followed up his season with strong showings in pre-draft camps and college all-star games. Teams around the league began inviting him for individual workouts before the draft, a sure sign that he was a hot prospect. But instead of jetting off to NBA towns, Robinson was filling his calendar with appointments at the Virginia Tech library. Final exams were coming up. He was not about to bail out before graduation. "Not that I didn't think about the NBA some, but I never really talked about it a lot," he says. "My education was very important. I knew I was going to get my degree first and foremost. If the NBA happened, great. But it was not part of my conversation with people in athletics or academics."

During exam week, Washington Bullets general manager Bob Ferry called. He told Robinson the Bullets might select him with the 14th pick in the first round. Then Philadelphia GM Pat Williams indicated he might take Robinson with one of his team's two first-round selections. This was critical information. All first-rounders earned guaranteed three-year contracts. Players selected in the subsequent rounds were guaranteed nothing. Still, Robinson opted for the books.

When draft day arrived, there was good news and bad news. On the plus side, Robinson was selected by the Los Angeles Lakers, a team on the brink of greatness. On the minus side, he was the eighth player taken in the second round. The distinction was lost on the rookie. "I just felt like if I could go and play hard, I would be OK," he says. "Maybe I was little naive. I was so glad that I got my degree."

Robinson had reason to feel good about his future with the Lakers. He knew that Los Angeles general manager Jerry West had watched him closely at the Portsmouth Invitational Tournament. But as soon as he joined the team in training camp, he felt a bit overmatched. "I didn't have a whole lot of good advice about how to handle that kind of environment," he says. "My attorney was experienced, but not as adept as others. When I got there, I just wasn't mentally ready to take the pressure. I didn't play as well as I could have." Making matters worse, he made a rookie mistake off the court. "I was late for a couple practices because I overslept. Not because I wanted to, but because I was so tense from one day to the next."

Robinson's learning curve was steep. So when Kareem Abdul-Jabbar proved to be a willing counselor, the rookie was all ears. "He was very cordial, but very much an introvert. He was very protective of his personal space. But he was always feeding me knowledge. One day we were having breakfast, and Kareem shared with me how important it was to watch my back—how you can never trust people. I'm sure that was a product of his own experience. He wanted me to know that you can't just assume that people like you, love you and want you to succeed. At this level, you have to take care of yourself and make sure that you are doing your best. Recognize that everybody wants to play."

Maybe Kareem was warning him about the politics of Lakers practice. Robinson recalls the lobbying of veteran power forward Jim Chones. At 6 feet 11 inches, Chones was the most suitable forward to guard Kareem in practice, but he wanted nothing to do with guarding the 7-foot-2-inch superstar. "And he didn't want to play backup center," he recalls. "He politicked tremendously not to have to play against Kareem every day. He wanted to play with Kareem."

Robinson played the full exhibition schedule with Los Angeles but was traded to the Detroit Pistons just before the start of the season. "Being traded was devastating. I didn't understand it. I didn't know it would happen so quickly. I had no reason to believe I wouldn't be on the team. But at the same time, it's a business. I began to learn about the grind and the dog-eat-dog attitude people have. You couldn't really trust people."

Although he was rattled by the trade, he received a vote of confidence from Lakers assistant coach Pat Riley on the way out the door. "Pat Riley said this to me—and I'll never forget it—'You're going to be a good player. You've got some good, raw talent. You just have to be in an environment that will allow you to develop.'"

Robinson was grateful for Riley's words of encouragement, but the trade left him fragile. "Obviously, the Lakers were a great learning experience, but certainly it hurt, feeling as though I was a failure. You have tears if you have any sensitivity, and I'm a pretty sensitive person. I wasn't overly emotional. I was able to quickly recover, and I was thankful to still be in the league. It didn't take but maybe a day or two to get re-acclimated and to begin the process of finding out that I could play at that level."

Detroit was coming off a 16-66 season. The Pistons roster was filled with middling NBA talent, giving Robinson the opportunity he needed. The only star player on the team was scoring legend Bob McAdoo. He and Robinson had both grown up in Greensboro, North Carolina and already knew one another. Robinson assumed he had found the perfect mentor.

"He didn't want to play for the Pistons at that point in his career. He felt the team was far beneath his abilities. He'd been a Buffalo Braves all-star and the NBA MVP in 1975. But Detroit was a bad experience for him. And I needed someone who could give me a deeper deposit, help me to become a little bit tougher. Obviously you'd like to think the guy from your hometown would provide something there. I was looking for it, being a rookie. But he was at a point in his life where he was looking for some stability."

On opening night of the 1980-81 season, Robinson did not look like a rookie in need of guidance. He scored 14 points and added eight rebounds, a performance worthy of player-of-the-game honors on Detroit's radio broadcast. "I'll never forget, I got this watch," he says, breaking out in laughter. "It was a cheap watch, but it was for the player of the game. You couldn't help but feel great. I'm competing against Wes Unseld, Bobby Dandridge, Elvin Hayes, Kevin Porter. This is a team that in 1978 won the championship, and I loved that team. My confidence started very high."

The Pistons got off to an 0-6 start. With many players struggling, Robinson had a chance to make an impression. He played nearly 20 minutes per night in 81 games as a rookie. He reached his personal best of 19 points against both San Antonio and New York. By the end of the season, he looked like a steal for the Pistons. Among the 30 players drafted ahead of him, only 14 topped Robinson's 7.9 points per game. The only disappointment was Detroit's 21-61 record. "I'd never lost that many games, but my enthusiasm and expectations were running high because I knew I played well," he says.

After getting married in the summer, Robinson returned to a team with renewed optimism. First-round draft picks Isiah Thomas and Kelly Tripucka gave the Pistons hope for an immediate turnaround. But after the last exhibition game, coach Scotty Robertson pulled Robinson aside in the airport. "He said, 'Rob, we're going to have to cut you. We're looking to make some moves.' Obviously, I had a huge well of emotions, but I didn't show it. I'm thinking, Who played better than I did? Just weeks prior he had said I was playing as well as any forward on the team.

"I was getting this double talk. I knew I couldn't change his mind. I just wanted to understand. When I saw that he was pretty much done with what he had to say—with very little emotion, very little compassion—I left. I went

back to my apartment. I wouldn't say I broke down, but I had to release my emotions. The next couple days I spent pretty much locked in my apartment. I was devastated."

Then came a phone call from former NBA executive Don DeJardin. He was looking to place experienced NBA players in the professional leagues in Europe, and he promised a job in Italy within 48 hours. When Robinson heard about the salary and the tax breaks—"I was an accounting and business major," he says—he was ready to sign on the dotted line. He could nearly match the $100,000 salary he would have made in Detroit. He called his wife and told her they were heading to Italy.

In his excitement over the new opportunity, Robinson overlooked the possibility of signing with another NBA team. When he first phoned home from Italy, he learned that his father had fielded offers from the Phoenix Suns and San Diego Clippers. "My dad was saying, 'Get your behind home! They're calling for you!' I said, 'I can't come back. I've got a contract. I'm loyal.'"

Playing in Italy put his NBA future at risk. Europe was for fringe players. Robinson was walking away from the best league in the world while he was still regarded as a top prospect. "I understand," he says directly. "But here again, I could have easily told my college professors my senior year, 'Forget about you guys, I'm going to these NBA tryout camps.' It came down to this: I'm loyal."

So Robinson suited up for Trieste, a team in the middle of the pack in the Italian league. After averaging 19 points and 11 rebounds, he signed up for another year. By the time he had two seasons under his belt, he was not pining to return to the NBA. "I thought about it and talked about it," he says, "but I had no master plan for how to get back." Besides, the European experience was giving him everything he wanted from basketball. After Italy, Robinson played three more years with Real Madrid, winning the Spanish national championship each year.

Finally, the NBA caught Robinson's attention once more. John Wetzel, a friend and fellow Virginia Tech grad, had taken over as head coach of the Phoenix Suns. He brought Robinson in to work out against Ed Pinckney and

Nick Vanos, a pair of two-year NBA veterans. "I was killing those guys," he recalls. "There was no question that these young guys were not at the level I was. My confidence was high. I was at the height of my career. So I sat down at the end of the mini camps and I said to Wetzel, 'I'll come back to veterans camp but you're going to have to guarantee me money because I am one of the highest paid players in Europe. You're going to have to come close.' I didn't need an agent to say that.

"But they couldn't do it. He had just gotten the job, so he didn't have a lot of clout. I really wanted that, but I wasn't willing to give up the guarantee."

Without hesitation, Robinson headed back to Europe, where he joined Barcelona for three years and closed out his professional career. "I always thought I would be done by the time I was in my early 30s, even when I was playing in the NBA. My goal was to go back and get my masters degree and go on with my life. I had not thought about getting rich."

By the time he retired, Robinson had grown indifferent about basketball. "By the tail end of my career, there was a void that couldn't be filled by playing basketball. The fun was gone. It was strictly a business. Making money, saving money."

He returned to Greensboro with an eye toward commercial banking. But on the short term, he was in demand as a motivational speaker in the local school district. "It really gave me that warm-fuzzy feeling to engage young people," he says. As he became more involved with school kids, Robinson developed a concern for at-risk students. As a result, he established the not-for-profit Center For Champions, an after-school program that focused on school work and decision making. Over the next seven years, more than 1,000 students came through the program. "My heart was entrenched in counseling, but there was a spiritual aspect. It was clear to me that the ministry was the next step."

Today, after 15 years in the ministry, Robinson has a keen sense of religious purpose. He recently founded the New Millennium Christian Center, a fledgling church with 50 adult members and 15 children. Services are held

in the clubhouse of a community golf course in Greensboro. "It is a non-denominational, interracial, multicultural ministry," he explains, easing into his sales pitch. "It is set up as a teaching and empowerment center. It is a Christian church. We believe in the full gospel and the literal translation of the Bible. We are plowing a lot of fallow ground. Most churches are segregated. We are about trying to break that up. Our objective is to create bridges whereby people can trust, where they can love, where they can build relationships regardless of race, creed or color."

The philosophy of the church draws from Robinson's teenage experience. In the ninth grade, he enrolled at Greensboro Day School, a nearly all-white, private school on the city's northwest side. Prior to that, he had known little of life beyond the segregated southeast side of Greensboro. "My parents saw something much larger in my future than I could see at the time. They were convinced that the environment would be more conducive for me as a student first, and then as an athlete eventually."

Some might say Robinson's pulpit presence differs from traditional black ministers. His speech is measured. You can hear happiness and poise in his voice. "I don't press emotionalism at all. I think it blocks people's hearing. Yet stereotypically, you think about how black preachers kind of evoke emotions." He preaches the way he feels it. Simple and straightforward. "It's about teaching the word and making it relevant, making it such that people can apply it every day of their lives."

With his life's work so meaningful now, Robinson has little concern over how his basketball days played out. He doesn't second-guess his decision to skip NBA workouts in favor of final exams. Nor does he wonder whether he should have come back to the NBA after a few seasons in Europe.

"I know beyond the shadow of a doubt that I could have competed in the NBA for 10 years," he says. "Some guys who didn't have the statistics, they could always say it in their minds. But you've got to have something to substantiate it. Game in and game out, I was guarding somebody and scoring on somebody and not being inhibited."

Robinson may not be inclined to feed his basketball ego, but he has quite a catalog of feel-good experiences. He recalls fondly his role in Detroit's first win of the 1980-81 season after the 0-6 start. He spent the fourth quarter battling Houston Rockets center Moses Malone, who was at the peak of his brilliant career. "I'm bellying him up. This guy is like a horse," he recalls. "I'm not just guarding him, I'm scoring on him, too. Those kinds of things let me know. Those are very fond memories, and it helped to validate who I was at the time."

When he looks at today's professional athletes, Robinson is concerned. His church work puts him at odds with the NBA lifestyle, replete with objectionable personal and moral behavior. Nothing bothers him more than the players who cannot practice what they preach.

"Some people have been in trouble, and they talk against it, but yet the next week you find out they're back in it," Robinson says. "I could name a bunch of guys who are like that. They come out and they try to preach, or they're advocates for no drugs and abstaining from sex, and they're still doing that stuff. That does the most damage. Positive role models are in short supply."

As he chats in the church's administrative offices, Robinson stretches his legs alongside a conference table. He's not about to get worked up over today's NBA players—any more than he does over yesterday's basketball career. That's just his style. There is no need for emotionalism.

"Do I regret any part of it? No. I really believe it was meant to be the way it occurred. I don't think it could have been altered at all. I have a different mindset because of my spiritual background. I just know it was the way it was supposed to be."

It begins with confidence

A college rival
helped Brian Rowsom
realize he could compete
in the pros.

It is T-shirt weather on a perfect October Saturday. Outside the Naomi Drennan Recreation Center in Charlotte, North Carolina, a few teenagers are working on skateboard moves. If you listen carefully, you can hear the squeaky sounds of basketball echoing inside the building.

For the young men pressing up and down the court, there is no such thing as a day too nice to be indoors. The players are hoping to make a modest dream come true. They are trying out for the minor league Charlotte Krunk of the American Basketball Association.

Today's ABA is nothing like the league that rivaled the NBA in the 1970s. The Krunk and their brethren are members of a low-budget league, and this tryout is strictly a bottom-feeding session. Some of these guys played in college, while others have been on the playgrounds since high school.

The man watching over the scrimmage is Charlotte general manager Brian Rowsom. You would be hard-pressed to find a better talent evaluator for the not-ready-for-the-NBA set. Before he came to the ABA, he operated his own business, placing American college players on professional European teams. So this Saturday in a stuffy gym is familiar territory.

"You can play in any rec center you want to," he says, "but if there's nobody there to scout you, all you're doing is working out."

For pure basketball ability, none of these hopefuls can touch the skill level of the GM. Rowsom played in the NBA, where his game was strong enough to crack the starting lineup at times. On other occasions, however, he struggled to keep pace in an unforgiving league. If Brian Rowsom knows anything about basketball, it is that talent is only part of the equation.

When Rowsom arrived at University of North Carolina Wilmington as a freshman in 1983, he brought with him a lightly-tested set of skills. He came from a small high school, and he felt a little intimidated at the start of his college career. In his sophomore year, he had no choice but to get over his

insecurities. Navy was joining the Colonial Athletic Association, led by 7-foot-1-inch center David Robinson, a budding star in the college game. At 6 feet 9 inches, Rowsom needed to fine-tune his skills for his new rival. "He helped elevate my game because I knew if I didn't play well against David, he would destroy me, which would embarrass me—which would prove to everybody that I wasn't a good player," he says.

Over the next three years, the two players met on the court eight times. Robinson averaged 22 points, Rowsom 17. But in his junior year, Rowsom briefly established the upper hand. In UNC Wilmington's 62-60 loss to Navy in the conference tournament, Rowsom outscored Robinson, 24-22. Former Celtics star Sam Jones was scouting the game for Boston, and he greeted Rowsom after the game with a simple comment: "You have NBA skills." Rowsom's lingering doubts were gone.

He averaged 21 points and 11 rebounds as a senior and was selected by the Indiana Pacers in the second round of the 1988 draft. He was in good company in Indianapolis, along with first-round pick Reggie Miller. "Reggie was so skinny coming out of college," Rowsom says. "We all thought he would last two weeks and be broken in half." While Miller was an immediate success, Rowsom was a project. Just as in college, he felt overwhelmed by the skill level of his teammates. His competition included Chuck Person, the NBA's reigning rookie of the year, and Wayman Tisdale, a solid third-year pro.

"I was such a sports fan that I knew too much about the NBA and the players," he admits. "It was to the point that it almost intimidated me when I watched us play. I was such a fan growing up in college. That's where it goes back to confidence. I didn't have the confidence, especially my rookie year, to go in and compete on a daily basis like I should have. I was too caught up in, Wow, I'm guarding Chuck Person, the rookie of the year. I should have thought, I'm a player just like everybody else. I have to prove that I can play, too. I didn't do that enough."

Rowsom made two mop-up appearances to start the season before facing the ultimate test in a November game at Utah. Jazz star Karl Malone, the gold standard among power forwards, was putting on a clinic against

Tisdale and center Herb Williams. Pacers coach Jack Ramsey turned to the kid, looking for someone who could slow down Malone. "I was shaking in my pants," he says. "But of course, I'm on the court with him and I've got to show everybody that I can play with this guy supposedly."

All night, Utah had torched Indiana with long passes to Malone for easy baskets. Nothing changed when Rowsom checked into the lineup. "They would throw the ball down court every time and Malone would score. He made it look easy. It was just like a man against a boy out there. It seemed like an hour." In reality, his go-round with The Mailman lasted just seven minutes of game action. When he returned to the bench, Rowsom plunged his head into his hands.

 **"When I got my first rebound or my first basket in every game, I became more confident. But going into the game, I had that question mark there. I shouldn't have at all. I should have said, 'I'm in the NBA. There's a reason why I'm here. It's because this team believes in me.'"**

"I just thought, Wow, I can't do this! I cannot play at this level against these guys. I remember specifically thinking that. If you lose your confidence as an athlete, you're shot. Other teams are going to prey on that."

Over the next few weeks, he struggled to regain his edge. Even practicing against his teammates did not come easily. "By then, I had been destroyed. It's like Mike Tyson when he fought Buster Douglas and lost. He was never quite as confident after that. That's how it was with me in Indiana that first year."

The Pacers waived Rowsom a few weeks later when a player returned from the injured list. "You learn quickly that it's a political business. My contract was not guaranteed. It's easier to cut me than someone who is

making $300,000 at the time." His Indiana career lasted four games. He played just 16 minutes, not nearly enough time to make a strong impression. "You need 16 minutes per game to demonstrate what you can do as a player," he says.

Indiana general manager Donnie Walsh suggested he make the best of the situation by finishing the season in Europe. Rowsom joined a French team, Pau-Orthez, and spent the second half of the season as a starter. With his confidence back in place after the European season, he returned home to jump-start his NBA career. He caught a break with the expansion Charlotte Hornets. Their coach, Dick Harter, had been an assistant for Indiana the previous season. He invited Rowsom to camp for a tryout.

When Hornets power forward Kurt Rambis went down with an injury, Rowsom stepped into the role and played well enough to earn a roster spot. With few top-tier players on the team, Harter gave everyone a chance to play early in the season. Rowsom made the most of the opportunity. In his second outing, he scored 16 points and grabbed seven rebounds against the Detroit Pistons, the defending NBA champions. But in his sixth game, he suffered a stress fracture in his foot. When he returned to the lineup in February, he scored a personal-best 17 points in 21 minutes against the New York Knicks. For the season, he reached double figures in scoring seven times.

"I was pretty confident. The only problem was that some nights I would be more confident than others," he says. "Some nights I would look across there and think, OK, I'm going against Charles Oakley or Horace Grant—I'm OK, I can handle that. But there were other nights I would play against Kevin McHale and Karl Malone and I'd be a little bit intimidated."

When he returned to the Hornets for the 1989-1990 season, his role was established. Rowsom was the guy who came off the bench to inject the game with energy, whether by diving for loose balls or making a defensive stop. But throughout the first month of the season, he continued to wrestle with self-doubt.

Then came a defining moment in his career. David Robinson, his former adversary in college, was lighting up the NBA as a rookie. But because

Rowsom had a history of holding his own against Robinson, he felt no anxiety as Charlotte prepared to play in San Antonio. The Hornets lost the game, but Rowsom responded with a career-high 20 points in just 26 minutes. It was all about confidence. "That's it right there!" he says.

Midway through the season, as the Hornets lagged behind their expansion-year pace, Charlotte fired Harter and replaced him with Gene Littles. The new coach shook up the lineup, cutting Rowsom's playing time in half. His season came to an abrupt end in late March when he was injured in a game against Phoenix. He was carried off the Charlotte Coliseum floor on a stretcher with a cervical vertebrae sprain.

By summer, he was healed and ready for the 1990-91 season, but his future with the Hornets was uncertain. The team offered another non-guaranteed contract, leaving Rowsom disappointed and willing to move on. His agent secured a deal for him to play in Nancy, France. Having played overseas once before, the decision was easy. "To be able to travel and see the world, it was almost like a paid vacation," he says. "When they bring American players over there, especially if you have the NBA on your resume, they roll out the red carpet. They make you feel like you're the Karl Malone or Charles Barkley in that particular town. I loved it. Everywhere I went, I got in free. I didn't have to pay for meals or drinks. I thought, This may not be a bad idea. I liked it, as opposed to having to come to NBA training camps every year and having to earn a spot."

He was no longer playing against the top players in the world, but he now had a guaranteed contract worth $400,000. His offer from the Hornets had called for $300,000—if he made the team and stayed on the roster.

After a year in France, Rowsom was ready for another global basketball adventure. This time he chose a team in Eilat, Israel, a resort town on the Red Sea. "It was hot, palm trees, hotels. It was like a mixture of Vegas and Atlantic City. The people were great, everybody spoke English. The first week I was there I was going out every night to the pubs and experiencing everything. I was getting caught up in the night life and going to the beach every day."

Rowsom came to love playing hoops in Israel. For four seasons, he earned

guaranteed contracts in the $250,000 range. The life was luxurious and it allowed him to spend half the year relaxing in the United States. But at the end of each season, his agent would suggest that it was time to consider a return to the NBA, with its high profile and big money. That argument was a tough sell. "You have the lap of luxury in the NBA. You don't have to do anything but perform. When you go to Europe, you're still getting good money, but you have to take your uniform home and wash it yourself. You don't have the penthouse, but you don't exactly have the outhouse."

Plus, there was the issue of all the Malones and Barkleys waiting back in the United States. Those guys weren't getting any softer. "I had less pressure to perform every night than in the NBA, looking over my shoulder," he says. "Every year I played in Israel, it made it easier for me to stay there. I was another year older, I saw my bank account growing."

In the summer of 1995, Rowsom got married and signed with a team in Manchester, England. Right away, he began to lose focus on his career. "Playing basketball was starting to become more of a job. It was tougher every day to get out of bed in the morning for practice, just like any job if you don't necessarily want to go. I had gotten married and had gotten a little lazy. I wanted to spend more time at home with my wife. Plus, I was getting older, and I was getting a few nicks and pains. Your sprained ankles and your back don't heal as fast."

Reality set in quickly on a January evening in London. Rowsom was playing poorly and he knew it. He finished the game with four points. "I thought, I'm better than this. I'm not into it as much, my body is breaking down slowly but surely. I remember putting the ball down right there on the court after the game was over." On the bus ride back to Manchester, Rowsom told his coach that he was finished with basketball. "I never really picked up the ball again to play," he says quietly. "For whatever reason, it was not as much fun for me anymore."

With many contacts in professional leagues around the world, Rowsom became a registered agent. At first, it was difficult to make the connection between American players and foreign teams. So he decided to bring the players and European coaches together for tryout camps on American soil. For several years, Rowsom made his living by pairing up the two sides. Players paid a $200 fee to attend the event, and the teams paid Rowsom a percentage of each contract signed. After a typical camp, 10 American players walked away with overseas deals.

In 2004, a friend convinced him to coach the Charlotte Thunder, the predecessor to the Krunk in the ABA. "I thought minor league basketball could work here, plus there were a lot of good players in the area." Under Rowsom's direction, the Krunk finished in the middle of their division. He then moved into the general manager's role, preferring to use his skills as a talent evaluator.

And that is his mission on this Saturday afternoon at the rec center—to find an overlooked gem who can play for the Krunk. If he finds one, Rowsom makes a dream come true, even though the weekly paycheck is in the neighborhood of $300. "When I see the young guys out here today going through the stuff I went through, this is where I feel like I can be of help to them. I can guide them and help them do certain things that will allow them to play for a long time. My dream was fulfilled by playing in the NBA and having a professional career. I want some of these guys to experience some of the same joy I have experienced."

He cannot help ABA hopefuls land a six-figure payday, but he can give them a start. After that, he hopes the players will listen to his message about life outside of basketball. The team's name, Krunk, is a useful starting point. The term (also, crunk) refers to a style of hip hop music that originated in Atlanta in the 1990s. The name provides a nice marketing tie-in for the fan base, but Rowsom wants his players to embrace something more meaningful than a cultural trend. "I try to be open-minded," he says with a deflated voice. "Everybody's into this hip hop culture. But I still think you're representing yourself and the league. If you want to get into corporate America, you can't have a do-rag. You're not going to go to an interview like that. Whether the players like it or not, there are kids that emulate what they do. I'd rather the kids emulate them doing something positive instead of negative."

At age 40, he has plenty of experience to share with young hoop dreamers. He could start with a message about confidence. He speaks on the subject with a clear and robust voice that belies his own struggle to find his footing in the NBA. "As you get older, you get wiser," he says. "You know stuff you wish you had known at 20 or 25.

"When I got my first rebound or my first basket in every game, I became more confident. But going into the game, I had that question mark there. I shouldn't have at all. I should have said, 'I'm in the NBA. There's a reason why I'm here. It's because this team believes in me.'

"Now looking back at it, I wish that I would have had a different mental approach to the game. Talent-wise, I could at least hold my own because I was a big guy who could handle the ball a little bit and I had a nice shooting touch. I could score in the low block, I could pass the ball well. Even back then, a lot of big guys were just rebounders or guys setting picks. They weren't as talented as me overall. But they believed in their heads that they belonged. That's something I didn't do enough of. Otherwise, I would have played longer."

But two-plus seasons in the NBA will have to do. Living in Charlotte, Rowsom is asked from time to time if he used to play for the Hornets.

"It makes me feel good to say, 'Yes I did.' I take pride in it."

The road leads home

Despite his low
profile, Donald Whiteside
was not about
to come up short.

When **Donald Whiteside** was a high school kid, thinking big was out of the question. At Chicago's Leo High School, he started on the freshman team at 5 feet 3 inches. By his senior year, he was a budding star at an underwhelming 5 feet 6 inches.

"When you're born into this situation," Whiteside says, "you adapt."

After leading his Catholic school to the Illinois Sweet 16 twice, he accepted a scholarship from Northern Illinois University, the only Division I school to come through with an offer. Whiteside's progress at NIU mirrored his high school career, peaking at the finish. He led the Huskies to the NCAA Tournament as a senior in 1991, where NIU came up six points short against St. John's in the first round.

At that point, Whiteside turned his attention to the future. He had grown to his full height of 5 feet 10 inches, but reaching the NBA was still a tall order. "I got a questionnaire from the New Jersey Nets and the Los Angeles Clippers," he says. "I personally didn't think I was ready for the NBA, so I didn't pursue it. I sent in the questionnaire, but not until months after I received it."

With his name on the wrong kind of NBA short list, he set his sights on playing professionally overseas. When he was offered a contract with the Hobart Devils in Australia, he jumped at it. The atmosphere was a bit like college, playing in front of 5,000 fans each night. And the pay—$25,000 for the five-month season—was enough to get started in life. "I just wanted to get some playing experience," he says. "I was making some money doing what I liked to do. The people of Australia were polite and generous. They received me really well. I had a great time."

After two seasons with Hobart, Whiteside learned the down side of playing Down Under. The level of competition in Australia is relatively weak among foreign leagues, so his two professional seasons had done little to entice the NBA. Whiteside's only route to the big time was through the

American minor league system. He joined the Rockford Lightning of the Continental Basketball Association for an exhibition game, hoping to take a baby step toward his NBA dream. "It was a far off goal," he says, "but I was working at it constantly." Once the game started, he quickly became disenchanted with the style of play. He was teamed in the backcourt with Jay Taylor, a former college rival at Eastern Illinois. "Any time I took a shot and didn't give it to Jay, he'd turn to the coach and yell, 'Coach!' And I thought I was taking an open shot. My take on the CBA at the time was it was extremely selfish. Everyone was out for themselves and trying to get to the NBA."

With no fondness for the CBA game, Whiteside looked for another opportunity to play abroad. "The whole thing about playing overseas is you're always waiting on a phone call," he says. "You stay in shape, keep practicing. Every now and then you get a job, and it keeps an inflow of money." In 1993, he took a short-term gig in Venezuela, playing for a team that did not want to be troubled with bookkeeping. "They gave me money in my hand and counted out $100 bills and $50 bills. That was amazing to me. I made $5,000 in a month and a half."

He returned home in June, in time for his wife, Petrice, to give birth to their daughter, Reigna. But by October, Latvia was calling. Another payday awaited, and now he had the added incentive of providing for a baby. When he returned after four months in Latvia, Whiteside realized he had missed a lot of family life. "My daughter was five months old when I left for Latvia. We were extremely close. It was a shock when I got back because she didn't know who I was. So I spent those next couple months having her get used to me again."

Not wanting to endure another long separation from his family, Whiteside put his playing career on hold. He accepted a job as the assistant basketball coach at Leo High School. The return to his old stomping ground involved more than just hoops. He taught theology classes, instructing teenagers in the basics of Catholicism. "I tried to relate it to everyday situations the kids were in. They took to it. I had their respect because I was the basketball coach. That kind of preceded me. So I didn't have a lot of trouble with the students."

Coaching them came easily too. But along the way to a 19-win season, he felt the itch to compete again. This time Whiteside pursued an opportunity in his own backyard. He joined a team in the Chicago Pro-Am summer league, where college and pro players gather to showcase their skills. The games are played at the Illinois Institute of Technology and often feature some of the top players in the NBA. "It's near the projects, and the gym is a heat box," he says. "It's like 100 degrees. It's packed. They turn people away at the door."

Whiteside did more than hold his own against the elite players. He led his team to the playoffs with just one loss. That's when his name began moving through NBA circles. Toronto Raptors general manager Isiah Thomas sent his brother to scout a playoff game. A couple weeks later, the Raptors invited Whiteside to Toronto for two days of workouts. After securing a leave of absence from the principal at Leo, he was headed for his first NBA tryout. Much to his surprise, the audition included a game of one-on-one against Thomas, who was just two years removed from his hall-of-fame playing career.

Whiteside returned to the high school halls and heard nothing from the team for several weeks. When Toronto finally extended an invitation to training camp, he realized he was at a disadvantage. Camp was already underway. He wondered if he was merely serving as an extra practice player. When he picked up a copy of the training camp roster, he figured he had his answer. Whiteside's name was not on the list of 18 players.

The Raptors were a second-year NBA franchise in 1996-97, with little hope of contending for the playoffs. At the top of the roster were young stars like Damon Stoudamire, Marcus Camby and Walt Williams. Several other spots were taken by veteran role players. But the Raptors had an opening for a backup point guard, so Whiteside went right to work. Paired with veteran guard Hubert Davis in a two-on-two drill, Whiteside stole the ball from Stoudamire, passed to Davis and eventually finished the play with a three pointer. "Everybody was like, Who is this? But I didn't know half of these guys either. As far as I was concerned, they were just basketball players."

Whiteside was steady throughout the preseason, but Toronto gave him no indication of where he stood with the team. Then a couple days before the season, he got a call from his high school coach. The opening day NBA rosters were printed in the newspaper in Chicago, and the coach spotted Whiteside's name. "It didn't even hit me. I just wanted to play. I was just looking forward to the next game. It was an opportunity to play against some of the best."

After a one-minute debut against the New York Knicks on opening night, he played 12 minutes at Charlotte. He hit all three of his field goal attempts, two of them from three-point range. He added two assists and a steal. With nine points, he proved what he had always believed—that he could play in the NBA. But that fact alone gave him no reason to celebrate. "I just felt like I was doing what I could to help the team. We weren't predicted to do very well. Honestly, it was no big deal."

For two months, he played just enough to give the starters a rest. For a rookie with a non-guaranteed contract, that role can be psychological torture. One night you play double-digit minutes and think you've earned the coach's trust. The next night you get two minutes and wonder if the front office is scouring the waiver wire. But Whiteside's worries went beyond the decision makers. He began to doubt whether his teammates supported him. In a game against Seattle, he played 19 minutes while paired with Doug Christie. "I felt like Doug would purposely overlook me when I was open," says Whiteside, who was 1-for-7 from the floor that night. "I just thought it was crazy. It was something that always stuck in the back of my mind."

Practice was worse. Forward Carlos Rogers liked to pit Whiteside against Stoudamire. "Carlos was always saying, 'Hey Damon! Whiteside said he's way better than you. He says he should be playing more minutes.'

"I said, 'Carlos, why would you say that?' I was just a guy who wanted to be on the team. I didn't want to make any waves."

With each passing day, he felt less in control of his NBA destiny. But all those periphery issues disappeared for one night in early December. Michael Jordan's Chicago Bulls were in town. During the pregame warm up, Whiteside watched Jordan's every move. "That's when it hit me that it was the NBA. That's who I tried to pattern my work ethic after. I found myself looking down the court during layups. Man, I'm here. That's him."

By late December, Whiteside was struggling to understand his role on the team. After a one-minute appearance at Washington, he earned his longest outing of the season, 31 minutes at Orlando. But instead of getting into the flow of the game, he found himself wrestling with distracting questions: Did Rogers and Stoudamire expect him to do nothing but set up their shots? Did coach Darrell Walker expect him to prove he could thrive with the extra minutes?

He began asking himself, What am I doing? Am I playing well enough? Am I stepping on toes? The result was extreme. He did not attempt a shot all night. "I kind of backed off. I passed up some shots in that Orlando game. Then I thought, OK, I should have shot the ball. I'm going to shoot the next game."

Two nights later at Detroit, he had a chance to let it all hang out. Whiteside made his debut in the starting lineup and played 36 minutes, more than any player on the team. But his new strategy backfired. He took nine shots but made just one. Usually one of the team's top three-point shooters, he missed all seven from long range. Most of his teammates shot poorly, too. Detroit pounded Toronto, 118-74. "Every shot I took, except for one or two, it was in the rim and out," he says.

But it was more than his shooting touch that was off. "I don't know if my fire to be there was the same. I didn't feel comfortable. And I got the sense the other guys weren't playing as hard as they could play. Damon was kind of joking around and going through the motions, and some of the other guys were too. I felt like they knew something."

Maybe the veterans sensed a shake-up was in the works. Toronto's record had fallen to 10-20, and the 44-point loss was the worst of the season. The next day at practice, Whiteside felt the same vibe. "I was getting dressed for practice, and Stoudamire had this little smirk on his face. It just seemed strange. And when I went out to shoot around, Darrell Walker called me in and sat me down."

Whiteside was released. Perhaps he was the scapegoat for the loss to Detroit, particularly since three other players combined to shoot 3-for-24 that night. But the Raptors had to try something to get back on track, and they started with a player whose contract was not guaranteed. For Whiteside, it was just as well. He was tired of the emotional turmoil. "Where other guys would have asked why, I was OK. I had prepared myself for something. I wasn't playing the way I could play. I wasn't even sure I wanted to be an NBA player. The biggest question I wanted to answer for myself was, Could I make it? And I had made it. At that point, I had a daughter and I wanted to be around her. The lifestyle takes you away from your family so much."

He packed up his Ford Explorer and drove his family back to Chicago. He joined the CBA's LaCrosse Catbirds, a job that allowed him to commute to practices and home games. But the drop-off from the NBA was a dramatic one. His monthly pay of nearly $36,000 was gone, replaced by $1,400 per month in the minor leagues. And the style of basketball in the CBA was just how he remembered it. "I already thought the CBA was extremely selfish," he says. "That just confirmed it." After two months, he quit and began focusing on the following season.

In the summer of 1997, he landed a tryout with the Atlanta Hawks. His main competition for a backup job was three-year veteran Eldridge Recasner. Like Whiteside, Recasner spent much of his early pro career in the minors and overseas. "I felt like he was the only guy I had to beat out, and I thought he was overrated. So I would have my way with him in practice, but it did no good," he says, noting that Recasner had a guaranteed contract. "You can make him look as bad as you want in practice, but that's the guy they're paying. I had pretty much gotten the gist."

Whiteside made the Hawks roster out of training camp, but he had no meaningful role. In Atlanta's second game, he played nine minutes against his old team, the Raptors, contributing two points. But after the first week of the season, he was cut loose. If you blinked, you missed him. In three games with the Hawks, he logged 16 minutes.

Although his NBA career had soured, the experience made him a more valuable commodity in foreign leagues. He played a season in the Czech Republic for $90,000, followed by a season in Spain. But with his wife expecting their second child, Whiteside came home to focus on his family.

He went to work for a friend's company. He spent his days piecing together billboards on a warehouse floor, then covering them with a weather-resistant gloss. The job was anything but glamorous, but the quiet time gave him a chance to think about where he was headed. After a few months, he took a job with a family center, working with kids who had been sentenced to home confinement. During high-crime hours, Whiteside was on duty. He kept the kids busy with study tables, meals and activities. He was satisfied with the work.

Whiteside rolled the basketball dice once more, playing the 2000 season with the Chicago Skyliners in the unheralded American Basketball Association. At the end of the season, he was offered a chance to make a clean break from his playing career. Northern Illinois coach Rob Judson offered him a job as an assistant coach. After a bit of soul searching, Whiteside said yes to his alma mater. "As a player, if you lose that drive and hunger, that's your edge. And I really enjoyed being a family man. This was an opportunity to spend time with my family and watch my kids grow up."

Now in his fifth year on the NIU coaching staff, Whiteside's responsibilities range from recruiting to game preparation. "I like showing guys how to approach things," he says. "I get instant gratification when guys have success. We've graduated three public-league guys, which is really good. They come from the same type of background I come from."

That background is rarely a fast track to success. As a kid on the streets of Chicago, Whiteside saw enough trouble to know he wanted to avoid it. "Like every kid, I hung out on the corners for a little while," he says, letting out a laugh. "But I always got home in time to go to bed. My mom was a single parent, and I didn't want to upset her. I'm a momma's boy. One of the most important things was making my mom proud."

Coaching at the college level is a good fit for now, but someday Whiteside might return to the high school ranks, where the need for mentors is urgent. "I go back to the city, and we're just losing so many of them. The role models they look up to now, they've got to be an entertainer or an athlete.

"I like having an impact on a person's life, starting first and foremost with my children. I want my children to look at me and say, 'When I become successful, I want to reach back and help some kids as well.'"

Whether Whiteside coaches teenagers or young adults in the future, he will do it with an extra measure of poise. His NBA career lasted just 30 games, but the achievement is a permanent one. "There's a certain level of confidence you carry when you're a professional player. And even when you're old and you slow down a little bit, it can still carry you through situations that other people mentally can't get through. You know you can will yourself to do things. It's a certain confidence that you keep the rest of your life."

The NBA may have been Whiteside's most enticing challenge, but he found rewards most everywhere he played. The work was fun and the money kept his family afloat, one foreign assignment at a time. "I feel like my life, my path, was already mapped out. It wasn't meant for me to be in the NBA for a long time. I'm not mad about it. A lot of people never have that opportunity, and it was a great experience. But it's a fast life, and I don't think it would have made my wife and family happy had I continued it. I don't know if I would have been able to handle it."

When Whiteside watches the NBA today, he pays particular attention to the young guys trying to make their way. Some will catch the right breaks, others won't. None of it is fair, he knows.

"Sometimes I get frustrated because I think, Man, they're giving that kid every chance in the world. I didn't have as many chances. But I'm not mad about that. I get a lot of breaks because of who I am. Maybe someday my son (Donald Jr.) will get a lot of breaks because of me."

Whiteside pauses and thinks about how that sounds.

"Hey, that's just people helping people."

journeymen

Photo credits

Baseball
Fireovid: courtesy of Steve Fireovid and Seattle Mariners.
Ingram: courtesy of Toledo Mud Hens.
Jennings: courtesy of Cincinnati Reds.
Lancellotti: courtesy of San Francisco Giants archives.
Polley: courtesy of Richmond Braves.
Pose: courtesy of Kansas City Royals.

Football
Bowers: courtesy of John Reid/Cleveland Browns.
Dilweg: courtesy of Green Bay Packers.
Flick: courtesy of Tom Flick.
Haggins: courtesy of Florida State University Sports Information Department
and San Francisco 49ers.
Oglesby: courtesy of Arizona Cardinals.
Perry: courtesy of Michael C. Hebert/New Orleans Saints.

Hockey
Eakins: courtesy of Jerry Thomas/Calgary Flames and Manitoba Moose.
Gruhl: courtesy of Scott Gruhl.
Jensen: courtesy of Darren Jensen.
Knipscheer: courtesy of Boston Bruins.
LeBoutillier: courtesy of Ken Babbitt/Lowell Lock Monsters.
Littman: courtesy of David Littman and Rochester Americans.

Basketball
Jepsen: courtesy of Golden State Warriors.
LaRue: courtesy of Utah Jazz.
Peplowski: courtesy of Michigan State University Sports Information Department
and Detroit Pistons.
Robinson: courtesy of Detroit Pistons.
Rowsom: courtesy of Indiana Pacers Sports and Entertainment.
Whiteside: courtesy of Northern Illinois University Sports Information Department.

Kurt Dusterberg has spent most of his professional career as a television sportscaster and freelance writer. He has covered Major League Baseball, the NFL, NHL and NBA while working in Ohio, Indiana, North Carolina and West Virginia.

Early in his career, he developed a fondness for journeymen professional athletes—the ones who often possess more determination than natural ability. He finds their humility refreshing and their stories inspirational.

His own journeyman sports career lasted through high school in his hometown of Cincinnati, where he played baseball and golf.

Dusterberg is married and has two children. He lives near Raleigh, North Carolina.